The Enriched Field

Leonardo Ramondetti

The Enriched Field

Urbanising the Central Plains of China

Birkhäuser
Basel

Crossing Luohe River in Luoyang, 2019.

Introduction

Since the economic reform of 1978, China has experienced a period of radical transformation: the population has increased from less than 1 billion to 1.5 billion, while annual gross domestic product (GDP) growth has ranged between 4 and 15 percent (China National Bureau of Statistics, 2020). One of the most obvious effects of these changes is the rise in urbanisation: the percentage of the population living in cities has rocketed from 18 to 60 percent, with 75 percent of this growth accounted for by net migration and reclassification of the household registration system (Chan, 2013; Liang, 2014; Miller, 2012). During this time, the Chinese territories have undergone a revolution in structure. The number of cities has increased from 190 to 674, all parts of the country have infrastructure, and land conversion to non-agricultural use has reduced China's farmland to only about one-tenth of the country's total surface area (China National Bureau of Statistics, 2020; Hsing, 2010). The first wave of urban development mainly affected the coastal regions and thus, urban policies are now being put in place to rebalance regional disparities. The central government is planning to use such policies to urbanise 25 percent of China, that is, an area inhabited by 63 percent of the Chinese population that accounts for 80 percent of China's GDP and is home to 64 percent of the nation's cities (Fang & Yu, 2016). To put this in perspective, China is currently urbanising an area approximately eight times the size of Italy, with a population about three times that of the United States, and a GDP almost twice that of Japan.

In this context, granting official status to the urban agglomerations that resulted from the massive and rapid urbanisation of the coastal regions soon after the economic reform simply rubberstamps existing metropolitan areas such as the Yangtze River Delta and the Pearl River Delta. The Central Plains, however, represents a new frontier in Chinese urban development and has a story that is different from most of China's inland territories. Apart from a few larger cities, which over the centuries have chiefly performed administrative functions, the region was characterised by minor agglomerations and a diffuse urbanisation, built up over quite a long period of time and using minor infrastructures to shape the land (Kirkby, 1985; Ren, 2013; Su, 2009). In the last three decades, the situation has rapidly changed as these territories have become testing grounds for new policies, practices, and forms of spatial development. Within this context, the Central Plains was first subjected to the urban entrepreneurial policies of major municipalities; then, since mid-2005, the area has experienced several initiatives undertaken by central and local governments to promote a more comprehensive urban development (Shepard, 2015; F. Wu, 2015). As a result, the Central Plains is now a regional urban agglomeration (Zhongyuan City Group) made up of 9 prefecture cities, 23 cities, and 413 townships, which produces 3.06 percent of China's GDP and is home to 45.5 million inhabitants (3.39 percent of the nation's population), of which 13.7 million (30 percent) are registered as urban citizens (Henan Province Bureau of Statistics, 2020). In this area of 58,400 square kilometres, the current policies aim to urbanise another 4,902 square kilometres to provide space for new inhabitants, new economies, and new ways of living and social structures (Fang & Yu, 2016).

Consequently, when looking out the window of a high-speed train today, the Central Plains of China appear to be a flat, wide-open expanse in the throes of a revolution. The ancient urbanisation pattern of scattered villages, small factories, and farms connected by a dense network of dirt roads and small canals is now being taken over by new forms of urbanity. Construction sites have sprung up everywhere, and the number of blue roofs indicating workers' shacks is greater than the red roofs of farmers' houses. Bridges, highways, and railways crisscross the entire area, and gridworks of four-lane roads partition the land into plots in preparation for the forthcoming urbanisation. Near the major cities, the infrastructural network intensifies; industrial sites and high-rise compounds fill the landscape; towers and skyscrapers appear on the horizon. This is the Central Plains of China today: a huge accumulation of heterogeneous urban materials.

Most current studies consider this area to be a "city of exacerbated difference" (Koolhaas, Chung, Inaba, et al., 2001, p. 29) located "between the exceptional and the ordinary" (Bonino et al., 2019, p. 20). The conditions have given rise to a variety of contrasting opinions, often in contradiction with one another. For instance, it has been described as the outcome of uniquely "Chinese characteristics" (Huang, 2008; Zhu, 2009), as well as one with multiple "materialisations of globalisation" (Ren, 2011; F. Wu, 2006), and even as a "third space" or "hybrid space", meaning the result of a mix of specific place conditions and international trends (AlSayyad, 2001; M. Y. Wang et al., 2014). The hypotheses on the prospects for Chinese urbanisation are even more divergent. The variety of scenarios ranges from deeming the Chinese city to be the "fix to absorb capital [...], [that reproduces] the inequalities within the world system [...] into the urban realm, further shaping inter- and intra-urban inequalities as new forms of 'uneven spatial development'" (F. Wu, 2007, pp. 9–16) to considering it "a test bed for some of the new industries, research facilities, innovation themes, quality assurance processing or a way of working that will lay the foundation for that modernising rebirth" (Williams, 2017, p. 203).

Despite this spectrum of positions, most of the research conducted in the field of urban studies in recent years has been based on non-spatial readings, discounting the materiality of urban space. By regarding Chinese cities as "theatres of accumulation" from where Western cultures and values are spread (Armstrong & McGee, 1985), physical space is seen merely as banal areas carved out by developers and designers who are blueprinting distorted replicas of transnational models and iconic symbols of global society (Bosker et al., 2013; King, 2004; Sklair, 2006). Based on this assumption, most research sees built spaces, cultural artefacts, landscape organisation, and the other physical features of Chinese development as undeserving of attention or, at best, worthy only of quantitative assessment.

As a consequence, despite the general consensus that China is "the largest construction site in the word today" (Zhu, 2009, p. 169), few scholars are investigating what is currently under construction. The materiality of Chinese spaces (e.g. architecture, landscapes, houses, streets, rivers, and all other physical elements) remains an elusive matter. This is due to the difficulty of grasping a phenomenon which is subject to continuous and abrupt change, the outcome of which is "unsteady terrain", constantly in evolution. Every time one goes to a place, it looks different. In light of this, as stated by Rem Koolhaas (2001), in the context of China, "the urban seems to be least understood at the very moment of its apotheosis" (p. 27). However, it would be a mistake to consider Chinese urbanisation as merely an above-ground phenomenon that affects the socio-economic sphere mostly because of quantities and ready-made imaginaries. On the contrary, space matters very much: new economies are closely linked to the emerging spatial organisation (new infrastructures, logistics platforms, industrial areas, and tourist sites), new practices and social structures are connected to changes in the everyday living environment (new housing, systems of mobility, recreation areas), and there are an increasing number of new policies addressing territorial issues (the need to preserve farmland, curb pollution, capitalise on specific sites). Based on this, investigating the physical space resulting from Chinese urbanisation processes is currently a vital issue. Its complexity can reveal a great deal about the contemporary city and calls for interpretations able to give depth to the reality observed.

However, this is not a simple operation. To do so, the ongoing urban transformations of the Central Plains of China must firstly be positioned within the wider body of knowledge, notions, words, interpretations, narratives, and techniques upon which a shared discourse to question the major urbanisation processes worldwide has been built up internationally over time. Relating Chinese urbanisation to other urbanisation processes means neither providing a coherent vision, nor putting the transformations observed in the Central Plains into perspective. It does not mean adopting a comparative approach either, given the impossibility of using traditional models and interpretative categories when researching urban China (Bonino et al., 2019; Governa & Sampieri, 2020). The research does not use the urbanisation occurring in China to prove, reject, or revise specific urban theories. On the contrary, by linking the urban transformations of the Central Plains to other urbanisation processes, the research attempts to define a common interpretative framework (made up of different times, places, and disciplines) to address realities which are still largely to be explored. This step is considered crucial. Indeed, retrieving this common discourse makes it possible to exchange knowledge and expertise on the urban transformations that occur in specific local places. One must, of course, bear in mind that "China is different", meaning that any theoretical framework, language, method, or tool adopted from another context will not perfectly fit the situations observed. However, they can indeed add another level of shared complexity.

As for any urbanisation process, the spatial transformations in the Central Plains of China are also a reflection of the socio-economic contingencies, political ambitions, and cultural values that are shaping new modes of building on, occupying, and using the land. The hypothesis of this book is that the space currently undergoing these transformations may be viewed as an *enriched field*, where the term *enriched* is a loose reference to the positions used to problematise the spatialisation of specific contemporary economies in the European context by Luc Boltanski and Arnaud Esquerre

(2020) in their book *Enrichment*. One must also remain aware that referring to transformation processes observed in contexts completely different from those in China is certainly a risk. It is thus important to clarify that the objective of the book is not to match processes, narratives, and outcomes with a coherent vision that perfectly fits the situation observed, but rather to find the words and images to describe and interpret what is (probably) happening. As with many interpretations, it is both rigorous and imaginative and thus cannot be considered neutral. Certain topics and themes that require further understanding and investigation are brought to the fore, while seeking to present an argument from which it is possible to further reflect on what Chinese urbanisation entails for the contemporary city, and more generally, for our way of building, living in, and perceiving cities.

Evidence for considering the Central Plains of China as an enriched field can be found in the new infrastructural systems, new housing, and new production spaces. The current expansion of infrastructure is not only equipping the entire area with a wide variety of facilities and conveniences, but is also disseminating a new type of environmental comfort that "reflect[s] China's newfound appreciation of quality over quantity" (Williams, 2017, p. 190), in turn producing an *enrichment of the environment*. Within this enhanced surface, every single artefact is rendered unique through the adoption of a specific imaginary. This is evident in the rich aesthetics of new housing which, by mixing global and local characteristics, exploits the power of symbols to produce branded living spaces. The result is an *enrichment of the everyday* that is created by the reciprocal differences between urban elements and the wide variety of unique spaces that make up the landscape. Similarly, by hybridising uses and functions, the new production sites become gigantic creative clusters capable of being performative, while exalting the latest advances in culture, technology, and art: in other words, an *enrichment of the experience*. These different forms of enrichment transform all parts of the landscape from raw space into clearly recognisable and legible places instilled with their own stories and identities. In light of this, the space of the Central Plains of China can be seen as *enriched*: in performance, materiality, and practices and, above all, in stories, images, and interpretations.

This book begins with an introductory piece discussing the three different urbanisation processes that have occurred in Europe, North America, and worldwide over the last 50 years. This helps to position the research on China's urbanisation within a broad international context, while highlighting the importance of developing new interpretations as a useful starting point for debate, for articulating broader discussions, and for further research. Following this overview, the main body of research is presented in three parts. The first is an iconographic section that explores the Central Plains of China using maps and data. The second is a diachronic narrative of the spatial transformations occurring in the Central Plains of China over the last century that focuses on the relationships between socio-economic trends, urban policies, and development planning. The final part examines how the space of the Central Plains is currently being developed and inhabited, focusing on the overlaying of infrastructural networks, the juxtaposition of different types of settlement, and the assembly of functions. These research findings help clarify the logic, structures, and features of this new space. Finally, the concluding chapter presents an interpretation that ties together current policies, the economy, and society with the transformation of the space, and highlights a path for future investigations and discussions.

To create a foundation for this book, it has been necessary to navigate between multiple disciplines, methods, and fields of inquiry. The path has been non-linear and guided by provisional findings that, while shedding light on the subject, also raised new questions that required still deeper understanding and further investigation. The displacement brought about by this research has been a great challenge, but I have been driven on by the conviction that the radicality of the Chinese city goes beyond the specifics of each observed case, and can help reveal specific characteristics of urban transformations affecting other contexts.

Therefore, my primary concern has been to trace the profound interactions between space and the ways that it is changing on the one hand, and cultural values, social imaginaries, and economic conditions on the other. These interactions are frequently elusive, and even more so in unfamiliar contexts such as China. The empirical studies conducted over the last four years through the joint research project "CeNTO—Chinese New Towns: Negotiating Citizenship and Physical Form" conducted by Politecnico di Torino, Tsinghua University (Beijing), and the École Polytechnique Fédérale de Lausanne (EPFL), which culminated in the book *The City after Chinese New Towns* published by Birkhäuser in 2019, have been vital to uncovering them. Thanks to this initiative, in January 2017 I set foot in China for the first time, spending ten days visiting several new towns, such as Zhaoqing New Area (Guangdong), Tongzhou New Town (Beijing, Hebei), and Zhengdong New District (Henan). After this initial survey, I decided to focus my research on the urbanisation processes of the Central Plains of China, a place I then explored over the course of several fieldtrips from September to December 2017 (during a three-month stay as a visiting Ph.D. at Tsinghua University in Beijing), and where I lived in April and May 2019. The gathering of data during these periods of fieldwork was demanding and involved exploring places, observing the ongoing transformations at different times, and monitoring them using photos, sketches, official documents, interviews, travel diaries, and every other method fitted to documenting what was happening. I then critically selected and processed this raw data into maps, datascapes, charts, and texts. This broad body of material blended both qualitative and quantitative information, providing an invaluable starting point for opening a discussion on the current practices of designing, modifying, and living on the land.

The following pages thus bear a striking similarity to the product of a craftsperson's labour: the sum of experiencing places, discovering as much as possible by gathering all the information yielded by every possible method, re-shaping it into new speculative materials, engaging with the literature to gain insight on the provisional findings, testing several interpretative hypotheses, and reflecting on these critically. Then, repeating the entire process over and over until a satisfactory result has been achieved.

This approach is common practice among urbanists, architects, and planners; however, in the field of urban studies, it is currently being called into question. On one hand, some claim it is too vague since it does not aim for *thick descriptions* and fails to demonstrate a comprehensive understanding of the research context. This implies that it is impossible to do "scientific" research in China unless one is Chinese or a sinologist. On the other hand, some criticise the approach for being too specific compared to *thin descriptions*, which are often used to confirm or reject global theories. In practice, the approach calls for deductive reasoning, the outcomes of which do not always fit into the pre-established categories of the mainstream discussion. While bearing this criticism in mind, such a working method does provide great advantages in terms of freedom and flexibility in conducting research. It is also helpful for avoiding a culturalist approach that all too often produces self-referential literature regarding Chinese studies. Moreover, it also supports the development of a personal reading of the phenomena observed, using all the tools available. This does not mean ignoring other theories or methods but rather enriching them with one's personal viewpoint from which it is possible to open a discussion on consolidated narratives and established models. This viewpoint must be firmly grounded in empirical research and requires great accuracy and meticulousness. For this reason, I have always measured my work not in terms of *thickness* or *thinness*, but, like any craftsperson would, in terms of precision, care, and detail.

Positioning the Field

Three Narratives

Although Chinese urbanisation has garnered increasing attention, it is not easy to frame the phenomenon within a more general body of research on contemporary urban transformations. The two contrasting readings that dominate the current literature on China do not help in this case. On the one hand, the Chinese city is regarded as a banal mix of emulations and distorted international models (Bosker et al., 2013; King, 2004; Sklair, 2006, 2006). On the other hand, Chinese urbanisation is seen as a sort of *Wunderkammer*: the result of "Chinese characteristics" that produce an accumulation of exceptions unrelated to any conventional definition of urbanity (Ebanks & Cheng, 1990; Furlong, 2021; Glaeser et al., 2017; Timberlake et al., 2014; Y. Wu et al., 2018). Both approaches, however, confine themselves to establishing how much China adheres or differs from pre-determined categories and consolidated interpretative models. Their result is "to acknowledge that Western urban theory is unsuited to narrate (and understand) Chinese cities" (Governa & Sampieri, 2020, p. 369), with little regard to the complexity of Chinese space. However, engaging with this complexity is vital, and helps us understand how to address issues that go beyond Chinese exceptionality (and, vice versa, how other contexts help us to comprehend the urbanisation processes in China).

Following this line of thought, another approach is employed: while provincialising and contextualising the research on China (Roy & Ong, 2011; Sheppard et al., 2013), the findings are also positioned within a wider genealogy of narratives which have sedimented around past urbanisation processes in other spaces. In this way, it becomes possible to form an interpretative hypothesis by recombining the similes and metaphors, ambiguities, and contrasts that arise from the interaction of different contexts. Here, a flexible and open interpretative framework emerges from studying three narratives: the formation of the middle landscape that has characterised the United States since the 1950s, the process of urban diffusion that has been taking place in Europe since the 1980s, and the emergence of logistics and infrastructure spaces from the overall globalisation of the last 30 years. As with Chinese urbanisation, these prove elusive and difficult to decipher. For instance, North American suburbanisation is often considered a "mega assemblage of urbanity [...] [where] the prefix mega- speaks to their scale, their incomprehensibility, and their resistance to be recognised as a stable or singular identity" (Thün et al., 2015, p. 2). Likewise, the European territories appear to be a jumble of heterogeneous fragments in which it is impossible to recognise any principle of rationality that may make it intelligible (Secchi, 2000). Similarly, the infrastructural space is said to be "a set of constantly evolving systems or networks, machinic assemblages which intermix categories like the biological, technical, social, economic, and so on, with the boundaries of meaning and practice between the categories always shifting" (Amin & Thrift, 2002, p. 78).

In a nutshell, no matter what the context, urbanisation processes everywhere put up stiff resistance to being described. They can, however, be carefully documented and interpreted, which helps us to construct narratives that form the foundation for a common theoretical framework for discussing the meaning of current and future transformations. This, while being conscious that the narratives of the urbanisation processes selected here stem from origins that are profoundly diverse in terms of time, place, and the imaginaries used to recount and mythologise them. However, this same diversity may prove useful in that it provides much-needed perspective by preventing the eye from catching sight of its subject too soon and allowing new prospects for research through novel interpretations.

Middle Landscape

In *International Perspectives on Suburbanization* (2011) Nicholas Phelps and Fulong Wu highlight how today's suburbanisation processes are taking place on a global scale. These centrifugal forces are turning the city inside out, creating a new space: the middle landscape. Its roots lie in the suburban expansion that has characterised North America since the post-World War II era. At that time, the middle landscape was based on precise principles: "the idea of median line between 'primitivism' and 'civilisation'" (Thomas, 2000, p. 38). The space where humanity and nature coexist in harmony, and where conflicting forces are merged into a new environment between nature and the city (Machor, 1987; Marx, 1964). Overall, the outcome is a "collective effort to live a private life" (Rowe, 1991, p. 290). Based on these principles, several North American projects theorised and built the middle landscape based on a modern pastoralism that seeks to overcome the urban–rural dichotomy through an agrarian urbanism, envisaging the entire landscape as a single ecosystem.

Modern Pastoralism. Machines in the Garden

Modern pastoralism refers to the effort to synthetise the myths of pastoral primitivism and utilitarian modernisation with a healthy, harmonious society in a way that combines the best of both city and country.[1] In North America, such aspirations led to the "suburban grand compromise" (Mozingo, 2011, p. 34). This was based on two main factors: the progressive displacement of businesses to the urban fringes, and the construction of housing developments outside of city centres that solidified race and class segregation. As a result, during the second half of the twentieth century, the American landscape evolved into an ensemble of independent cultural artefacts, including retail areas, corporate estates, and residential settlements (Easterling, 2001; Rowe, 1991; Tunnard & Pushkarev, 1964). These tame the land, operating as "machines in the garden" (Marx, 1964).

Modern pastoralism was initially driven by pastoral capitalism, causing most industrial and commercial activities to abandon overcrowded and unsafe urban centres. Supporting this decentralisation, new corporate campuses, business estates and office parks revived the myth of pastoral progressivism, "[the] civility of bucolic small towns, technological modernity in service to life-enhancing progress, and the nuclear family ensconced in material comfort" (Mozingo, 2011, p. 42). These developments were reminiscent of the imaginaries and rhetoric of the welfare capitalist factories and company towns of the previous century (Rowe, 1991). Thus, the idyll of the Lackawanna Valley painted by George Innes in the mid-eighteenth century (village, factory, and railway) found its correspondence in the General Motors Technical Centre by Eero Saarinen (suburbia, corporation, and highway) in the 1950s. This decentralisation of industries characterised North America for the entire second half of the twentieth century, to the point that by the 1990s, the suburban economy had reached critical mass (Fishman, 1990). Indeed, not just blue-collar factories, but also headquarters and companies had moved out of the city centre (Lang, 2003). Moreover, the number of suburban shopping malls exploded from 2,900 in the late 1950s to 42,048 in the 1970s, draining commercial activity from urban areas (Koolhaas, Chung, Jeffrey, et al., 2001).

The decentralisation of industries and workspaces fed suburban sprawl: "low density, scattered, urban development without systematic large-scale or regional public land-use planning" (Bruegmann, 2006, p. 18).[2] Similar to the corporate estates, this new trend exploited the rhetoric of modern pastoralism: an updated version of the great bourgeois houses in a tamed countryside (Banham & Day, 1971; Wigley, 1999). Here, the pastoral myth of the first pioneers who moved westward in search of untouched land was transmuted from the exodus from the cities into the quasi-pastoral landscape of suburbia. The spirit of modernity was to be found in the mass produced goods such as prefabricated houses and cars used to build one's own personal paradise (Hayden, 1979; Marx, 1991; Teyssot, 1999). These commodities were also the signals of a precise symbolic code, conforming each user to "appropriate cultural norms of formal and figure appearance" (Rowe, 1991, p. 105). In this way, it was ensured that suburbia was a simulacrum of genteel rusticity founded on autonomy, privacy, and segregation (Krieger, 2019; Mozingo, 2011). The situation was celebrated in pop-culture, art, and design: in the sitcoms of the 1950s (*Father Knows Best, The Donna Reed Show* or *Leave it to Beaver*), the paintings of David Hockney, and private villas designed by architects such as Philip Johnson, Frank Lloyd Wright, Pierre Coening and Craig Ellwood.

Under the influence of modern pastoralism, the American Dream took shape as an ensemble of cultural artefacts spread across a common garden: "the American lawn, [where] the entire social order is seen to rest on neatly trimmed blades of grass" (Wigley, 1999, p. 156). In other words, a collection of everyday urban materials repeated itself all across North America, without, however, forming a clear composition. This antitechnocratic order generated "[a] landscape [which] is not a scenery, it is not a political unit; it is really no more than a collection, a system of man-made spaces on the surface of the earth" (Jackson, 1984, p. 156).

Agrarian Urbanism. Overcoming the Urban–Rural Dichotomy

Based on the conviction that "grass-roots democracy has its home in the suburban town" (Tunnard & Pushkarev, 1964, p. 19), during the twentieth century, several anti-urban projects envisioned new ways of inhabiting the middle landscape. Some of the most significant were *Rush City Reformed* (1910) by Richard Neutra, *Broadacre City*

(1934–1935) by Frank Lloyd Wright, *The New Regional Pattern* (1945-1949) by Ludwig Hilberseimer, *The Linear Metropolis* (1956) by Reginald Malcolmson, and *Mesa City, Arcology* and *Arcosanti* (1959–1969) by Paolo Soleri. These scenarios promoted a type of agrarian urbanism in which city and countryside were "dissolved in favour of a third term, a proto-ecological landscape urbanism for the industrialised North American modernity" (Waldheim, 2016, p. 126).

To achieve this, each of these projects relies on mobility systems, the infrastructural network, and the organisation of open spaces to define a macro-scale structure that establishes clear relationships between individual elements and the composition as a whole. In other words, a spatial layout capable of dispersing urbanity and encompassing different environments and urban materials, guaranteeing freedom within a general order. In middle landscapes such layouts can take on different patterns: Hilberseimer's ladders, the organic forms of Soleri's cities, and even Thomas Jefferson's grid to uniformly organise the heterogenous landscapes of North America (Corner & MacLean, 2000). Despite claiming to be systems of freedom, these projects were still rooted in modernist principles. They expressed the same inherent tensions as the rationalist urban approaches attempting to guide society through the designing of physical spaces. This conviction emerges when considering one main spatial layout or infrastructure as the best way to organise an entire landscape according to specific values. A perfect example of this is the rectangular grids that organise North America, which have been deemed the perfect spatial expression of the republic's democratic imperative because they distribute power equally across space without privileging any one point above another (Cosgrove, 2000). Similarly, the mobility system has also been idealised (Banham & Day, 1971). Private cars and public freeways constitute household networks: individual micro-geographies created by the free assemblage of spaces operated by each inhabitant (Fishman, 1990). So, the North American landscapes "have a diagrammatic clarity in their constituent parts that suburban residents link together as coherent experience as they move through the suburbs by automobile" (Mozingo, 2011, p. 218).

Such claims make it clear that agrarian urbanism still focuses on the American myth of "the road" as a means of traversing and taming the vast North American landscapes. Like many projects envisaged in agrarian urbanism, these become the keystones of an all-encompassing ecological system, "a fundamental determinant of America as landscape rather than as landscapes" (Cosgrove, 2000, p. 8).

Landscape Urbanism. The Ecology as Common Ground

In the 1970s, Fordism went through a crisis, and people's unconditional faith in progress waned. The American lawn turned into *Suburbicon*: where appearances are deceiving, and everything is wild and dangerous. As in Gregory Crewdson's photographs, the machine is now broken, and the garden has taken on a hostile air. The urban elements are unable to adapt to the changes brought about by the economic crisis, and all of North America is strewn with drosscapes: industrial sites fallen into disuse, abandoned mining sites, and deserted suburban areas (Berger, 2002, 2007). The cities depopulate, and all that remains is a fractured landscape of ruins, vacant lots, and rubble. Detroit is exemplary: a city that has turned into a "'non-site' for the architect in the same sense that Certeau's dead body ceased to operate as a 'site' for the physician's attention" (Waldheim, 2016, p. 92). Landscape urbanism emerged from these ruins: a means "to absorb the shocks of the economic restructuring and to insulate urban populations from the worst social and environmental impacts of these transformations" (Waldheim, 2016, p. 69).

Landscape urbanism is based on the assumption that the city "can no longer be thought of only as a physical artefact; [...] [but as] dynamic relationships, both visible and invisible, that exist among the various domains of a larger terrain of urban as well as rural ecologies" (Mostafavi & Doherty, 2016, p. 29). The movement attempts to synthesise the natural and artificial environments into a unified metabolism in which city and countryside act as mutual infrastructure to one another. Middle landscape thus becomes a fluid and holistic ecology, organised by uncovering the identity of each place, producing new images and managing transformative processes (Corner, 2006). Different from the modernist approach, such a new paradigm emphasises the relationship patterns between the elements that compose the environment. These are considered on the basis of the dynamics that they establish within the entire ecology (Berrizbeitia, 2002; Thün et al., 2015). This caused attention to shift from the design of fixed forms and structures to the guiding of flows and processes to ensure "the irrigation of territories with potential" (Koolhaas et al., 1995, p. 969), that is, the establishment of a flexible landscape to support everchanging relationships between actors, elements, and spaces.

As a result, the middle ground is no longer perceived as a stable social construct based on a clear spatial layout and coherent symbols. On the contrary, it becomes "terra fluxus" (Corner, 2006, p. 21): a horizontal field of action open for future appropriation. Here, like the environmental work of art *Wheatfield, a Confrontation* (1982) by Agnes Denes, abandoned and undefined spaces are seen as resources to be exploited for their flexibility and ambiguity. These characteristics enable the new landscape to "engage multiple systems of signification at different scales" (Berrizbeitia, 2002, p. 125). In other words, to avoid permanent socio-political designation, allowing new collective dimensions on the basis of temporary communities. This fluid condition is a strategy to avoid tension and conflict, a means of fostering an organic landscape able to encompass all cultural attitudes. Landscape urbanism reinterprets "the middle ground as fragmented spatial capital and as an agent of transformation, as a support and a place of potential" (Viganò, 2014, p. 79).

Urban Diffusion

In parallel with the American middle landscape, a new form of urbanity emerged in Europe starting in the 1980s. It is "both urban and rural; [...] neither city nor landscape, but [...] has characteristics of both" (Sieverts, 2003, pp. 2–3). Indeed, the new European landscape appears continuous and homogenous, depolarised from main centralities yet saturated with minor centres. These conditions are primarily evident in the areas that make up the Blue Banana: the Flemish Diamond, the Ruhr, and the lower Po Valley (De Geyter, 2002; Grosjean, 2010; Sieverts, 2003). These areas are "characterised by a horizontality of infrastructure, urbanity, relationships, and by closely interlinked, co-penetrating rural/urban realms, communication, transport and economic systems" (Viganò et al., 2018, p. 1). Such horizontality supports a society of minorities, composed of a multitude of individuals no longer able to construct a grand narrative (Secchi, 1989). Thus, urban diffusion is an isotropic space, studded with mutually heterogenous fragments, whose wealth lies in the *mixité* generated by the melting pot of identities, customs, and traditions.

Isotropy. A Porous Ground

Driving across the Netherlands, Flanders, or the Ruhr, it comes as no surprise to see a ship sailing over your head. This is an area where highways pass beneath water bridges, tunnels pierce the hills, and energy pipes traverse the ocean. This thick infrastructure network connects all places, and the entire landscape is inhabited: a continuum of single-family homes, private gardens, open spaces, fields, woodlands and small towns. There is neither a centre nor a periphery, and "each and every node is equally connected to each other node" (Viganò et al., 2016, p. 35). Urban diffusion thus occurs across a homogenous and non-hierarchical expanse where the properties of the whole are evenly distributed among the parts. This is the result of two main factors.

First, there are numerous infrastructural capillaries in the dense fabric of human settlement: tiny roads, railway networks, and small canals. This allows the landscape to act as a "sponge": a space within which movement between areas occurs via percolation and osmotic exchange (Secchi & Viganò, 2014). This porous system mitigates the differences in positional values and alleviates socio-economic polarisation (Secchi, 1989). Its ubiquity helps avoid discontinuity, fracturing, and separation, that is, spatial injustice (Bianchetti, 2014; Soja, 2010).

The second factor is the frequency of open space. These public spaces act as a technical support, providing opportunities for individual and collective appropriation. Indeed, such *terrains vagues* are the space of possibility: a blank canvas deprived of all meaning and urbanity, ready to be used for different purposes (de Solà-Morales, 1995). They form a neutral and malleable landscape that mediates between different urban materials without providing a fixed sense of unity (De Geyter, 2002; Viganò, 2016). Indeed, such a substrate may host "any diversity of settlement and built form, so long as [...] [they] remain embedded as an 'archipelago' in the 'sea' of an interconnected landscape" (Sieverts, 2003, p. 9).

These isotropic systems of minor infrastructures and in-between spaces are considered key elements in shaping urban diffusion for political, ecological, and economic rationality (Sieverts, 2003; Viganò, 2016). This assumption is the foundation of works and theories such as *Il Progetto di Suolo* by Bernardo Secchi, *After-sprawl* (2002) by Xaveer De Geyter, *Zwischenstadt* (2003) by Thomas Sieverts, and *La Ville Poreuse* (2008–2009) by Bernardo Secchi and Paola Viganò. All share a common understanding of urban diffusion as a song in which greater attention is given to the pauses, to correct spacing between the notes, to providing structure and orchestrating the parts to produce a coherent melody.

Fragments. A Collection of Singularities

The isotropy of urban diffusion has its counterpart in the fragmentation that characterises the same landscape, the result of the post-Fordism economy and post-modern culture.

The economy of urban diffusion is mainly one of molecular capitalism based on self-entrepreneurship, which led many individuals to set up their own business (Bonomi, 1997). This trend exploded in countries such as Italy, where in the 1990s, under the motto "lean enterprise, fat society", the number of companies with less than 50 workers grew to make up more than 50 percent of manufacturing industries (ISTAT, 1994). This multitude of small and medium enterprises progressively modelled the land, giving rise to highly specialised productive landscapes, such as the textile cluster in Prato, the furniture cluster in Brianza, and the so-called "packaging valley" in Emilia Romagna. By establishing strong relationships with specific territories, these industries were able to exploit local cultures, traditions, and landscape imaginaries; to the point that location became an extremely important factor for the economic development of specialised manufacturing.

As with the economy, the post-modern society of urban diffusion also underwent fragmentation, something which can be clearly seen when looking at shifts in practicing and designing public and collective spaces. These no longer represent the universal values of the community, rather, they are conceived as spaces to welcome each individual's lifestyle, culture, and customs. This trend is recognisable in projects such as West 8's plan for Borneo Sporenburg (1993–2000) and BIG's Superkilen Park (2009–2012), where houses can be customised and public spaces are a means to celebrate the plurality of the inhabitants. The emphasis is placed on personal singularity rather than on the collective dimension, which leads to the progressive fragmentation of the public realm. This is indicative of the fact that urban diffusion is a space where the "do it yourself" paradigm more often than not implies "do it alone".

Such economic and cultural conditions have greatly influenced European design culture, which has regarded urban diffusion as a stratification of elements selected progressively over time: a sedimentation that turns the landscape into a palimpsest of contiguous urban materials existing side by side, even if in contradiction with each other (Corboz, 1983). These pieces of memory make up "the analogous city", that is, a city composed of different parts, each one with its own positional, representative, and symbolic values (Rossi, 1982). However, such a divided landscape is not stable. Each relic becomes the inspiration for new formal configurations through its state of undefinedness (Cattoor & De Meulder, 2011; Gregotti, 1966). This led to urban projects which act mainly through a multitude of minimal interventions, such as the plan for Barcelona (1981–1992). This urban acupuncture envisioned each European territory as a landscape that acquires its meaning within a more generalised social project, to be enhanced through light urban planning and sensitive architectures (Secchi, 1989). Based on this, urban diffusion took shape as a collection of fragments: a space whose parts have been progressively modelled to accommodate the habits and customs of each individual.

Mixité. The Ensemble of Diversities

Urban diffusion is thus a tailor-made landscape where every person contributes to the porosity of infrastructure, the dispersion of functions, and the maintenance of a widespread commons. The result is a space characterised by a constant intermingling of populations and activities.

Indeed, such a *mixitè* is radically different from those pursed in late-modernist projects which postulated the establishment of appropriate standards based on a well-balanced combination of different functions, inhabitants, and urban elements. On the contrary, the *mixitè* of urban diffusion is created by the malleability of in-between spaces. These spaces act as thresholds: places of mediation in which the "right distance" is constantly negotiated through trial and error, refusing any rigid and formal regulation. This condition is evident in urban diffusions where all places are versatile spaces that accommodate multiple functions. Houses, for instance, that are dwellings, workshops, factories, shops, and warehouses all at once. This mix, rather than suggesting peace and stability, creates spaces that must be contested and struggled for (Sennett, 2009).

However, despite being a space in constant flux, lacking coordination, filled with anachronisms, and permeated by tension, urban diffusion is also "a system which permits the widest variety of action, spaces, and connections, or as a 'menu' with the help of which its inhabitants can put together for themselves a life *à la carte*" (Sieverts, 2003, p. 71). Indeed, this atomised way of life gives rise to light and provisional aggregations of different persons who work together, step by step, to pursue a common goal (Bianchetti, 2014). In other words, while being a space of individuality, urban diffusion also allows people to converge in more complex and articulated configurations. This, without establishing lasting relationships, but recognising the fluid and flowing status as having value.

This state has been implemented in several urban projects, for instance the plan for Eindhoven (2000) by Andrea Branzi, or for Almere Oosterwold (2011) by MVRDV. These consider urban diffusion as a place for a "weak and diffuse modernity", where the overcoming of morphological constraints has led to the dissolution of the relationships between form and function (Branzi, 2006). Hence, based on a minimum of shared rules, it is possible to freely colonise each space, with people practicing their right to *habiter autrement*, that is, to stay at and be kept at a safe distance.

Infrastructures and Logistics Spaces

In the late 1980s, Jean Gottmann (1987) declared that "modern cities are better viewed not in isolation, as centres of a restricted area, but rather as part of a 'cities system', as participants in an urban network revolving in widening orbits" (p. 57). With an enormous increase in scale, this network has gone global in just a few short years and the urban agglomerations which comprised it have dissolved into what has been described as planetary urbanisation (Brenner, 2014; Castells, 1996; Soja, 2000). This has led to a global urbanism centred on the pervasiveness of new infrastructure and logistics spaces. These socio-technical forces have rewritten consolidated spatial configurations, done away with relationships of proximity, and brought about the separation and re-alignment of spaces into global networks of processing, wellbeing, and social segregation. The resulting space is characterised by clusters of specialised production, spaces regulated by standards and norms, and zones in which heterogeneous populations and urban materials are temporarily allocated to meet contingent demands.

Global Zoning. Clusters of Specialised Production

On July 2018, a decision by the Chinese government to apply a 25 percent tariff on US soybeans directly affected 362,286.6 square kilometres of American land that, over the last century, had been turned into a highly specialised landscape for the production of soy and corn.[3] This event brought to light the many areas of the planet that are now "specialised regions of production, extraction and circulation where land, energy and labour are invested in the exploration, harvesting and operationalisation of all physical and material substances that sustain contemporary urbanisation" (Katsikis, 2018, p. 43). These operational landscapes are everywhere: lithium mines in the Atacama Desert (Carlisle & Pevzner, 2019; Romero et al., 2012), massive palm oil plantations in Malaysia (Bablon et al., 2019), and great swathes of greenhouses in the Almeria (Easterling, 2002; Tout, 1990).

Such clusters of specialised production result from a pervasive infrastructure network that acts on a global scale. It turns landscape into a fungible asset, allowing the vertical fragmentation of productive activities, and their horizontal spread to seek the most suitable locations for specific manufacturing tasks (Jones & Kierzkowski, 2001). Together with trade liberalisation, new infrastructures ensure cost-effective access to all markets, promoting a new division of labour based on "the increased specialisation, internationalisation, and dispersion of production processes" (Donaghy, 2012, pp. 396–397). As a result, productive activities can freely exploit these locations based upon the best performance that is offered (Weller et al., 2017).

However, to make such global supply chains work, each territory must be organised according to the principles and the rules of logistics. These constitute "a set of instructions for an interplay between variables, [in which] design acquires some of the power and currency of a software" (Easterling, 2014, p. 80). Hence, every space has to constantly upgrade its organisation and all components to meet ever-changing requirements. This can be clearly observed in the impact of retail corporations such as Walmart, low-cost airlines such as Ryanair, or even digital platforms like Airbnb. In providing tangible and intangible infrastructures to places generally considered off the map, these networks establish "an alternative spatio-geographic indexing" (Lyster, 2016, p. 22). As a result, the landscape is transformed into an open platform.

The combination of specialised production zones and plug-and-play infrastructures results in a sort of compromise between the visions of Buckminster Fuller and Constantinos Doxiadis: a space in which an interconnected system of flow and information zones the land in order to optimise resource management (Katsikis, 2014). This new landscape claims to be ephemeral and kinetic: "a place where designing functional arrangements is more important than the construction of the architectonic body, where openness prevails over rigidity and flexibility is valued over rigor" (Mehrotra et al., 2017, p. 11). However, as highlighted in research such as the *Atlas for the End of the Word* (2017) by Richard Weller, this infrastructure-driven urbanism is anything but shapeless and evanescent. It exploits local contingencies, often affecting the land irreversibly. Hence, the space that emerges appears to be closer to the Lefebvrian space of commodities: "both abstract and concrete in character: abstract inasmuch as it has no existence save by virtue of the exchangeability of all its component parts, and concrete inasmuch as it is socially real and as such localised" (Lefebvre, 1991, pp. 341–342).

Performative Standardisation. From Landscape to Datascape

Until the end of the last century, modern infrastructure had been regarded by national governments as an instrument for ensuring territorial cohesion and standardising customs and practices (Entrikin, 1989; Goodchild, 1990). Neo-liberal agendas changed this however, and now "the monopolistic infrastructural grids start giving way to multiple, separate circuits of infrastructure which are customised to the needs of different (usually powerful) users and spaces" (Graham & Marvin, 2001, p. 100). What emerges is a splintered landscape made up of premium networked spaces in which dominant groups and powerful locations reject less powerful users and bypass fragile territories (Graham, 2000; McFarlane & Rutherford, 2008). Being part of such elitist networks means having access to the "right infrastructure", where the "right infrastructure" is the infrastructure that enables each space to meet precise performance indicators and regulations.

This condition is epitomised by the new eco-cities in the Asian region. In the UAE, Masdar Eco-City was planned as the world's first sustainable metropolitan development, designed to host the "transnational capitalist class" (Sklair, 2005). To achieve this, the new development had to comply with the requirements established in the political agenda *Vision 2030*, based upon principles established by the private consultancy company Bioregional and the World Wildlife Fund (WWF). These guidelines greatly influenced how Foster + Partners envisioned the city, as a low-rise, high-density laboratory for designing, manufacturing, and testing new technologies (Cugurullo, 2016). Similarly, the urban layout of the Sino-Singapore Tianjin Eco-City in China relies on "eco-cells" designed to suit precise size, function, and residential density criteria in order to meet

61 different performance indicators established by the national government (Caprotti, 2014; J. Liu et al., 2017; Williams, 2017).

Standards and regulations (e.g., SEED, LEED, and ISO 37120) thus actively shape contemporary spaces: they "constitute an extensive yet mundane and, to now, rather silent force of social rationalisation across the globe" (Mendel, 2006, pp. 162–163) since they "format the performance and calibration of many components of infrastructure space at every scale, from the microscopic to gigantic" (Easterling, 2014, pp. 171–172). To make this possible, the space and its components are synthesised into a set of measurable, comparable, and manageable variables (Ben-Joseph, 2005; Cantrell & Holzman, 2017; Picon & Ratti, 2019). Perfect examples of this type of datification are the recent space matrix, mixed-use index, and space syntax methods, the extensive implementation of responsive technologies, and the establishment of global city indicators to perform computational analyses of a city's performance. All these enshrine "the passage from concrete, material things to ephemeral signs—the dissolution of objects into flows of information" (Allen, 1999, p. 49). Such a process reduces urban complexity, often in order to "make ownership of the city available to those who can pay for the data" (Easterling, 2021, p. 71). However, this body of regulations is also a new site of negotiation and can be challenged through design and everyday living practices (Ebbensgaard, 2020; Simone, 2004).

This emphasises the disputed nature of contemporary infrastructural spaces, which are inhabited socio-technical systems where the hegemonic forces of standardisation and the subversion thereof vie for control (Anand et al., 2018; Coutard & Rutherford, 2015). Hence, infrastructural spaces are filled with tensions and conflicts that, above all, rely on their promises of progress, modernity, and development.

Customisable Zones. Living the Logistics Platforms

In October 2010, while the first six buildings in the Masdar Eco-City were being moved into, Sheikh Ahmed bin Saeed Al Maktoum was inaugurating the Dubai Logistics Corridor about 100 kilometres to the north-east. This oasis of global trade aims to be much more than just a series of technical spaces for handling goods and passenger transport. The 200-kilometre-wide area includes the Dubai Internet City, the Dubai Health Care City, the Dubai Maritime City, the Dubai Industrial City, the Dubai Media City, the Dubai International City, the Dubai Textile Village, and the Dubai Knowledge Village (Akhavan, 2017; Easterling, 2014). Considering that expatriates make up 99 percent of the private work force in the UAE, the Dubai Logistics Corridor is planned to be a lively space, hosting a large variety of functions, and inhabited by a heterogenous population (Cowen, 2014).

The Dubai Logistics Corridor, like other logistics zones worldwide, is emblematic in revealing how infrastructural spaces are redefining their status. Even in the late 1990s, these were still considered to be places without urbanity, nothing more than technical enclaves spread all across the world for the purpose of seamlessly integrating the global economy. Today they are regarded as composite sites that encompass an ever-wider range of activities, in other words, they are fully-fledged cities (Easterling, 2014). These new urbanities are shaped according to the rules of logistics: they are secluded spaces, internally organised to be suitable for the accommodation of different urban materials, practices, and morphologies that, eventually, can be easily replaced. The Dubai Logistics Corridor is a perfect example. Here, it is possible to rent a plot of land, starting at a minimum of 5,000 square metres for an annual fee of 10 to 30 U.S. dollars per square metre.[4] The rental fee includes access to communal facilities (road network, electricity and water, telecommunications infrastructure, and 24-hour security), and each plot is completely customisable. Hence, this space is equally suitable for a variety of uses: industrial zones, warehouses, tertiary activities, or even residential. As a result, in Dubai "the entire vision for the city resembles a computer motherboard" (Cowen, 2014, p. 172).

Zones such as the Dubai Logistics Corridor are flourishing everywhere: from the Murmansk Economic Zone above the Arctic Circle to the Suez Canal Economic Zone in the Sahara Desert. These logistics landscapes are the outcomes of an urbanism on-demand where every space is modelled based on an assemble-to-order strategy, that is, the provision of a standardised infrastructural layout within which the space is customisable to a certain extent. Hence, in such zones, infrastructure plays the role of hardware, storing and supporting the correct functioning of the different programmes which rarely interface with one another. It allows "the division, allocation and construction of surfaces; the provision of services to support future programmes; and the establishment of network of movement, communication and exchange" (Allen, 1999, p. 54). As a result, to paraphrase Noel Greis (2004), the city is no longer selling spaces with services attached, rather it is selling services with spaces attached. In other words, the city has turned into a space to be freely used at will, whose value is set by the capacity to be manipulated or modified over time. Indeed, such new urbanities are continuously evolving and require constant maintenance, reconfiguration, and upgrading (Barry, 2006). Just as they easily enable the technologically enhanced replication of landscapes, these landscapes can also be easily replaced, since no single part is indispensable to the whole. These zones are thus an updated version of the *replascapes* described by Louise Wyman (2002), where the prefix "repl-" refers to the capacity "to reply" to specific input, "to replicate" specific conditions, and (if necessary) "to replace" specific objects.

Chinese Urbanisation as an Operational Space Open to Interpretation

The three narratives presented above do not provide an exhaustive overview of the multitude of transformations and diverse forms of urbanity that characterise the contemporary urban realm. They are selective and partial, and other narratives may be admitted. However, it is not a question of numbers, nor is this an attempt to construct a comprehensive picture. What is vital here is the leverage that these narratives provide in the quest to shed light on themes and issues relevant in the ongoing urban transformations occurring both globally and in the Central Plains of China.

First, there is the discussion about commonly occurring phenomena. Above all, about the underlying tension of being torn between the fear of hypertrophic urban growth on the one hand, and the disappearance of the city on the other (Secchi, 2005). These processes of implosion/explosion are shaping new forms of urbanity by breaking down the distinctions between city and country, rewriting spatial organisations and land uses, and reshaping economies and societies (Brenner, 2014). Today, this trend is taken to the extreme by the spread of infrastructure networks, the emergence of economies of agglomeration, the international division of labour, and an unprecedented polarisation of wealth. These phenomena, which are occurring globally, are even more dramatic in China. Here, their manifestation is so extreme that it may help to better understand the spatial implications and to formulate new interpretative hypotheses.

Second, it is important to note the uniqueness of each case study. The three narratives examined above clarify how, by formulating a well-defined interpretative hypothesis, it is possible to rescale the processes observed, to rearticulate specific subjects, and to relate them to other cases, issues, and disciplinary discourses. In other words, how it is possible to overcome local specificities and establish connections between various phenomena. This helps to construct a common language for discussing the ongoing urban transformation processes across multiple fields of study. Thus, to position Chinese urbanisation within this common framework, it is necessary to find new words to interpret the reality observed, to reject a merely culturalist approach, and to question pre-established models.

Finally, the rethinking of design-oriented research is another crucial aspect. In recent years, there is a growing consensus that there are limits to the efficacy of urban and architectural projects when defining policies, directing economies, and fostering new ways of living. Bearing in mind that the role of design has changed since the positivist assumption that urban projects are the foundations of future humanity and society, the three narratives emphasise how a design-oriented approach is still fundamental to opening up new trajectories, categories, and figures. Design-oriented descriptions still have a fundamental role to play in considering the project as a hermeneutic operation of understanding and interpretation (Corner, 2014). By adopting this approach, the current processes of urbanisation, including those in China, can be regarded as operational fields that make it possible to envisage new relationships between site and programme, form, and function, and aesthetics and meaning.

Positioning Chinese urbanisation within the wider framework provided by these narratives ultimately enables us to explore the infinite number of paths, possibilities, and trajectories created by the collision, juxtaposition, and interaction of multiple interpretations. What emerges is a deep and complex system of relationships between processes occurring in different areas of the planet, the implications of which are never linear, nor easy to follow. By eschewing the simplified affirmation of every place being unique with specific characteristics to be addressed alone, it is possible to discover more about this system of reciprocal influence—while remaining aware of the risk of generalisation. As with design, all assertions can be questioned and contradicted with strong arguments, eventually opening the way to new trajectories and interpretations.

---

1 More specifically, modern pastoralism is described by Peter Rowe (1991) as third term between humanity and nature, resulting from an operation of "moral gardening": "a complex formulation of [...] the dialectic of two inherent terms that gives it its power, as well as the possibility of staring straight at the dark side of one perspective from the temporary safety of the other" (p. 247). In a similar manner, Leo Marx (1991) highlights how the pastoral myth in America is a synthesis of the anthropocentric utilitarian myth developed in the seventeenth century by Protestant migrants who considered it necessary for man to overcome nature; and the primitivist myth, developed by the Romantic thinking of the late eighteenth century, that considered nature as a moral refuge from the corruption of modern civilisation. **2** While Robert Bruegmann's (2006) definition is probably one the most common ways of defining sprawl, many other descriptions of North American suburbanisation have been provided in the last 70 years. Indeed, according to a survey conducted in 1992 at Columbia University, there were more than 200 terms used for describing American (sub)urbanisation, and many others have undoubtedly been coined since then (Lang, 2003). **3** Nowadays, soybean production is mainly concentrated in the United States (119,518,490 tons), Brazil (114,599,168 tons), and Argentina, together accounting for 80 percent of total global production. China imports more than any other country at more than 85 million tons in 2016, and the European Union imports about 19 million tons (Food and Agriculture Organization of the United Nations, 2019). **4** See http://jafza.ae/ (accessed on 15th December 2021).

Exploring the
Central Plains of China

Maps and Data

Delving into historical Google Earth imagery, one soon realises that the urbanisation process in the Central Plains of China is all-consuming. Cities that were mere pinpoints in the mid-1980s start to expand, spreading to take up the entire screen. With the same impetus, even small towns that were once barely visible become major agglomerations. New infrastructures stretch, covering the land with a web of highways, railways, and canals. Even in the mountainous areas, new dams form huge reservoirs that penetrate the valleys for kilometres. Zooming in on any area and moving across the timeline bar shows a landscape that is a constantly changing patchwork: the same site morphs from fields into villages, then into a demolition site, then workers' shacks, and today, a high-rise compound. This incredible remoulding of the landscape has occurred in parallel with radical changes in production, population, energy, and land occupation. Maps and data are thus the first step in deconstructing the transformation of the Central Plains of China.

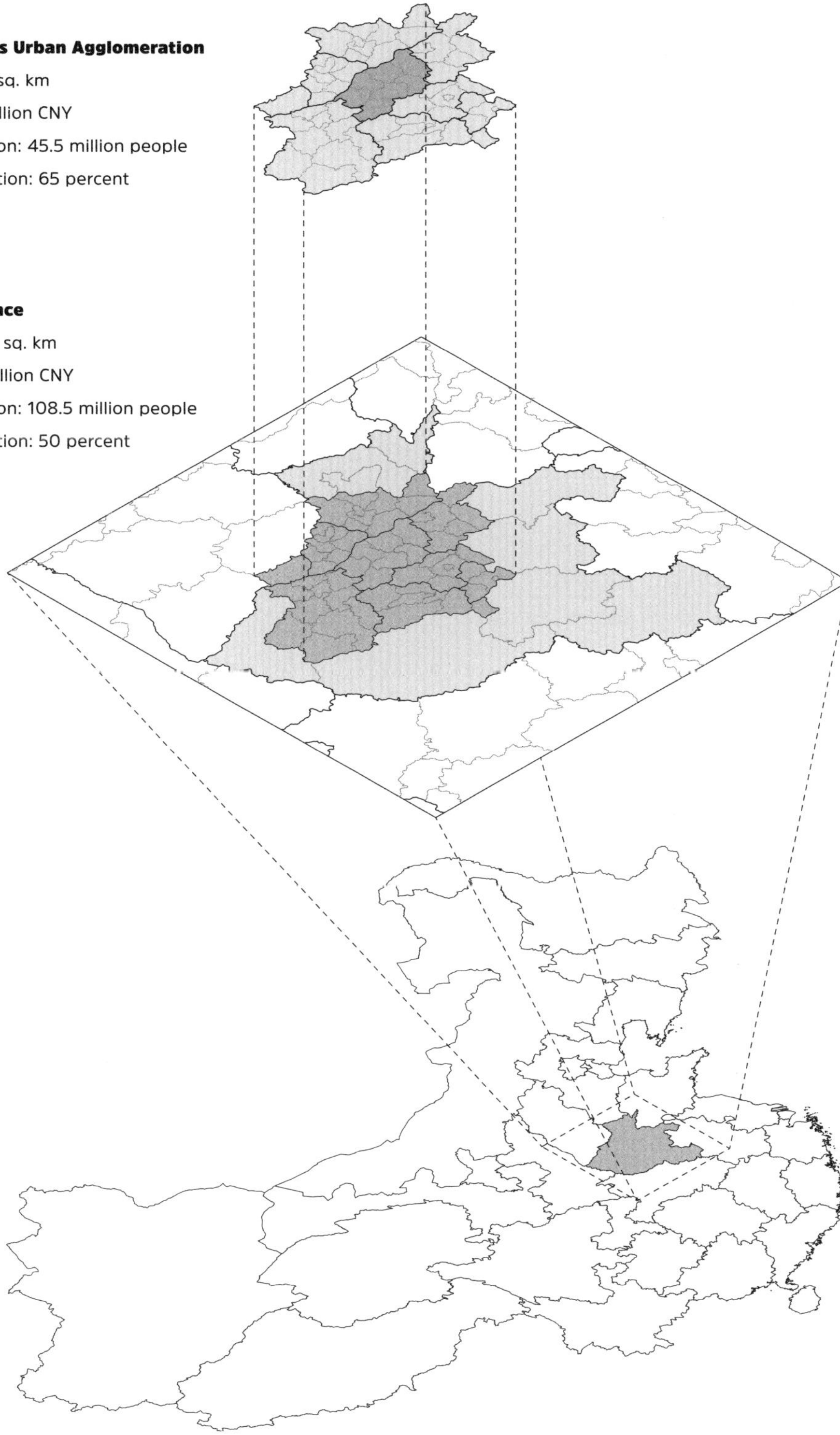

Fig. 1. China and the Central Plains.

Fig. 2. The Central Plains of China.

Administrative Divisions

Legend

- provincial borders
- municipal borders
- district and county borders
- municipality
- county
- Central Plains urban agglomeration

Graphic Scale

100 km

新乡市
Xinxiang
焦作市
Jiaozuo
济源市
Jiyuan
许昌市
Xuchang
漯河市
Luohe
郑州市
Zhengzhou
开封市
Kaifeng
南阳市
Nanyang
安阳市
Anyang
平顶山市
Pingdingshan
鹤壁市
Hebi
信阳市
Xinyang
周口市
Zhoukou
商丘市
Shangqiu
Linzhou
Taiqian
Fanxian
Puyang
Huaxian
Changyuan
Lankao
Minquan
Ningling
Suixian
Tongxu
Weishi
Xinzheng
Dengfeng
Yuzhou
Ruzhou
Fugou
Taikang
Zhecheng
Xiayi
Yongcheng
Luyi
Dancheng
Shangshui
Xiping
Shangcai
Xiangcheng
Shenqiu
Fangcheng
Wugang
Biyang
Tanghe
Tongbai
Xincai
Zhengyang
Xixian
Huaibin
Huangchuan
Gushi
Guangshan
Shangcheng
Xinxian

Fig. 3. The Central Plains of China.

Urban Areas

Legend

infrastructure network

built-up areas

elevation

Graphic Scale

100 km

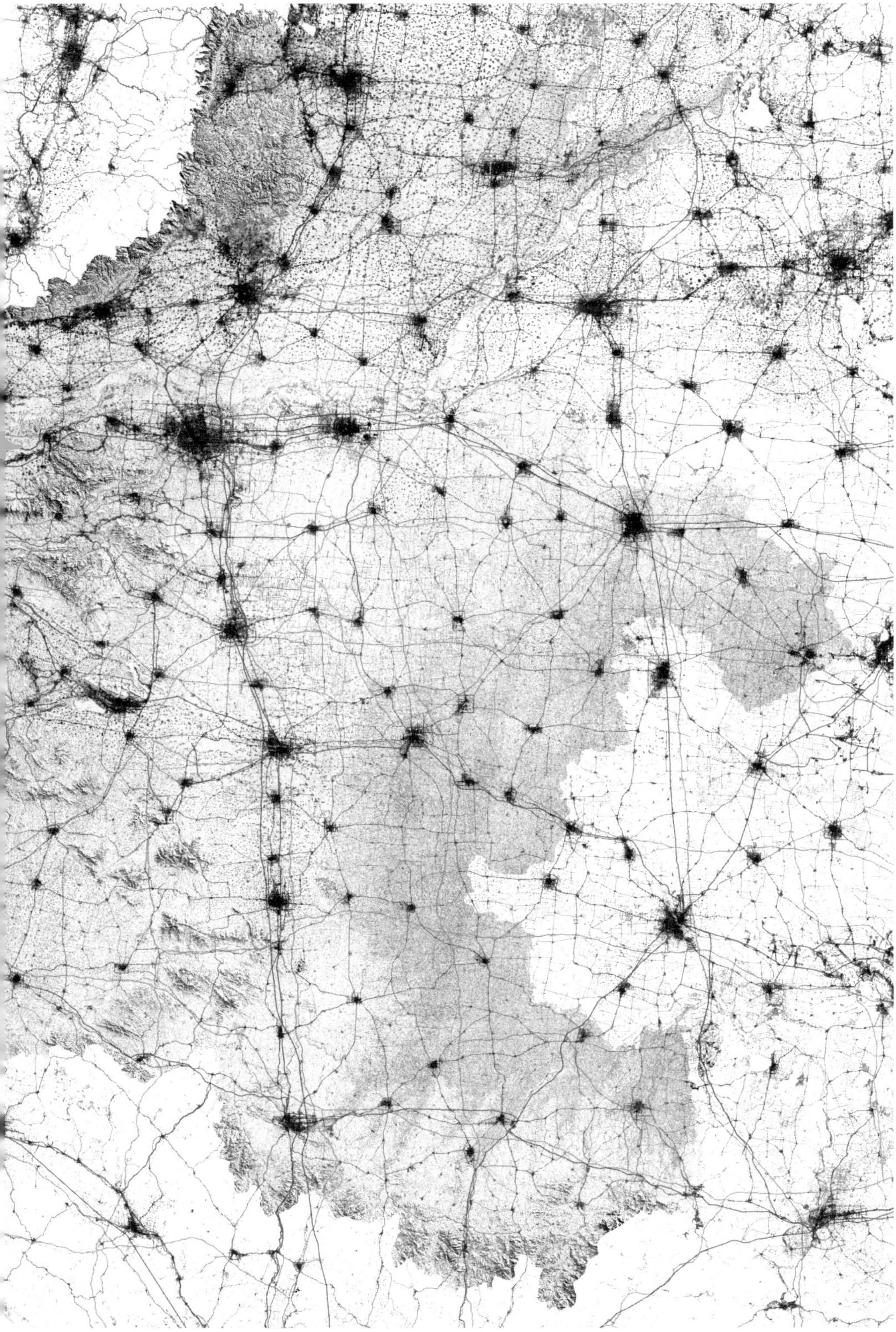

Fig. 4. Urban and rural population per municipality.

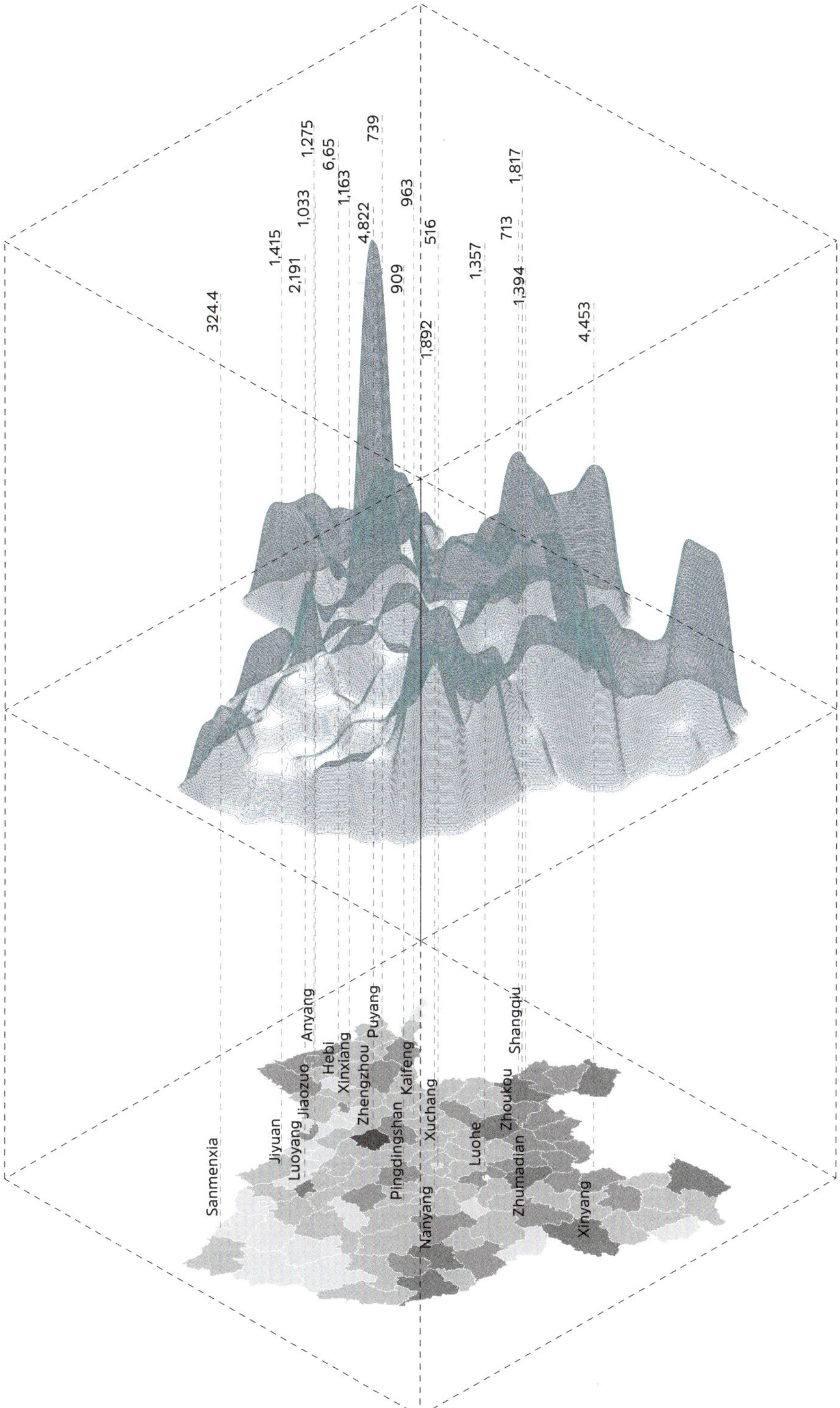

Fig. 5. Population per county in thousands of people.

Fig. 6. The Central Plains of China.

Urban Expansion and Areas Under Construction

Legend

waterways and river basins

infrastructure network

major urban centres

new districts and new areas

new urbanisations

elevation

Graphic Scale

100 km

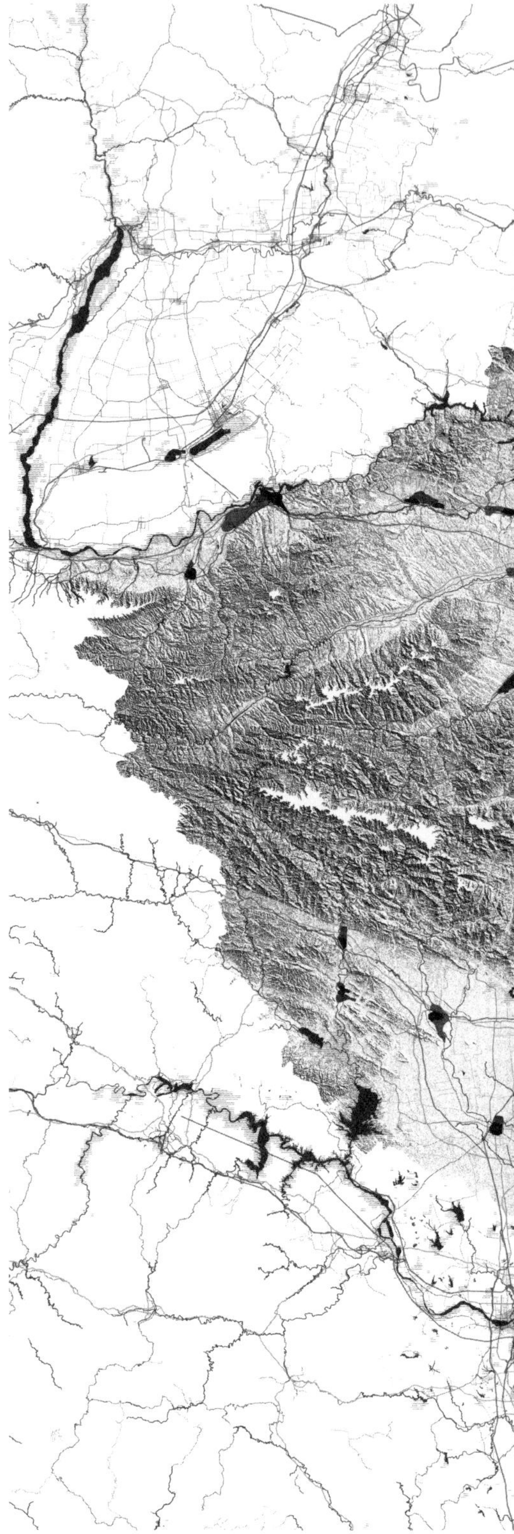

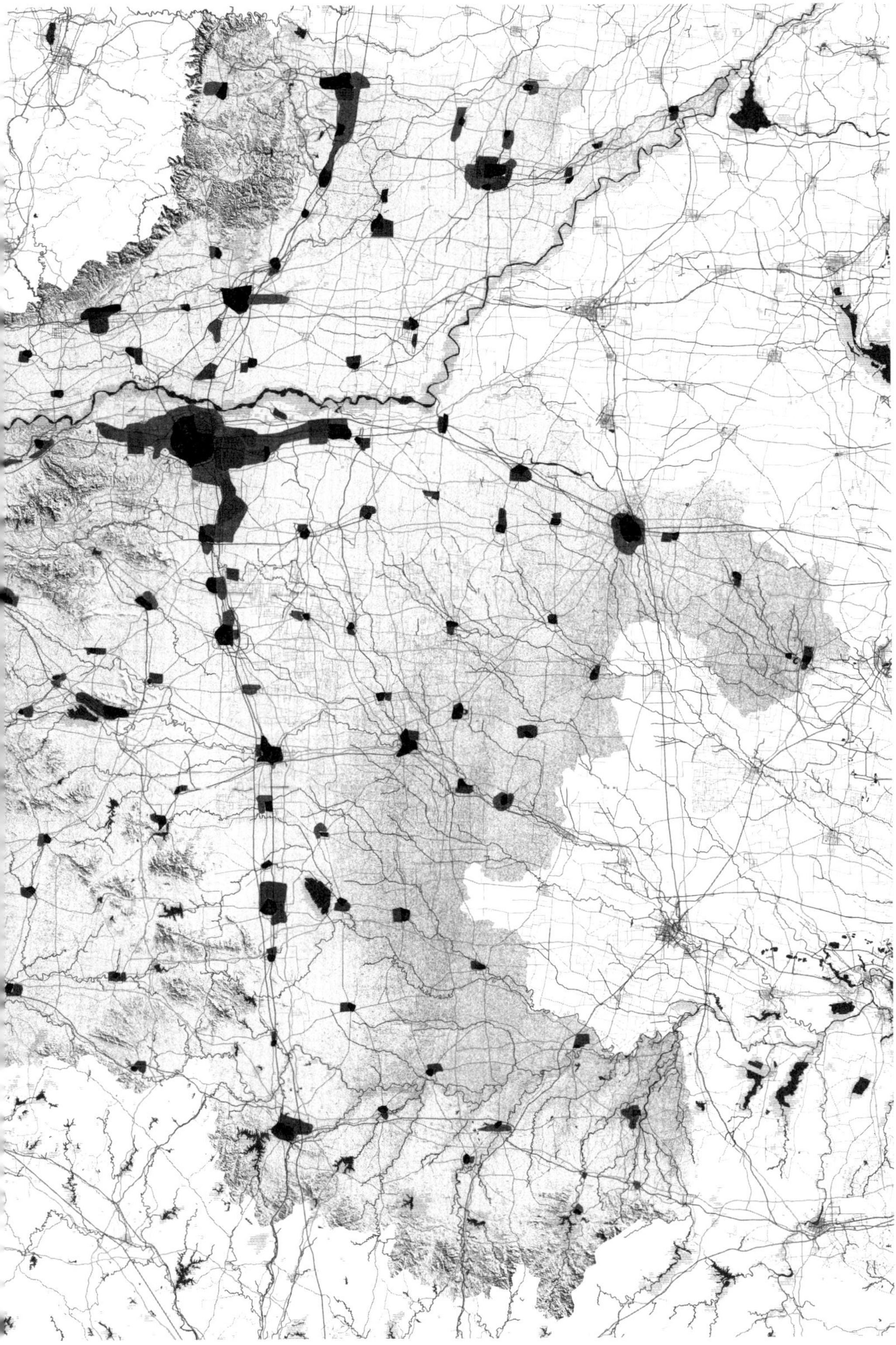

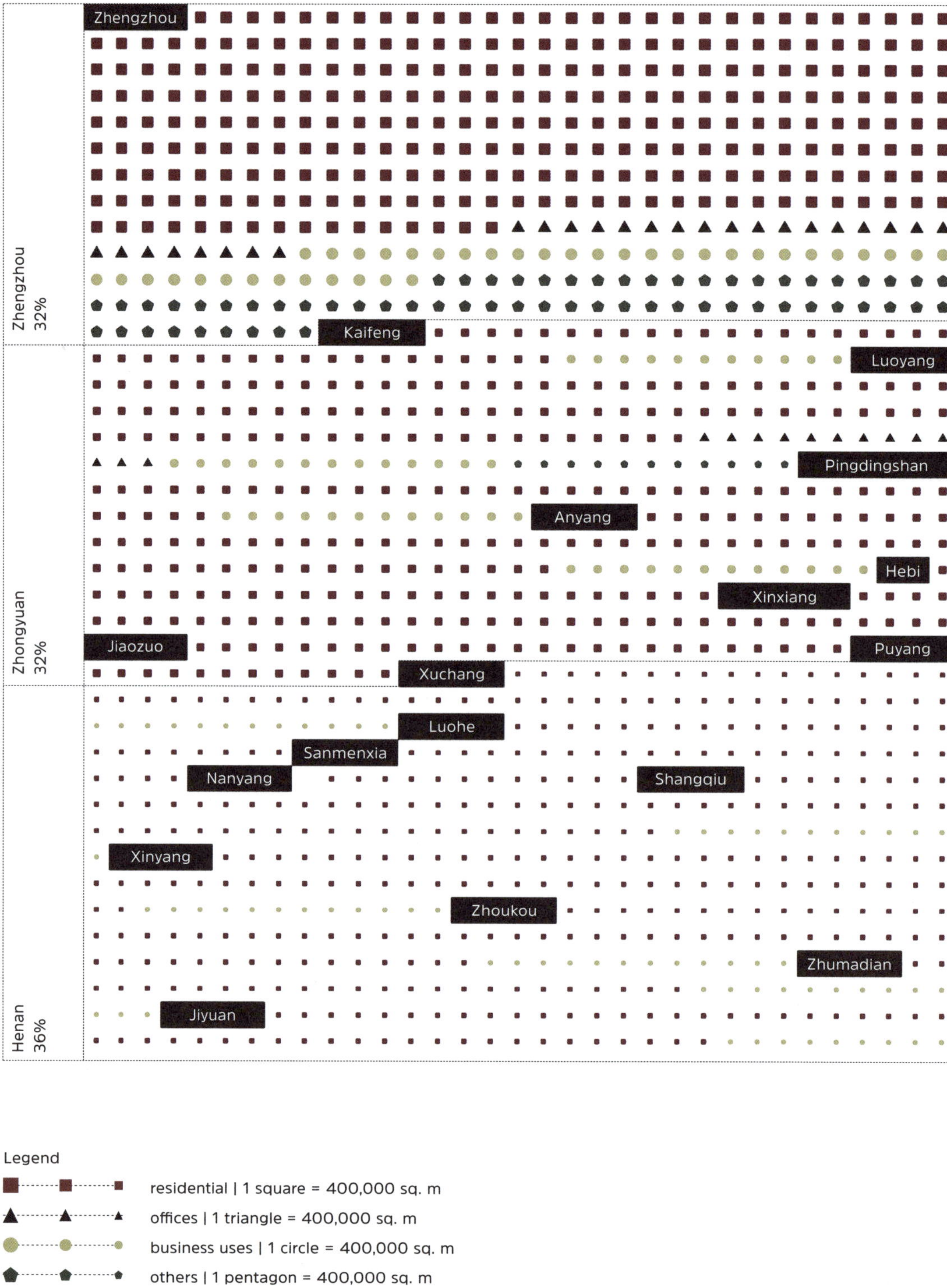

Fig. 7. Floor space of buildings under construction per city.

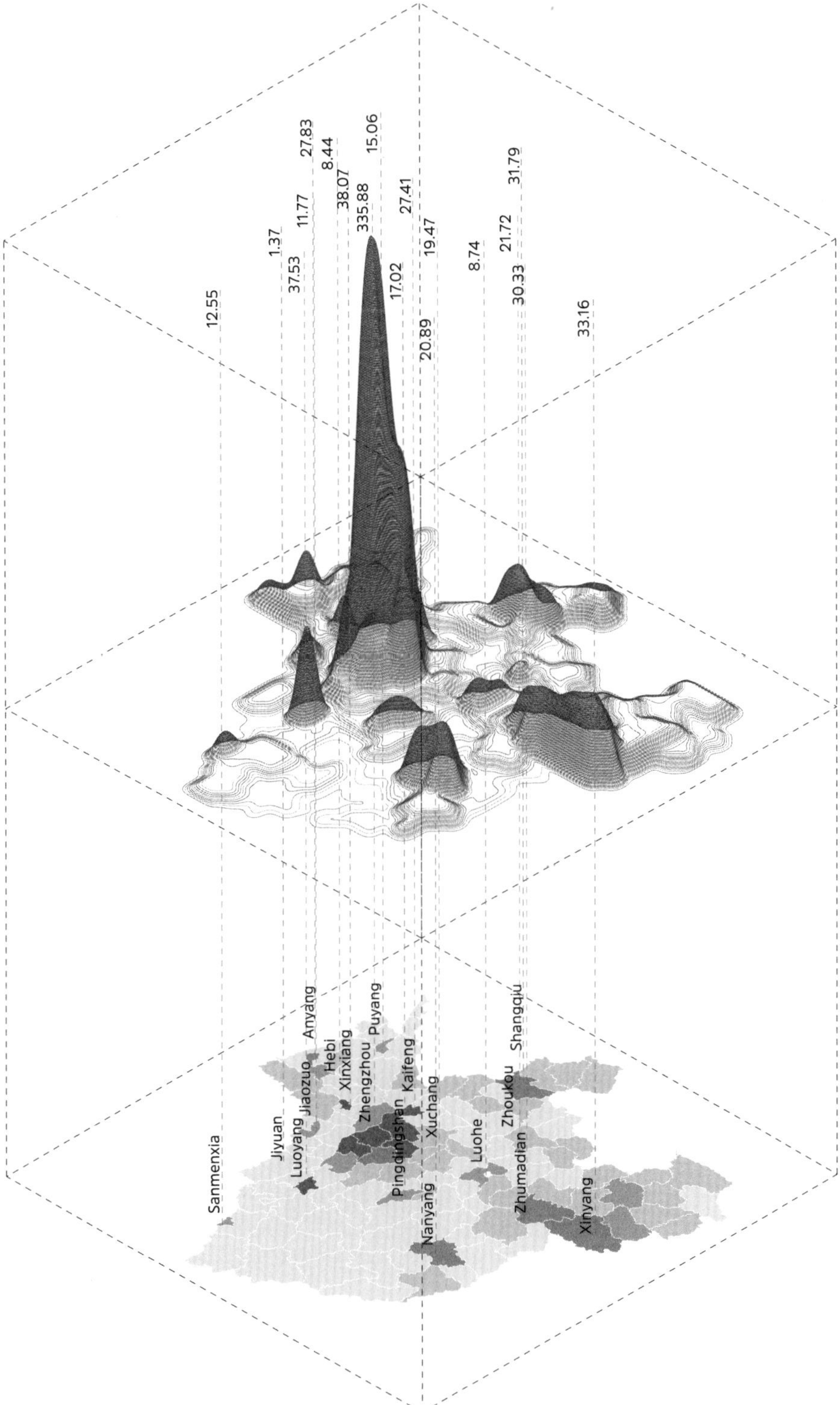

Fig. 8. Real estate investments per county in billions of CNY.

Fig. 9. The Central Plains of China.

Infrastructure and Energy Network

Legend

waterways and river basins

major road network

minor road network

railway network and stations

water reserves and dams

orography

airports

Graphic Scale

100 km

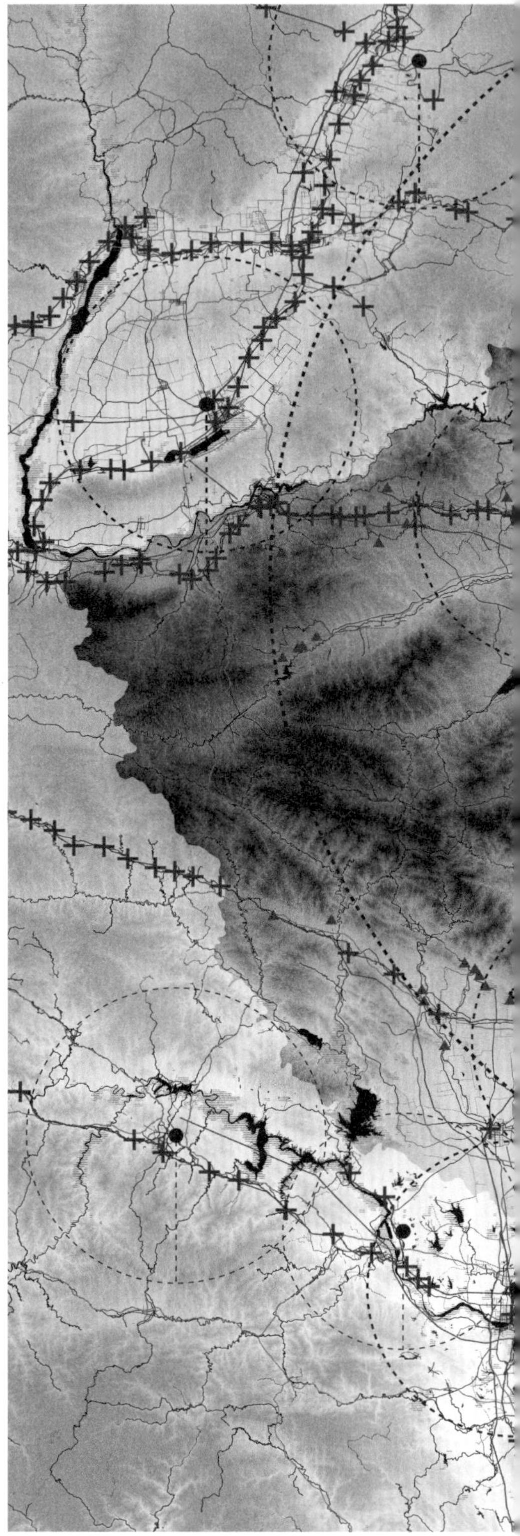

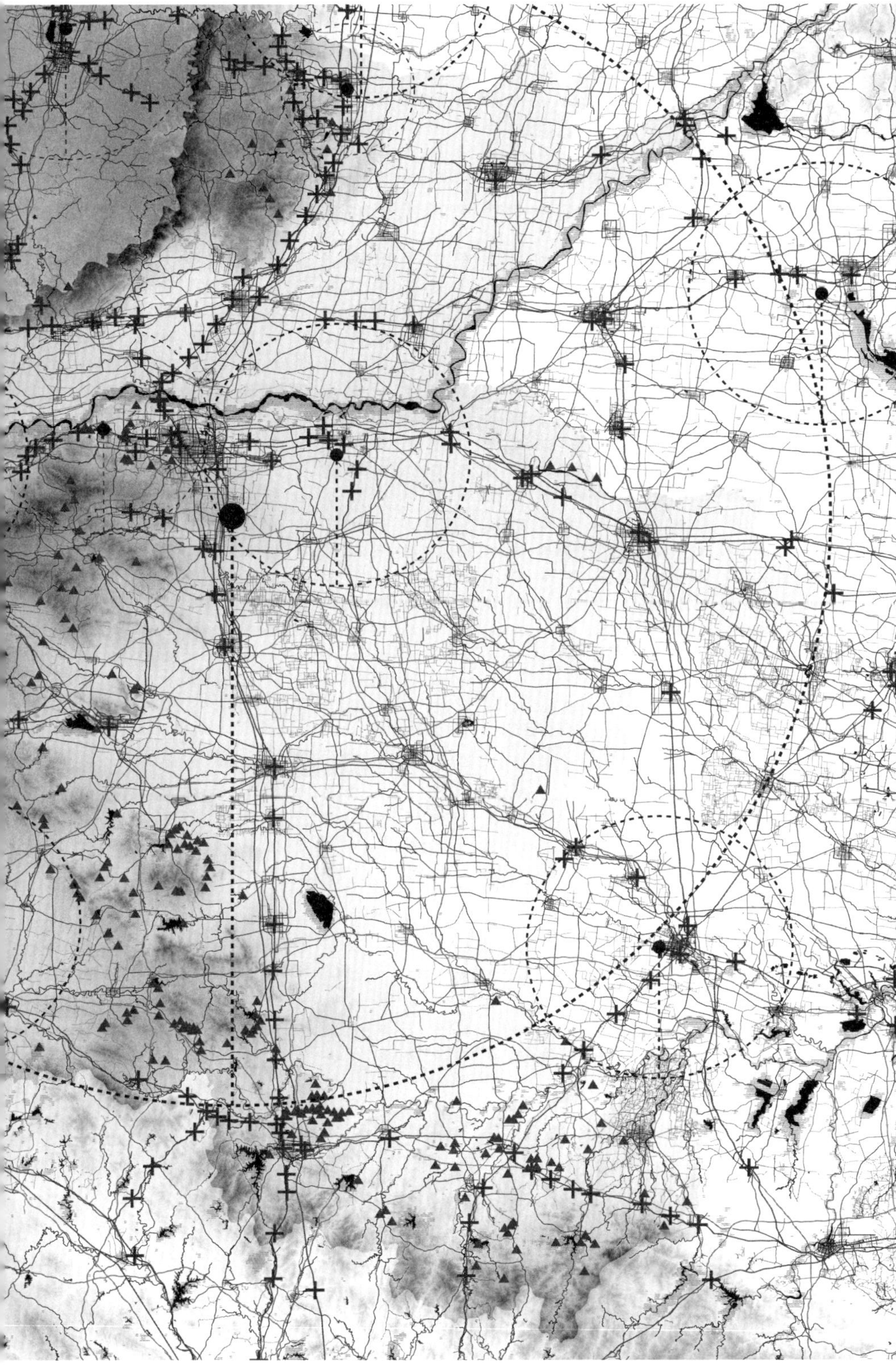

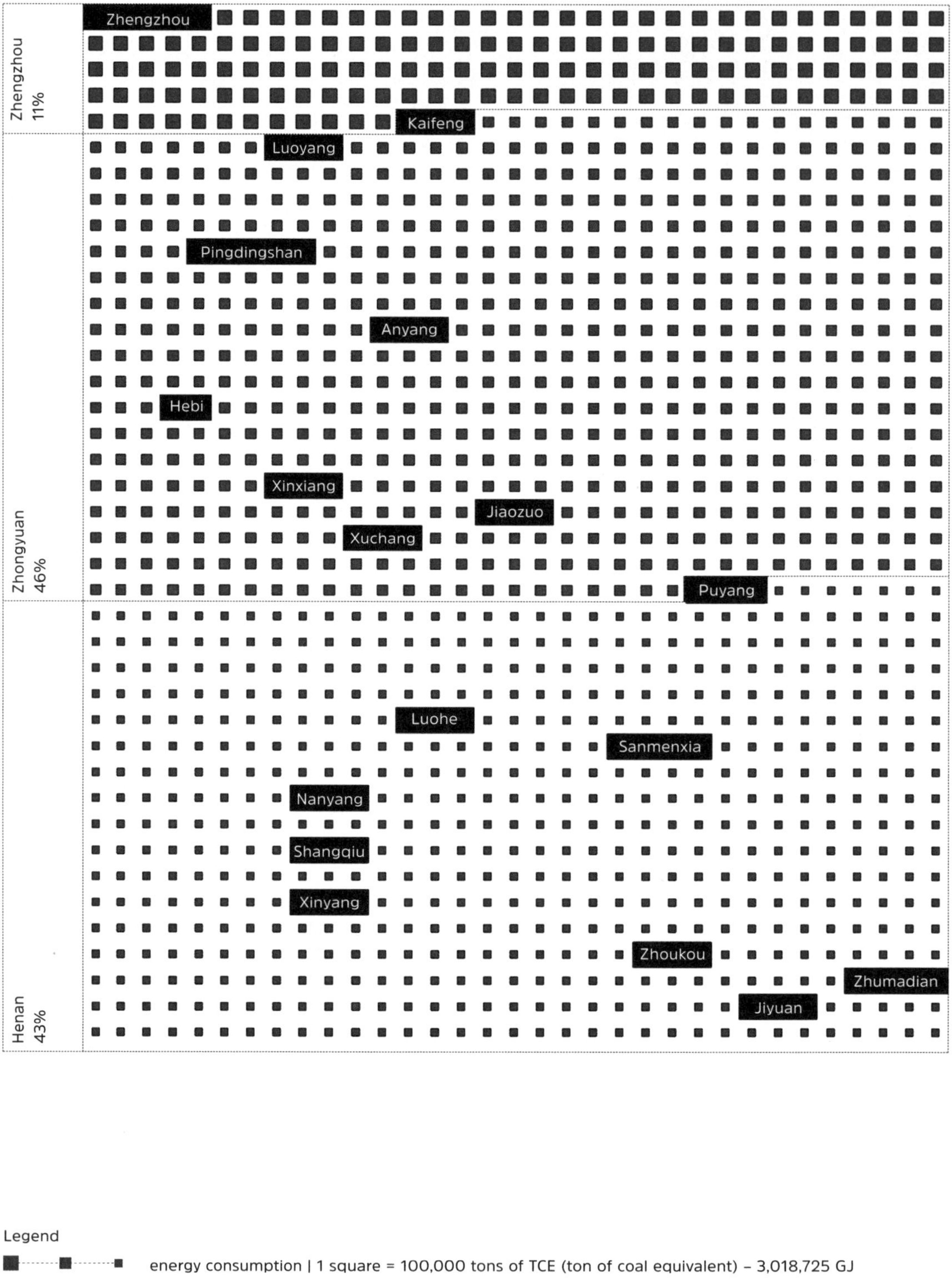

Fig. 10. Energy consumption per city.

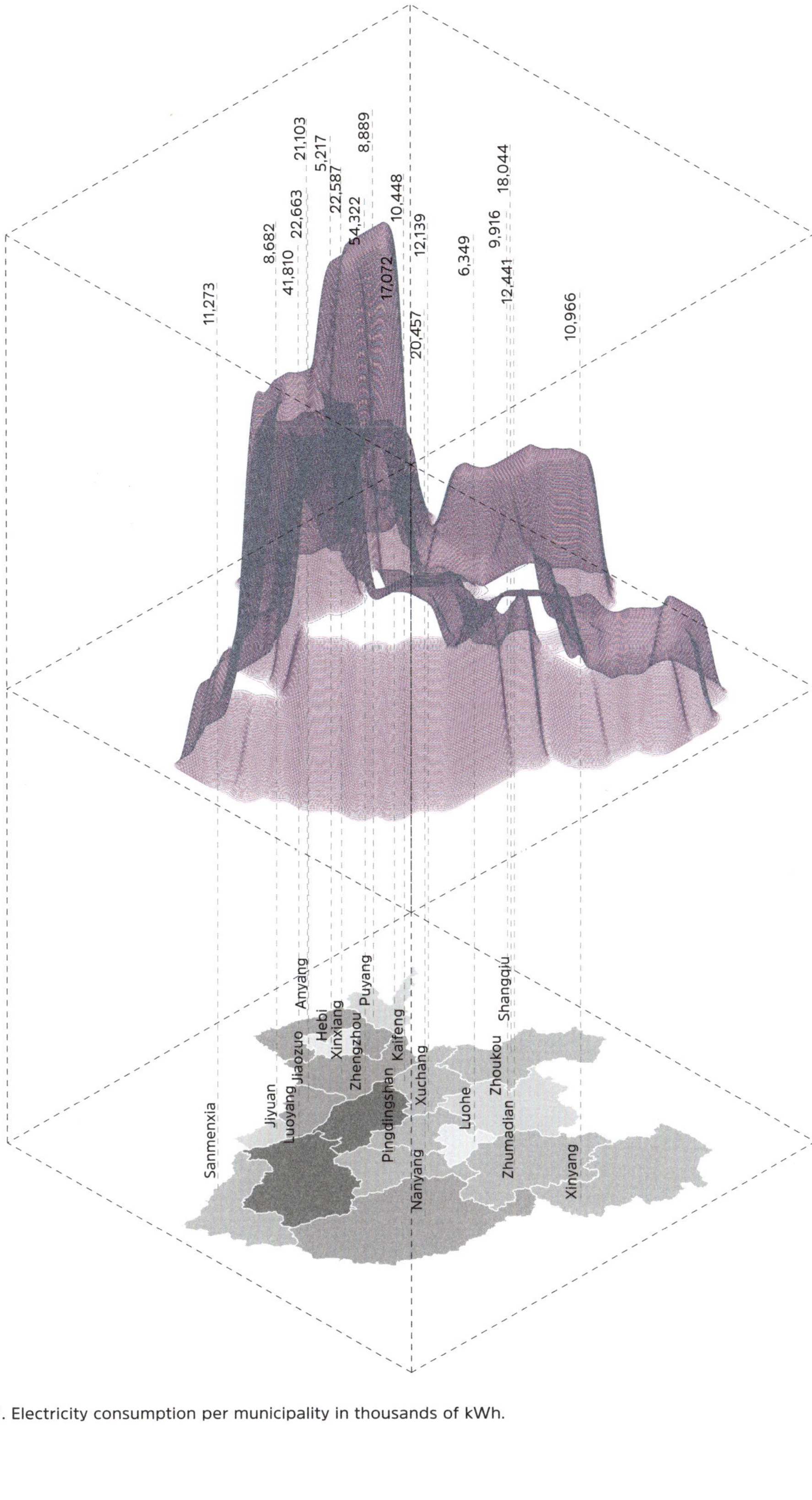

Fig. 11. Electricity consumption per municipality in thousands of kWh.

Fig. 12. The Central Plains of China.

Agricultural Land and Vegetation

Legend

- waterways and river basins
- mountainous areas
- forests
- meadows and shrubs
- crops and arable land

Graphic Scale

100 km

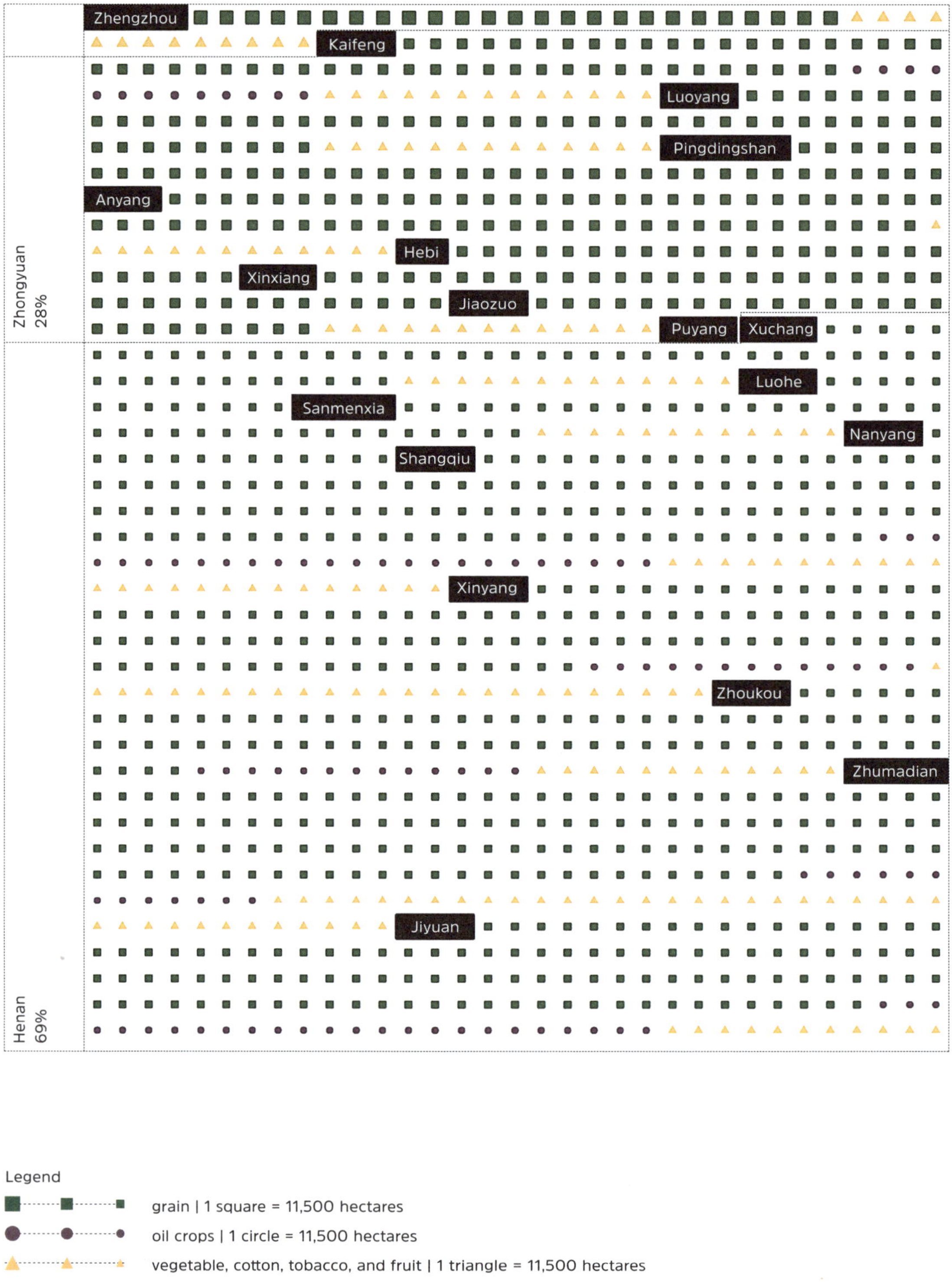

Fig. 13. Cultivated area per municipality.

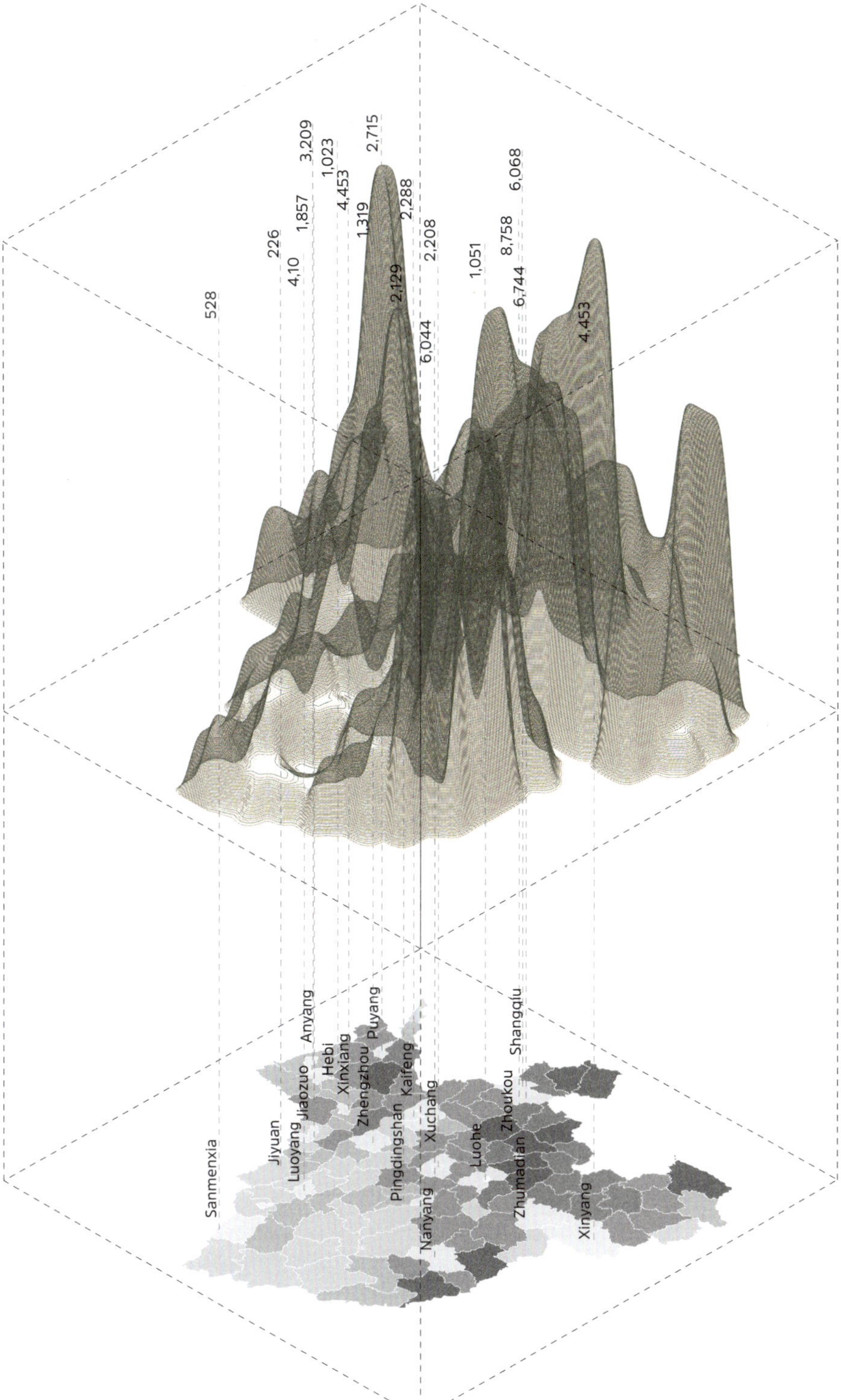

Fig. 14. Grain production per county in thousands of tons.

Fig. 15. The Central Plains of China.

Industrial Areas

Legend

waterways and river basins

infrastructure network

industrial zones

main urban centres

elevation

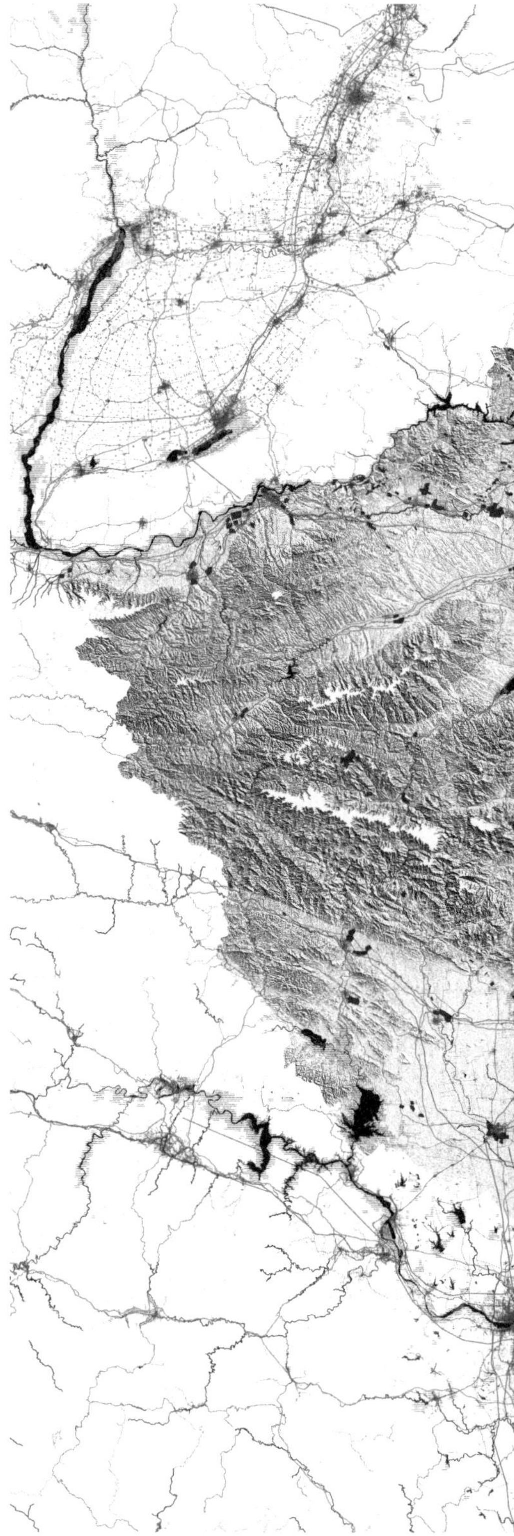

Graphic Scale

100 km

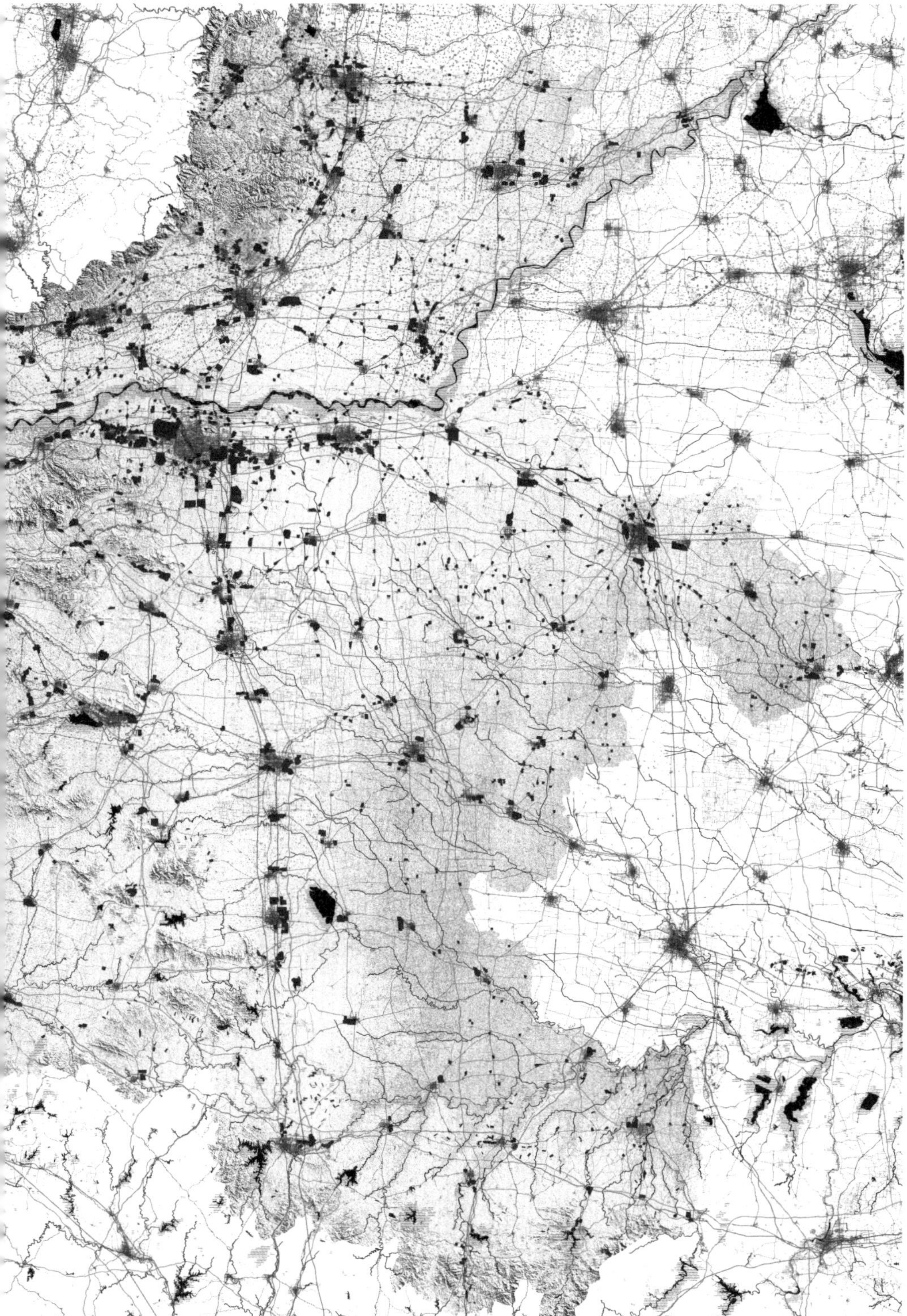

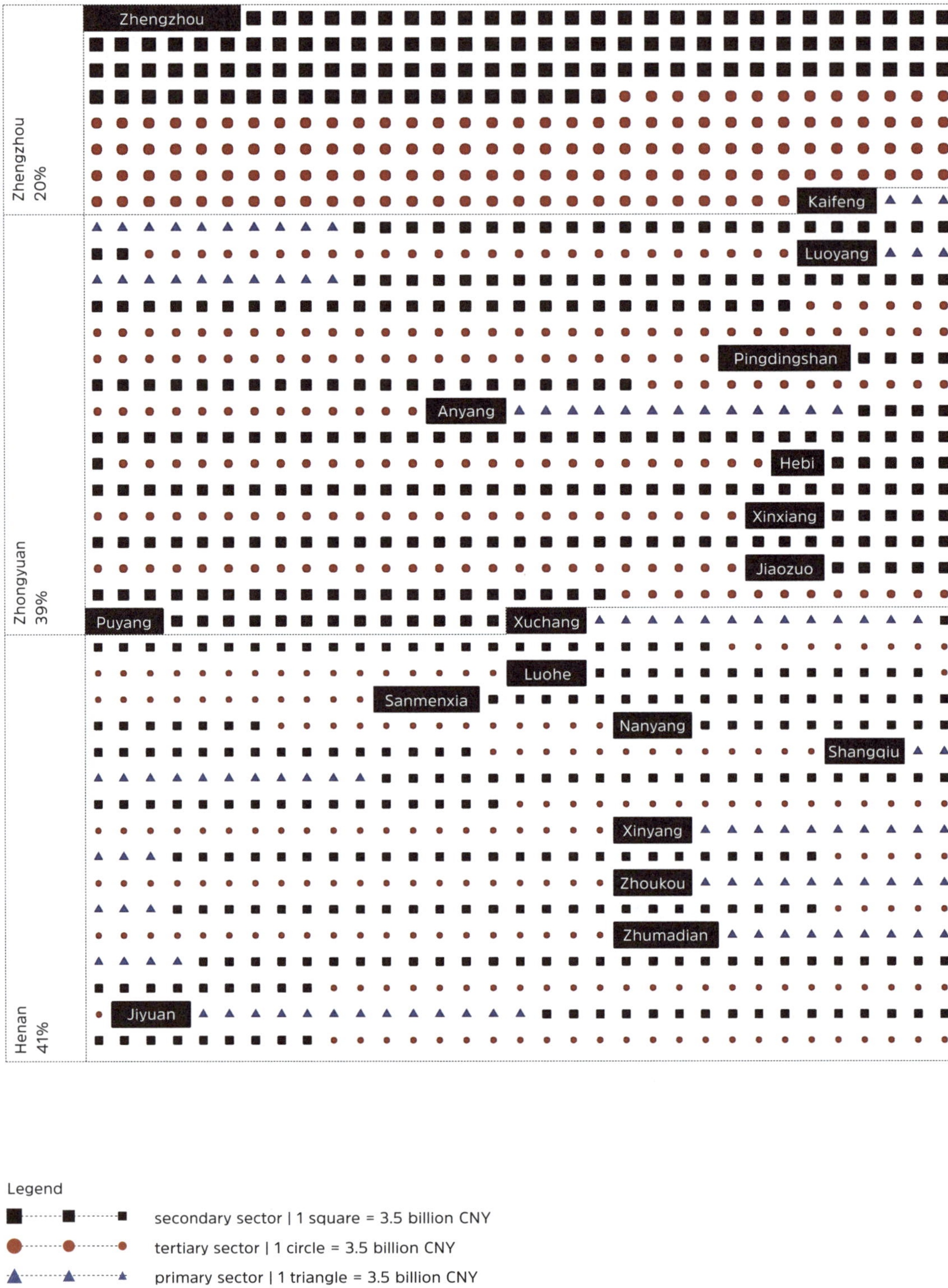

Fig. 16. Gross domestic product per city.

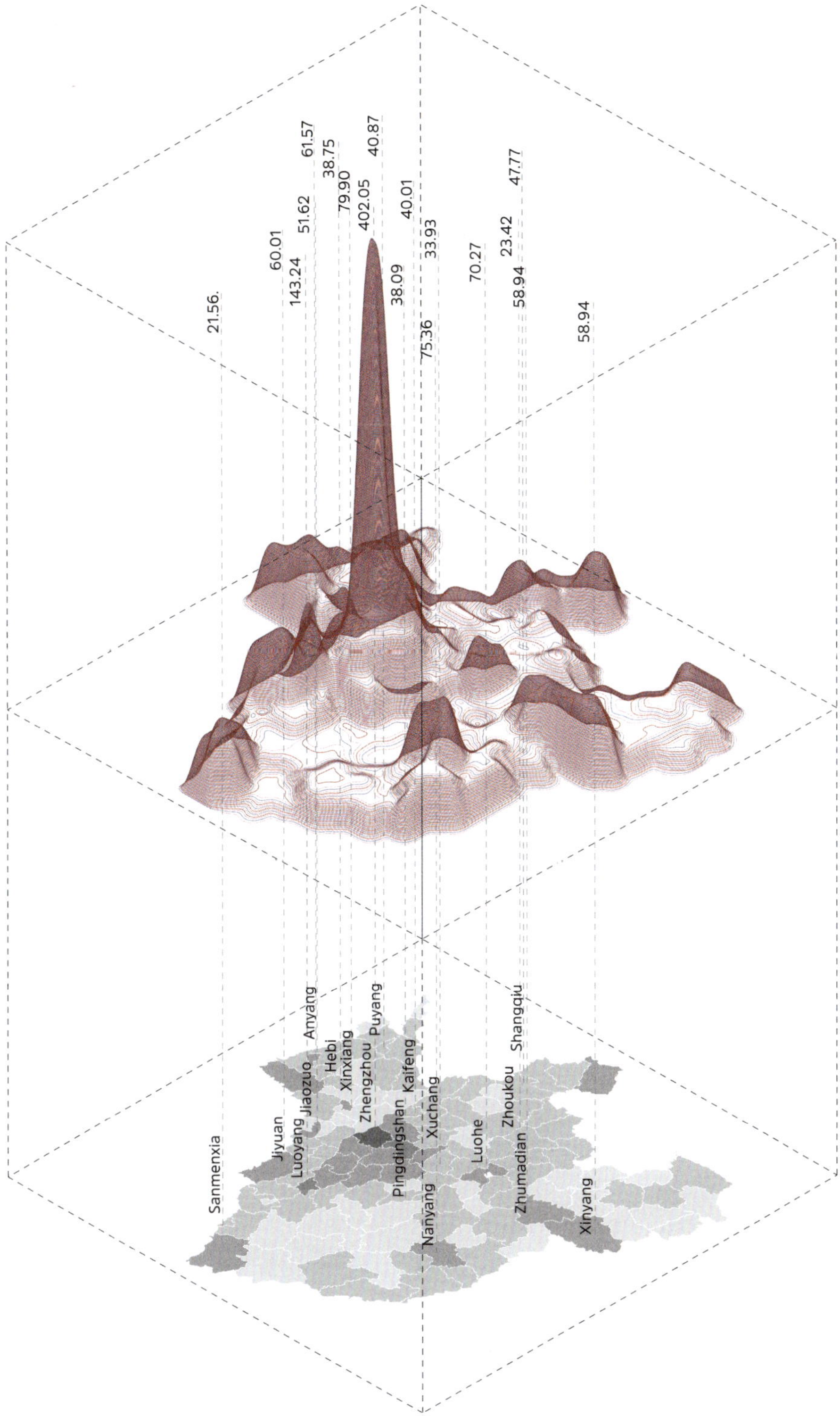

Fig. 17. Gross domestic product per county in billions of CNY.

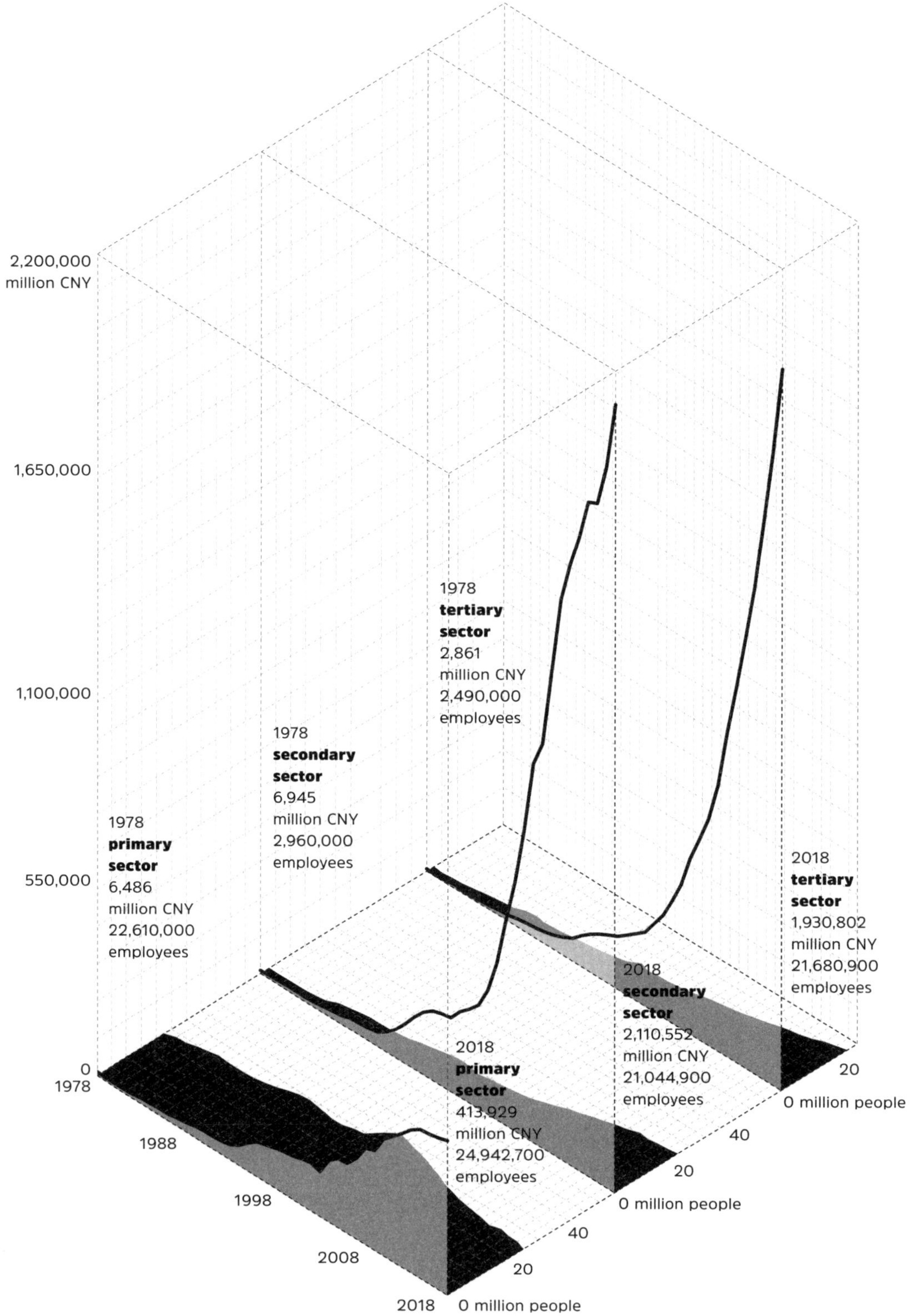

Fig. 18. Henan province workforce and GDP per sector over time.

Policies, Plans, and Projects

A photo exhibition on the top floor of the Erqi Memorial Tower documents the surroundings over the decades. In the 1970s, the structure towered over a neighbourhood of low courtyard houses immersed in lush vegetation. In the 1990s, it stood at the centre of a huge crossroads looking down on the frenzied activity of excavators, cranes, and multi-storey buildings under construction. Finally, in the 2010s, the monument itself is dwarfed by commercial buildings, hotels, and gigantic billboards lit up by colourful lights. These pictures sum up the radical transformations that have characterised the Central Plains of China since the last century. From the early 1900s to the late 1980s, the modernisation policies undertaken by the republican and socialist administrations strengthened the infrastructural networks, in turn boosting commerce and driving industrial production in major cities such as Zhengzhou. The same municipalities were also at the core of urban entrepreneurialism in the 1990s, which led to a centripetal urbanisation by establishing free zones, new towns, and new districts like Zhengdong. In contrast, starting in the mid-2000s, a centrifugal urbanisation took hold, which is now reorganising the entire landscape by spreading urbanisation through huge polyform urbanities, such as Zhengbian.

Zhengzhou. Building the Chinese Modern City

Historically, China was an agrarian society with the majority of the population living in rural areas and an economy based on agriculture (Kirkby, 1985; Kuhn, 2002). Chinese cities were chiefly consumer-oriented administrative centres, their authority based upon political and military power, rather than commerce and industry (Haiyan & Stapleton, 2006; Skinner, 1977). If not for the Opium Wars, China would have continued to reject foreign trade. However, that event, followed by the construction of an infrastructural network, fostered interregional integration and boosted commercial activity (Ren, 2013). Canal cities, treaty port cities, and railway cities flourished along these commercial routes, spurring local governments to commence planning. These, influenced by the garden city movement and other modern theories, led to a polynuclear development based on organic urban patterns and low-density settlements (Cody, 1996). However, the wars of the 1930s and the Japanese occupation interrupted this urban growth, preventing the implementation of most of the plans from that period.

After the establishment of the People's Republic of China, planning activities regained momentum. From 1945 onward, industrialisation policies sought to transform the major cities from "centres of consumption" to "centres of production" (Lo, 1980). With the financial support of the Soviet Union in the early 1950s, the central administration promoted 156 key industrial projects. These were based on large stated-owned enterprises that, by providing infrastructure and services to their workers, were more influential than local governments in the urban and economic development of the cities. This, however, led to disorderly urban growth. The Urban Construction Committee was established in 1953 to counteract this trend, and several Soviet experts were asked to collaborate in planning activities. This cooperation resulted in a decentralised industrial development based on satellite towns, the implementation of cellular urbanism through the construction of independent *danwei* (work units), and the adoption of socialist monumentality to celebrate workplaces and public institutions (Bonino & De Pieri, 2015; Fisher, 1962; Liang, 2014). Such operations were at the core of numerous plans drafted both for minor centres (such as Zhengzhou and Luoyang) and major cities (such as Beijing and Shanghai).[1]

Despite these initiatives, the industrialisation campaign did not achieve the desired results. Consequently, the second Five-Year Plan (FYP) (1958–1962) and the Great Leap Forward (1958–1961) rejected the Soviet model of development in favour of an agropolitan strategy that fostered industrialisation without urbanisation. Instead of siting heavy industries in large cities, this policy promoted economies based on light industry in small to medium-sized centres (Craciun, 2001; Su, 2009). This was behind the establishment of 26,425 communes, encompassing more than 98 percent of the 122 million rural households in the country (Knapp, 1992). The successive FYPs (1966–1975) exacerbated this anti-urban bias, which had been at the core of the Third Front Movement (1964–1978) to decentralise major industries into the mountainous and desert areas of China. Furthermore, several policies to restrict urban growth and to stem migration from rural to urban areas were adopted, above all, the establishment of the *hukou* (household registration system) (F.-L. Wang, 2005).[2] The Cultural Revolution (1966–1976) added to this trend and during that period all planning activities were progressively abandoned. As a result, by 1976, the number of cities and towns had decreased to 169 and 2,902 respectively, and the urbanisation level (i.e., the percentage of the population living in cities) had dropped to 17 percent (China National Bureau of Statistics, 2020).

The planning institutions were finally re-established in the early 1980s. Just after the economic reform, China was characterised by rural industrialisation resulting from fiscal decentralisation, institutional reforms, and overseas investment (Gonghao & Ma, 1999). This led to a grassroots urbanisation that was based on the local-government corporatism of small-scale production clusters known as Towns and Village Enterprises (TVEs) (Oi, 1992).[3] Due to their economic performance, these clusters were supported by the central government, which fostered the development of medium-

Fig. 1. Farmers in Zhengzhou, 1960.

sized and small townships and restricted the growth of large cities. Hence, most of the planning activities in the 1980s attempted to curb the development of the major centres, whereas the expansion of small and medium towns remained mostly unplanned. In spite of this, the urbanisation level rose to 24 percent, or 9,140 towns and 324 cities, by 1985 (China National Bureau of Statistics, 2020).

This brief overview is relevant to understanding how the Central Plains of China was shaped by changing concepts across successive time periods. These greatly influenced the entire area and, above all, the city of Zhengzhou. Zhengzhou was developed as a major inland trading port in the republican era, then as a major industrial centre in the socialist period, and finally, as a major infrastructural hub for inland China.

Fig. 2. Bridge on the Yellow River, Zhengzhou, 1960.

The Republican Plans. Building the Inland Trading Port

Although Zhengzhou was founded in ancient times,[4] at the end of the nineteenth century it was only a minor centre with 20,000 inhabitants spread across 2 square kilometres (Cao, 2019; Y. Liu, 1988). This changed in 1905, when the Qing administration built the Beijing–Hankou and Lianyungang–Lanzhou railways. The two lines connected China along the north–south and east–west axes respectively, intersecting in Zhengzhou. As a result, the city developed into the largest marshalling yard of the National Railway Administration and the most important hub of the Chinese cotton supply chain (Busquets & Yang, 2019).[5] In just a decade, the population increased threefold, and numerous trading companies and textile factories were established. This led to a disorderly urban expansion along the railway infrastructure of more than 3 square kilometres (C. Zhang, 2007; Zhu, 2012). To bring order to this development, the Zhengzhou municipality drew up the *Zhengbu Design Plan* (1927) and the *Plan for Zhengzhou New Urban Construction Area* (1928).

The *Zhengbu Design Plan* aimed to reconfigure the uncontrolled development east of the railway lines by urbanising an area of 10.5 square kilometres to host 250,000 inhabitants. The proposal adopted a radial layout spreading northward from the station. Within this circular pattern of roads, the area was supposed to be the site of commercial, cultural, and residential facilities necessary for improving trading activities and the inhabitants' living conditions. The *Plan for Zhengzhou New Urban Construction Area* strove to develop a new town over 35 square kilometres west of the railways to accommodate 200,000 inhabitants (Y. Liu, 1988). Based on a grid layout, the plan envisaged a low-density urbanisation with commercial and industrial activities near the railways, residential areas in the western section, and cultural and recreational facilities to the north. These were to be connected by a system of large parks spreading from the centre to each corner of the new town. The combination of the two plans would have led to a massive urbanisation of over 47.7 square kilometres that would have been the home of 450,000 inhabitants. Zhengzhou was to have three separate, but interdependent, nuclei: the ancient city, the trading port, and the new town.

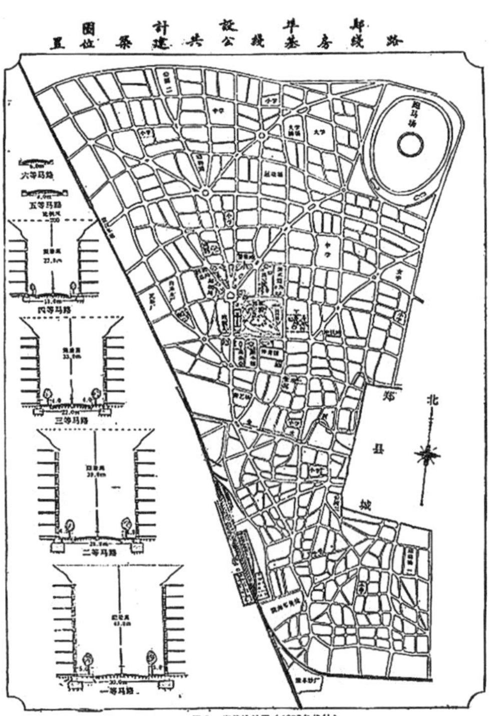

Fig. 3. *Zhengbu Design Plan*, 1927.

Despite these municipal efforts, the proposals never came to fruition. Over the following decade, the Central

Plains War caused an economic and demographic crisis that greatly affected the main urban centres, while the western extension of the railway lines resulted in the relocation of numerous cotton factories (C. Zhang, 2007). The Japanese occupation worsened the situation. A strategic railway junction, the area was bombed and occupied several times. Numerous key infrastructures were destroyed, causing enormous damage to agriculture, industrial production, and commercial activities. The situation did not stabilise until after World War II, when Zhengzhou municipality established the Revitalization Planning Steering Committee tasked with drawing up the *Preliminary Planning of Zhengzhou City* (1947) for reconstructing and maintaining the existing facilities, while offering affordable housing to cope with the shortage. Furthermore, when reorganising the urban fabric, the plan also promoted the construction of open spaces and large boulevards to facilitate evacuation in case of future conflicts. However, because of financial constraints and weak authorities, even this plan was only partially implemented (Y. Liu, 1988).

The planning activities that characterised Zhengzhou during the republican period are exemplary of the initiatives carried out across the Central Plains of China. Kaifeng, the provincial capital at that time, experienced similar developments. Influenced by the modernist approach, a plan to organise the city into three nuclei was drafted in 1928: the historic centre, the new town south of the railways, and the trading port close to the station. This layout was adopted in several cities where urban development was driven by railway networks boosting commerce. Outside of these major centres, the Central Plains largely remained a constellation of small agricultural villages.

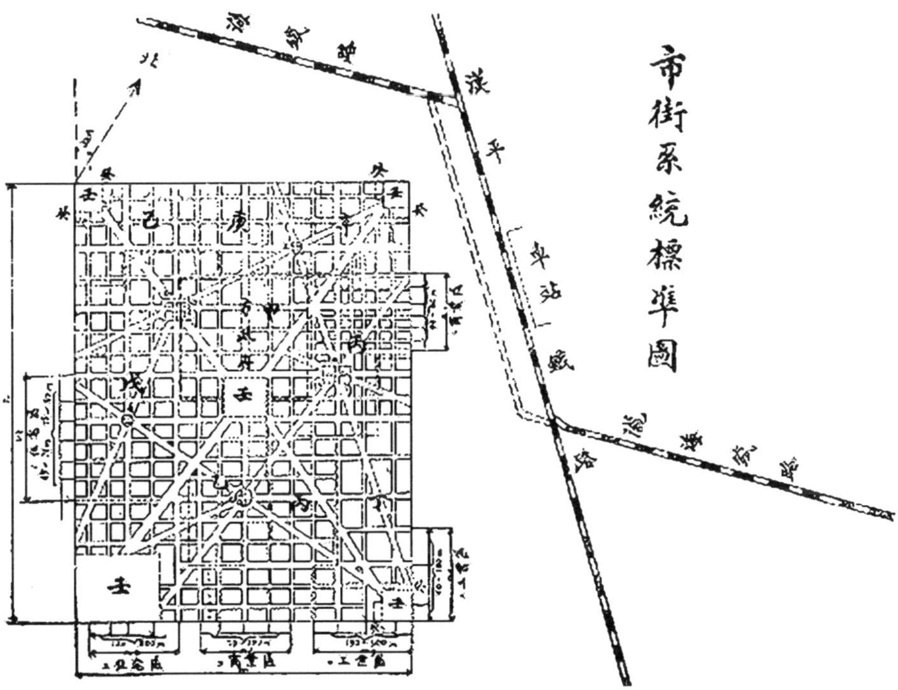

Fig. 4. *Plan for Zhengzhou New Urban Construction Area*, 1928.

In October 1948, the Central Plains became part of the People's Republic of China. At that time, Zhengzhou covered 5.23 square kilometres and had 164,000 inhabitants (Zhengzhou Municipal Bureau of Statistics, 2019). In the post-revolutionary period, the new local government mainly provided emergency housing and infrastructure (C. Zhang et al., 2010). This stage of recovery came to an end only after the political stabilisation of China in 1950. The following year, the Beijing Municipal Commission drafted the *Plan for the Future Development of Zhengzhou Municipality (1951–1981)*, which foresaw Zhengzhou becoming a city of 1 million inhabitants on over 108.9 square kilometres (Hao, 2006). This plan was soon set aside for two reasons. First, just after its completion, the city was chosen as the provincial capital of the Henan province, leading to the construction of new government offices. Second, in 1952, the State Financial Commission established Zhengzhou as one of the "fourteen cities to be restructured for major industrial development" (Hsu, 1996, p. 898). Consequently, the municipality hired Prof. Huxiong Wen from the Shanghai Federation of Industry and Engineering to draft a new proposal. The *Zhengzhou General Plan (1952–1972)* envisioned a population of 1.1 million inhabitants over 87.64 square kilometres (Y. Liu, 1988). Influenced by the garden city movement, Wen proposed a radial organisation of the road network with the railway station at its centre. Based on this, the layout proposed to locate factories and warehouses along the railways, new administrative facilities on the western side, and residential zones in the eastern part. These areas were supposed to form a compact urban core surrounded by a green belt.

Even the *Zhengzhou General Plan (1952–1972)* was never implemented. In 1950, the Sino-Soviet Treaty of Friendship led to growing Soviet influence in financial policies and urban planning activities. To foster heavy industry, Zhengzhou was planned as one of the six national cotton manufacturing centres (Yeh & Wu, 1999; Zhu, 2012).[6] Five massive cotton processing factories were built, and two industrial districts with agricul-

Fig. 5. Zhengzhou textile factories, 1970.

tural machinery and steel production plants were established (C. Zhang, 2007).[7] In order to regulate this development, the municipality promoted a new urban plan in 1952, which was drafted by the State Administration and Construction Committee under the guidance of Soviet expert Xin Mu (Y. Liu, 1988; Zhu, 2012). To prevent the infrastructure from dividing the city, Mu proposed not expanding the city west of the railways. However, since the new textile factories were already under construction on the western side, this decision was problematic. The plan was thus deeply modified in 1955 by the Ministry of Construction and Civil Engineering of Shanghai in collaboration with Soviet expert Bal Jin. The revised plan would urbanise 63.6 square kilometres to house 580,000 inhabitants (Y. Liu et al., 2008; C. Zhang et al., 2010), with residential areas located on both sides of the railways. The municipal offices would be built in the western part, while the new provincial government would be situated in the northeast part of the city centre. Finally, industries and warehouses were to be located along the railways, with green belts separating them from the residential nuclei. The overall organisation emphasised the morphology originating from the rail track intersection, which became the main element in structuring the new urban layout. This choice had a strong influence on future development and is still recognisable within the urban fabric today.

The number of plans drafted during the socialist period demonstrates the efforts to foster industrialisation via large-scale urbanisation. In the Central Plains, this policy influenced the urban development of most of the medium-sized and large centres. The case of Luoyang is emblematic. In 1954, the city was identified by the State Financial Commission as one of the eight major beneficiaries of national investment in industrialisation, and five factories were built across an area six times larger than the existing city (Hsu, 1996). Luoyang, Zhengzhou, and many other cities in Henan demonstrate how important the Central Plains was as a site for the industrialisation campaign of the 1950s which initiated great changes in the urban and social fabric of the cities.

Fig. 6. Zhengzhou textile factory, 1970.

Fig. 7. Zhengzhou heavy machinery factory, 1960.

Fig. 8. Zhengzhou textile factory, 1960.

During the late 1950s, in the wake of this rapid industrialisation, Zhengzhou experienced a large-scale migration that, coupled with natural disasters, caused great difficulties in supplying basic services. To address these problems, the municipality redefined growth expectations and updated the urban plan drafted in 1955. While retaining the previous zoning, the new version attempted to relieve overcrowding by expanding the city to 94 square kilometres. However, the Great Chinese Famine (1958–1961) and the economic difficulties caused by the Great Leap Forward (1958–1960) meant that the strategy was poorly implemented. In 1961 the situation deteriorated to the point that Zhengzhou municipality decided to decentralise 191,600 people. After this mass eviction, all planning activities were interrupted and the planning agencies were completely disbanded during the Cultural Revolution (1966–1976).

Under the anti-urban policies of the 1960s, the focus shifted from the cities to the countryside. The rural areas of the Central Plains were subjected to radical landscape restructuring through the collectivisation of land and the building of new rural settlements. Within this agropolitan strategy, most of the planning activities centred on the construction of people's communes. An example of this is the Weixing People's Commune, in Suiping County. The planned development, drafted in 1958 by the South China University of Technology (SCUT), was to be home to 8,000 people divided into eight brigades and a production centre. The layout was organised along a main road running north–south and flanked by administrative offices and public services (i.e., medical centres, sports facilities, and orchards), with four residential nuclei made up of rows of terraced houses behind. The industrial and farming zones were situated to the east and west of the residential areas. The plan was partially implemented and, despite being criticised by the Architectural Society of China as too expensive and using too much land, its layout was adopted for the design of most of the new rural settlements in Henan province (Knapp, 1992).

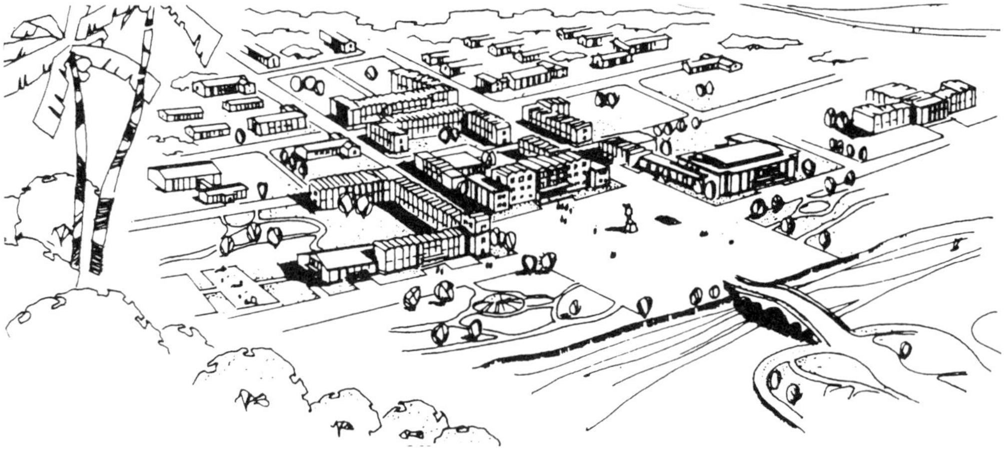

Fig. 9. Project of Suiping People's Commune, 1958.

The situation in urban and rural areas alike changed radically with the opening of China and the economic reform. In 1978, urban planning was reintroduced to the administrative system in order to restrict growth of the major cities, while promoting the development of small centres and towns (Zhengzhou City Planning Administration, 1989). As part of this, Zhengzhou municipality drew up a new plan in 1982 that was approved by the State Council two years later. The *Outline of the Urban Masterplan for Zhengzhou City* was aimed primarily at capping urban growth. In 1981, Zhengzhou was home to 780,000 inhabitants on 65 square kilometres. The plan established a limit of 1 million people on 105 square kilometres by 2000, with an expected 850,000 inhabitants on 71 square kilometres by 1985 (C. Zhang, 2007). To meet these targets, the proposal would redevelop historical neighbourhoods only and improve the connections between the eastern and western parts of the city, without allowing any further urban expansion. Despite this, the city overshot its targets by the early 1980s. At that time, both commercial and industrial activities were gaining momentum, causing Zhengzhou to experience an influx of migrants. Consequently, in 1985 the city had more than 904,000 inhabitants on 72.2 square kilometres (Zhengzhou Municipal Bureau of Statistics, 2019). In the following years, despite upping growth forecasts several times, urban development was consistently underestimated. This brought about an uncontrolled expansion that led to the formation of several suburban areas, loss of agricultural land at the urban fringes, and a failure to develop the city's greenbelt (Hao, 2006; Y. Liu et al., 2008).

The housing boom also involved rural areas to such an extent that the number of houses built between 1979 and 1985 exceeded the total number constructed in the previous three decades, "adding more than 5 square metres of housing stock per person" (Knapp & Sheng, 1992, p. 63). To check the loss of arable land, numerous efforts to introduce a land-use planning system were made at different levels of administration. As a result, by the end of 1985, urban development plans had been drafted for 98 percent of villages

Fig. 10. Telecommunications offices, Zhengzhou, 1970.

Fig. 11. Telecommunications offices, Zhengzhou, 1985.

and 85 percent of towns (Knapp, 1992; Su, 2009). Most of these recommended consolidating dispersed hamlets and standardising housing patterns in order to reduce land consumption. However, they were in large part ignored. Thus, like the major cities, the minor rural centres also experienced uncontrolled growth and indiscriminate land occupation.

Although both rural and urban areas experienced great development, the role of the Township and Village Enterprises (TVEs) was not as strong in the Central Plains as in the southern provinces of China, and thus, most economic growth was concentrated in urban areas. Zhengzhou, for instance, retained the industrial activities established in the pre-reform period while gaining further importance as an infrastructural hub. In the 1980s, the city became one of the trans-shipment centres for the new Eurasian Continental Bridge, and one of the major cities of the Yellow River Economic Belt. This had a major impact on the entire region and its organisation. The main cities came to depend on industrial and commercial activities; however, most of the population still relied on agricultural livelihoods. Thus, at the end of the 1980s, the Central Plains was made up of large cities sited along the main transport infrastructures (railways and highways) and surrounded by a diffuse urbanisation composed of towns and villages evenly distributed across the entire area.

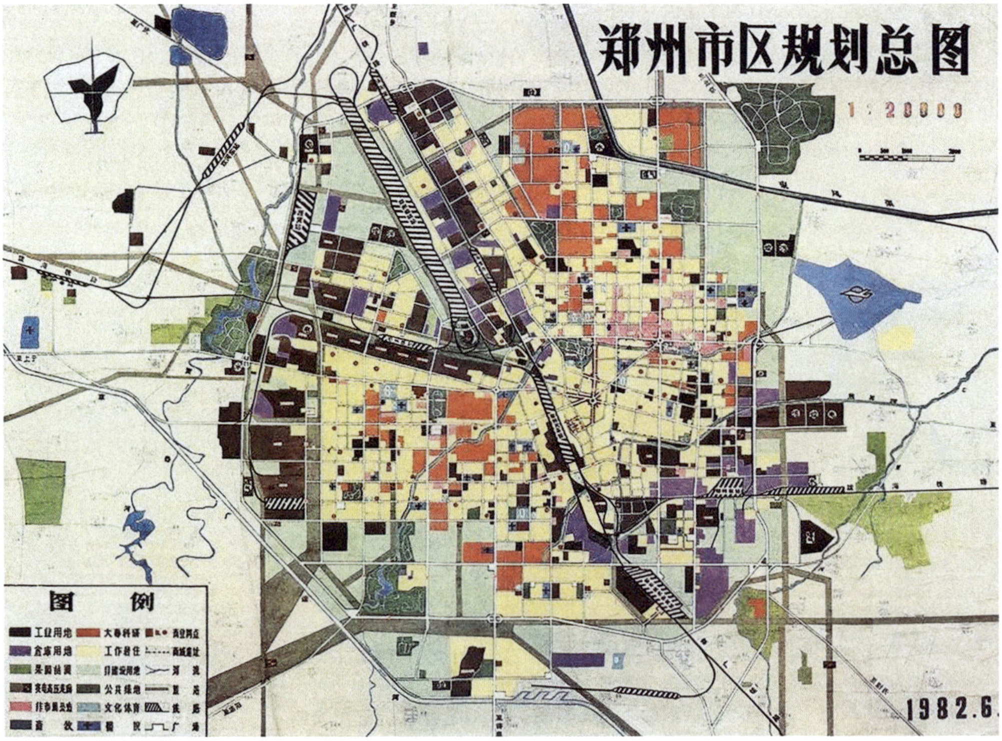

Fig. 12. *Zhengzhou City Urban Masterplan*, 1985.

Zhengdong. Doubling the City

From 1990 to the mid-2000s, China entered a new phase of economic and urban growth. While the process of administrative and fiscal devolution underway since the previous decade continued, the pace of integration into the global economy accelerated after China joined the World Trade Organization (WTO) in 2001. Unlike the industrial restructuring of the first opening-up period, these phenomena pervasively affected the entire urban realm. In shifting "from state-led industrialisation to urban based accumulation" (F. Wu, 2007, p. 9), land become the most important asset for local governments, and the major municipalities competed to encourage urban development and boost the real estate market. Thus, the urbanisation level rose to 29 percent in 1995 and the number of cities increased from 479 to 640 (China National Bureau of Statistics, 2020). This trend continued despite the Asian economic crisis, and in 2000, the urbanisation level reached 36 percent. During that period, several cities implemented urban entrepreneurial policies to attract foreign and domestic investment. These self-promotion initiatives relied on the ubiquitous replication of emblematic spaces, such as Central Business Districts (CBDs), economic and technological development zones (ETDZs), and university towns (King, 2004; Ren, 2011; Sklair, 2006). Consequently, the tenth FYP (2001–2005) advocated a "diversified and coordinated development of large, medium and small cities and townships" (Fang & Yu, 2016, p. 91). Despite this diversification, such an approach continued to fuel the urbanisation process and by 2005, 40 percent of the Chinese population lived in cities (China National Bureau of Statistics, 2020).

Such unprecedented growth greatly affected the Central Plains. As affirmed by Arata Isozaki (2012), washing over China, "the global tsunami deposited an archipelago of cities" (p. 3). Under this great wave of globalisation, these cities competed with one another to stay afloat. Such a phenomenon also characterised Zhengzhou. From the mid-1990s, the municipality made significant efforts to break into the national and international arena by promoting the city as the major infrastructural hub for inland China. To achieve this objective, four ETDZs were established in the 1990s, and in the early 2000s the municipality promoted the construction of Zhengdong New District.

Fig. 13. Zhengzhou central railway station, 1970.

Fig. 14. Zhengzhou airport, 1970.

China has been characterised by increasing economic and administrative devolution since the economic reform (Ma, 2005). Between 1982 and 1998 the central administration's share of public expenditure was reduced from 53 to 30 percent (Chien & Gordon, 2008). This caused financial problems for local governments, which were affected by increasing fiscal deficits. To overcome the situation, a tax-sharing reform was enacted in 1992. The new fiscal system allowed lower administrations to collect income derived from land management and extra-budgetary revenues (Wong, 2000; Xu & Yeh, 2009). This turned the land market into a major source of revenue for local governments. The strategy was implemented by reforming the land administration system using two laws: the Land Administration Law (1986, revised in 1998), that authorised local administrations to expropriate rural land, to merge cadastral parcels, and to supply infrastructures (Xu & Yeh, 2005); and the City Planning Act (1990), that allowed local planning authorities to change land use directly at the land parcel level (F. Wu, 2015).[8] Thanks to these laws, local governments controlled both the ownership of and the development rights for urban space (Xu & Yeh, 2009). Furthermore, a dual-track land management system was established in 1988 that separated land ownership, which remained public, and land use rights, which could be leased to private enterprises (Ren, 2013). The resulting leasehold system (similar to that of Hong Kong) allowed municipalities to distribute land rights through tender, public auction, and negotiation (F. Wu, 2003). In order to maximise the benefits, most land transactions occurred via closed-door negotiations.[9] By adopting this system, between 1987 and 1994, local administrations collected 241.8 billion CNY from land conveyance (G. C. S. Lin & Ho, 2005). The reliance on land sales intensified in the following decade, to the point that income from land sales increased from 9.3 percent of total revenues in 2000 to 74.1 percent in 2011 (Shepard, 2015). In other words, local governments need to ensure that cities kept expanding to make the fiscal system work.

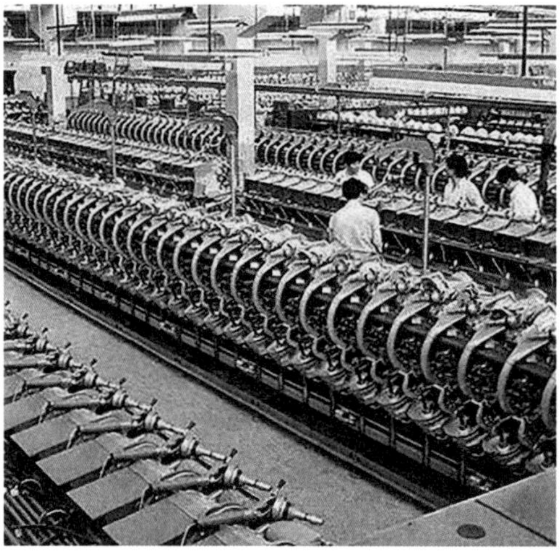

Fig. 15. Zhengzhou textile factory, 1970.

Fig. 16. Zhengzhou textile factory, 1980.

These administrative and financial conditions boosted urban entrepreneurialism, which became the main driver of a great landscape transformation centred on the major cities and their fringes. Since land was valued according to its location, the cores of major cities had been radically restructured (S. He & Wu, 2007; Shin, 2007; Tian & Wong, 2007). Many factories and work units moved onto the urban fringes and the vacant land was sold to real estate companies (Yeh & Wu, 1996). This process was supported by local administrations responsible for converting land use, coordinating relocation, and assisting with site clearance. Moreover, each local cadre adopted "a new discourse" to brand and promote its own city. Such "discourses" relied on planning activities, particularly the drafting of non-statutory plans and the promotion of international competitions. The new plans legitimised urban transformations based on the replication of iconic spaces, such as ETDZs, CBDs, TODs, and university towns. Consequently, a great urban expansion occurred on the urban fringes (Hsing, 2010). This was not only supported by incentives to factories and business enterprises, but by the provision of infrastructure. Large-scale infrastructural networks were realised both by local governments, as an initial condition for urban development, and investors, as a form of tax relief (F. Wu, 2003).

Urban entrepreneurialism led several local authorities to act as property speculators, promoting large-scale urban projects to attract domestic and foreign investment, and increasing land consumption. Indeed, these policies caused a tremendous loss of arable land. By the mid-1990s, this ranged between 130,000 and 97,000 square kilometres per year, that is, an area equal to the Beijing municipality (G. C. S. Lin & Ho, 2005). Furthermore, such a "growth machine" produced a skewed development that increased disparity among the different regions of China and exacerbated the inequalities between urban and rural areas, resulting in fierce territorial competition.

Fig. 17. Schoolchildren in Zhengzhou, 1970.

This territorial competition emerged in the 1990s as a result of strong administrative and fiscal decentralisation. Putting Deng Xiaoping's statement "let some regions and people get rich first" into practice, the central government promoted a "step-ladder-step approach" by relaxing redistribution policies at the national level, while pursuing a process of administrative devolution (Chien & Gordon, 2008; Xu & Yeh, 2005). Within this framework, local leaders became de facto managers of urban activity, competing with one another to secure the highest revenue from land administration. As a result, from the 1990s to the mid-2000s, a host of bottom-up initiatives driven by the entrepreneurialism of villages, towns, municipalities, and prefectures gave rise to a patchwork of urbanisation. This phenomenon occurred in two stages.

The first, during the 1990s, was the "land-enclosure movement", a redistribution of land resources via non-market measures that boosted the creation of Economic and Technological Development Zones (ETDZs) (Q. He, 2000). These were established to attract international investment, facilitate trade, and encourage new industries by adopting special finance and taxation policies (J. Liu & Xu, 2019). Although established by statute soon after China opened up, ETDZ construction did not gain momentum until the rise of urban entrepreneurialism in the early 1990s (Yeh & Wu, 1996). In just two years, from 1990 to 1992, about 40 percent of all converted rural land was designated for ETDZs, increasing their number from 1,874 to 2,700 (G. C. S. Lin & Ho, 2005). In 1996, development zones exceeded 15,000 square kilometres: more than the urban area of all existing cities in China (J. Liu & Xu, 2019). This exponential growth was driven by the lower tiers of administration (townships, villages, counties, and municipalities) that conducted both legal and illegal transactions to squeeze the utmost revenue from land management.[10] Although the central government promoted several initiatives to cool this development zone fever, the trend continued nonetheless, so that by

Fig. 18. A street in Zhengzhou, 1970.

Fig. 19. A street in Zhengzhou, 1985.

2003, development zones had expanded to cover more than 36,000 square kilometres. However, only a few of the 3,837 registered ETDZs were effectively operational, and in the early 2000s only 13.5 percent of the total area designated for ETDZs was under development, while more than 85 percent lay idle. Thus, in most cases, the promotion of ETDZs was just a means to convert farmland to other land uses. Consequently, in 2004, the Ministry of Land and Resources (MLR) abolished 4,813 ETDZs, that is, 70 percent of development zones nationwide. In terms of land area, this converted about 24,900 square kilometres (i.e., 64.5 percent of the total area earmarked for development zones) into state land reserves (Hsing, 2010).

While the development zone fever had cooled down by the early 2000s, a second stage of grassroots urbanisation was growing. Instead of converting counties into cities, the administrative restructuring of the mid-1990s launched policies of "city administering counties" and "annexation of suburban counties".[11] This encouraged major municipalities to seize control over their urban fringes by developing new towns, a strategy that relied on market-driven urban mega projects (Hsing, 2010; Yeh & Wu, 1996). Due to the changeable nature of land policies, these initiatives were undertaken by municipalities to convert as much land as possible as quickly as possible. The land reserve was then used as collateral to obtain the bank loans necessary for infrastructural provisions and, once the infrastructural network was in place, the new towns became "backup spaces" that could easily be modified to meet the needs of different stakeholders over time (Sampieri, 2019). This urban expansion led to a metropolitanisation process with satellite towns, industrial centres, and vast rural areas being turned into suburban zones of unified global city-regions (Bonino et al., 2019; F. Wu, 2016a). Within this picture, new towns treated the totality of urban space as a commodity: planning, zoning, marketing, fiscal benefits, and infrastructure supply were combined to build global centres to attract investment within a context of competing cities.

Fig. 20. A market in Zhengzhou, 1970.

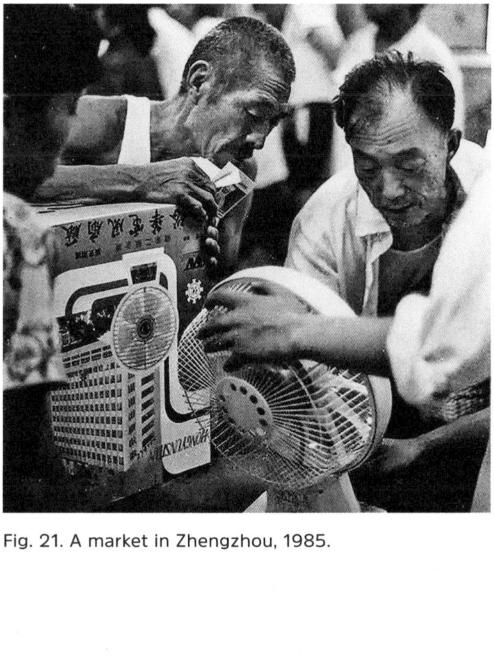

Fig. 21. A market in Zhengzhou, 1985.

In the early 1990s, Zhengzhou entered a new phase of growth. Under the development zone fever, the *Zhengzhou General Masterplan (1995–2010)* adopted a decentralised multicentre strategy based on four ETDZs situated around the city centre (Chen et al., 2017). These were to be home to factories and industrial activities, with just a few residential and commercial areas. The southern ETDZ (9 square kilometres) was planned for the relocation of the textile and electronics factories sited in the city centre, while the northern one (9.5 square kilometres) was intended for leisure and tourism industries. East of the urban core, another 12-square-kilometre zone was set up for automotive plants, while the Zhengzhou High-tech Industrial Development Zone was established on 18.6 square kilometres on the western side. At the end of the 1990s, the plan was partially implemented: the old textile factories were relocated and new industrial plants were built in the western cluster (C. Zhang, 2007). These transformations stimulated investment in fixed assets, which rose from 2,010 million CNY in 1990 to 15,940 million CNY in 2000, with investments in real estate increasing from 90 million to 3,420 million CNY (Zhengzhou Municipal Bureau of Statistics, 2019).

These economic trends encouraged the local government to continue along the path of urban expansion. Moreover, in 2000, Zhengzhou was included in the national infrastructural policies to develop the city as the main infrastructural hub of central China (F. Wu, 2015). Thus, the municipality commissioned local planning institutes to draft a plan for a new town to the east of the city centre (Xue et al., 2013). This was not considered satisfactory and, in 2001, the governor of the Henan province, Li Keqiang, launched an international competition for Zhengdong New District: a new town of 1.5 million people centred around a Central Business District (CBD), a technology park, and a high-speed railway station. This would increase Zhengzhou's population by more than a third, while doubling the size of the city by urbanising a new 150-square-kilometre area. The international competition involved the PWD Engineering Group (Singapore), Arte Charpentier (France), COX Group, SASAKI Corporation (Australia), Kisho Kurokawa Architects and Associates (Japan), and the China Academy of Urban Planning and Design (CAUPD) (K. Li et al., 2010b). Each of these firms was asked to draft a non-statutory plan to be evaluated by a Chinese jury composed of the chief planner of the Ministry of Construction, experts, planners, and professors in the field of urbanism and architecture (K. Li et al., 2010b; Xue et al., 2013).

Kisho Kurokawa Architects and Associates won the competition, proposing a metabolist-style project for a symbiotic city (W. He & Zhang, 2007). The plan adopted a poly-nuclear layout designed to evolve over time by adding further nuclei.[12] Based on this, Zhengdong New District is organised into five areas separated by ecological corridors accommodating the major mobility infrastructure. The main nucleus (40 square kilometres) is located in the north-western part of the new town. This is home to the main CBD (south), a sub-CBD (north) and most of the residential areas. Both CBDs consist of a double ring of high-rise buildings connected by a pedestrian, air-conditioned shopping street. While the main CBD (3 square kilometres) is 1 kilometre in diameter nestled in a park separating it from the existing city; the sub-CBD (1.5 square kilometres)

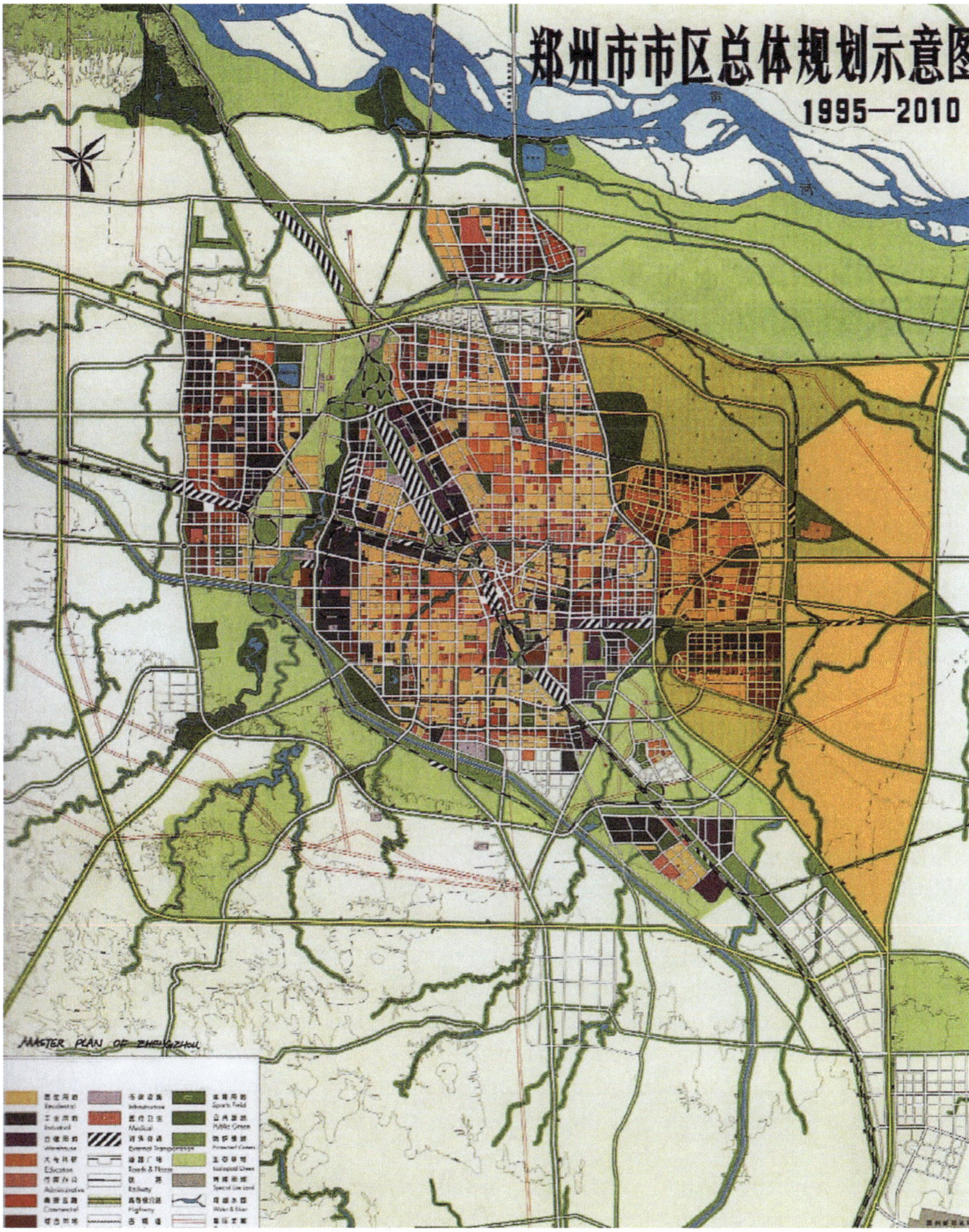

Fig. 22. *Zhengzhou General Masterplan (1995–2010)*, 1995.

is on an artificial island 0.7 kilometres in diameter at the centre of an artificial lake. The two CBDs are connected by the north–south axis of the new town: a 3.7-kilometre canal bordered on either side by commercial strips and buildings for tertiary activities. The remaining land is parcelled into future residential settlements by a road grid. The second nucleus extends across 50 square kilometres in the south-east of the new town and is bordered by existing road networks leading east from the city centre. Kurokawa's project envisages a new railway station being constructed there to separate the residential area to the north from the High-tech Industry Development Zone in the southern part of the section. The three remaining clusters, located along the eastern green belt, are the Sport City Cluster (north), the Resort Residential Cluster (centre), and the Research City Cluster (south) (K. Li et al., 2010c).

The original plan underwent several revisions during its implementation. From 2002 to 2009, the new town suffered from a severe shortfall in funding. The administrative committee generated 1.05 billion CNY from land compensation and took out a 5.55 billion CNY loan from banks (Xue & Wang, 2010). Together with other funds, it invested a total of 18 billion CNY (Xue et al., 2013). These were used to supply the basic infrastructure, boosting land prices to 4,000 CNY per square metre, the highest in the Henan province. During this phase, while Kurokawa designed the convention and exhibition centre and a residential compound, several Chinese design institutes began to work on the different nuclei. In the meantime, international designers competed for the construction of buildings and parks (almost always in partnership with a constellation of state institutes and groups of local architects).

At the end of this process, the main cluster and the layout of the two CBDs were the only parts of the original project that remained. The others had been repeatedly modified: the ecological corridors were downsized, the south cluster was revamped to host a new high-speed railway station, and the two clusters along the eastern green belt were redesigned by the Zhengzhou Urban Planning and Design Institute as a single 22-square-kilometre nucleus where the university town is now located. Finally, a grid layout was adopted for the remaining land.[13] In 2010, three years after Kisho Kurokawa passed away, the Administrative Committee of Zhengdong New District entrusted the completion of the project to Arata Isozaki & Associates, who are currently working on the sub-CBD and the eastern area of the main railway station.

Soon after the construction of the main CBD, Zhengdong New District came to fame as one of the most notorious ghost towns in China.[14] In the meantime, Kurokawa's design was sharply criticised for the overexploitation of water resources due to its extensive system of canals and lakes, traffic congestion due to the road layout, and the non-human scale of the living environment (Gui, 2012; Qin, 2009). Despite this criticism, nowadays the new town is filling up (Miller, 2012; Shepard, 2015). The main CBD is home to 821 enterprises and more than 25,000 employees; industrial and commercial activities provide work for more than 75,000 people, and the university town is home to 15 campuses accommodating more than 240,000 students (Henan Province Bureau of Statistics, 2020). In 2017, Zhengdong New District absorbed 72,130 million CNY in real estate

Fig. 23. Kisho Kurokawa's proposal for Zhengzhou Masterplan, 2001.

Fig. 24. Kisho Kurokawa's proposal for the main nucleus of Zhengdong New District, 2001.

investments, the highest in Henan province (more than the combined total of all other districts in Zhengzhou municipality) (Henan Province Bureau of Statistics, 2020). However, there are still doubts about the financial benefits of the new town, which have fallen short of the original predictions, and the development would not be viable without government backing (Zhao, 2013). Thus, in 2016, the municipality decided to expand the area of Zhengdong New District by adding another 110 square kilometres, creating a new development called Baisha Town.

Zhengdong New District is still under construction; however, no sooner had the plan been drafted than national policies began to change, in turn affecting the methods employed in urbanising new areas. Nowadays, the new town appears to be the product of an outdated concept that considered the construction of monumental centres as a means of empowering vast regions. Within this framework, urban plans and iconic buildings were tools to promote the city: "window displays" prepared by international architectural firms to provide precise images where every scale and every detail is meticulously controlled (to the point of being extremely inflexible). Thus, Zhengdong New District stands today as an enigmatic monument open to a variety of interpretations. On the one hand it could be the apotheosis of urban entrepreneurial policies (F. Wu, 2015). On the other, it can be regarded as an experimental site where international design culture engages with the challenges of a newly fledged globalised society, just as Kurokawa did in envisioning Zhengdong New District as a new urban environment for the *Homo Movens* of the twenty-first century.

Fig. 25. Kisho Kurokawa's view of Zhengdong New District, 2001.

Zhengbian. Spreading the Urbanisation

From the mid-1990s, the consequences of territorial competition and urban entrepreneurialism began to appear. Despite the adoption by central government of a variety of measures to curtail land speculation, the skewed urban development was causing great social and economic disparity among different areas of the country and segments of the population. To tackle these problems, the central authority has taken various measures since the early 2000s to reorganise land management and to promote regional patterns of urbanisation (F. Wu, 2015; Xu & Yeh, 2009). This new approach is driven by the current international and domestic conditions and has three main purposes. First, to reduce the geographical and social disparities caused by the "global tsunami" that has been underway since the opening-up (F. Wu, 2006). Second, to reduce internal migration by stimulating depressed regions (Chan, 2013; Miller, 2012). Finally, to produce and redistribute wealth by boosting domestic consumption and internal demand (Garnaut et al., 2013; J. Y. Lin, 2011; Rozelle & Hell, 2020). In order to achieve these objectives, a new generation of leaders headed by President Hu Jintao and Premier Wen Jiabao launched the so-called "scientific approach to development" in 2003. Distinct from the previous "growth-first approach" adopted by Deng Xiaoping, the new strategy called for greater coordination between the main stakeholders in the urbanisation process (F. Wu, 2015, 2016a). This became the cornerstone of the eleventh, twelfth, and thirteenth FYPs (2006–2021) which advocated for a rational development of large, medium, and small cities and townships. These policies fostered urban agglomerations: conurbations of mega-cities established to spread economic growth throughout their surrounding areas (Fang & Yu, 2016). This hub-and-spoke development is being pursued through two initiatives: the adoption of national and regional planning activities, and the enactment of policies to develop rural areas, such as the Building New Socialist Countryside programme (BNSC).

Fig. 26. Panoramic painting of Splendid Central Plains, 2010.

Nowadays, these initiatives are reshaping the Chinese landscape. By adopting a top-down approach, the national and regional planning determines the requirements for infrastructural networks and establishes basic guidelines for any future urbanisation. On the other hand, bottom-up policies such as the BNSC are the main drivers of landscape transformation at the lower levels. Thus, the urbanisation of the previous decades has radically changed. Instead of being centred on the major cities and their fringes, these initiatives are carrying out a comprehensive process of territorial restructuring by equipping large tracts of land with new infrastructure and distributing services across the entire territory.

Such operations lay the foundations for a space that can be indiscriminately occupied by different programmes, morphologies, and urban materials (Governa & Sampieri, 2020). As a result, "when we look at the new map of China, we will no longer see large independent cities functioning as singular urban entities, but a continuous amalgamation of interconnected urban zones that blanket the country" (Shepard, 2015, p. 87). These are a relational space "where every scale (and every space) is not an independent entity" (Governa, 2019, p. 224). In other words, this will be a new landscape in which the formal distinctions between urban and rural, city and countryside, and global and local are increasingly blurred.

Since the final outcome of these transformations are still unclear, several questions arise: what are the spatial implications of these policies? What are the features of the emerging urbanisation? What will the relationship between the new urbanities and the existing environment look like? Once again, the urbanisation process in the Central Plains of China is a case study. In fact, since the establishment of the Central Plains urban agglomeration in 2006, several projects have been undertaken to foster integrated and coordinated development.

Since the mid-2000s, one of the major changes in urban policy has been the re-appearance of regional planning to encourage and coordinate large-scale infrastructural and urban development. Regional planning is not new to China. During the socialist period, several policies were adopted at the regional level; however, they mostly focused on the allocation of financial resources with little regard for spatial conditions (Fan et al., 2012). Only after the economic reform was a "territorial planning notion" introduced into the planning activities (Xiao, 2016). In spite of this, urban entrepreneurialism and territorial competition progressively weakened the top-down system, until the drafting of territorial plans completely ceased in the 1990s (F. Wu, 2015).

This changed in the early 2000s, when national and regional institutions started promoting a process of governance upscaling centred on land policy (Xu & Yeh, 2009).[15] This led the Ministry of Housing and Urban Rural Development (MoHURD) and the China Academy of Urban Planning and Design (CAUPD) to draft the *National Urban System Plan (2005–2020)*. The plan emphasised the role of "urban clusters", that is, large urban agglomerations evenly distributed within the national infrastructural system. However, because of MoHURD's lack of instruments for implementing regional-level policies, the plan was published in 2010 without a statutory status. In spite of this, in 2006 the State Council required the National Development and Reform Commission (NDRC) to prepare the *National Main Functional Area Plan*, which was drafted in collaboration with the Chinese Academy of Sciences (CAS) and published in 2010. This plan is similar to the *National Urban System Plan (2005–2020)*. Both layouts are based on the "two horizontal, three vertical axes" network of infrastructures, which is considered the backbone of the "axes link agglomerations, while agglomerations support axes" strategy (Fang & Yu, 2016). The two horizontal axes are the Yangtze River corridor, which connects Shanghai to Chengdu; and the Eurasian Land Bridge, which links the Shandong Peninsula to Urumqi. Among the vertical axes, two of them connect northern China to the Pearl River Delta, one going through the coastal areas while the other crosses the inland regions. Finally, the last vertical axis links Inner Mongolia to

Fig. 27. View of Zhengbian New District, 2009.

Yunnan province, passing through the cities of Xi'an and Chongqing. Based on this infrastructural network, the *National Main Functional Area Plan* adopts a classification of zones based on optimised, prioritised, constrained, and forbidden development areas (Fan et al., 2012). The final group includes "natural and cultural protection zones", which consist of minor heritage areas all over the Chinese territory, coupled with large nature reserves in the western regions. The "constrained development areas" are ecological zones in western and northern China and major food-production regions in central and southern China. The Yangtze River Delta, the Pearl River Delta, and the Jing-Jin-Ji Region are "optimised development areas"; while the "prioritised development areas" consist of 17 urban agglomerations located along the main infrastructural axes. Based on this layout, in 2014, the State Council approved the *National Plan of New Urbanisation (2014–2020)* that, while adopting different categories to classify the territory, is basically a carbon copy of the *National Main Functional Area Plan* (J. Liu & Xu, 2019), which establishes 20 urban agglomerations encompassing more than 25 percent of Chinese territory and 64 percent of Chinese cities. These areas, already inhabited by 63 percent of China's population, are expected to be the main drivers of economic and urban development by absorbing 75 percent of newly added urbanities (Fang & Yu, 2016).

While regional plans establish the overall layout for the forthcoming urbanisation, several forces are actualising these initiatives. Infrastructure policies such as the Belt and Road Initiative (BRI) and the Go West programme are fostering "free trade zones" in the western provinces (such as Kasghar and Khorgos Gateways), "airport cities" in the central regions (such as Zhengzhou and Chengdu-Tianfu Airport Cities), and "port cities" in the undeveloped coastal areas (such as Dalian and Fuzhou Port Cities) (H. Liu et al., 2015). Moreover, since 2014, 106 large-scale urban projects, drafted within the framework provided by the regional plans, are now under construction. While those at national level are in the coastal and western regions, central China hosts the majority of new municipal and provincial urban projects. The new large-scale developments are different from the urban mega projects promoted under the impetus of urban en-

trepreneurialism. Two-thirds of those currently under construction are larger than 100 square kilometres, and 19 exceed 1,000 square kilometres (Fang & Yu, 2016). To reorganise such large sections of territory, new plans involve different levels of administration and engage with multiple spatial features. This comprehensive approach has turned planning activities into a "soft institutional space" where official levels of governance (such as provinces, municipalities, and counties) and organisations without a specific administrative status (such as regional associations, city-region bodies, and mayors' forums) may negotiate the future landscape transformations (F. Wu, 2015, 2016b; Xu & Yeh, 2009). Within this inclusive spatial and institutional framework, new urban projects are rearranging urban and rural areas, new cultural and industrial zones, new facilities, and natural resources. Hence, even though differentiated regional policies and zones of exception still exist, these planning activities are increasingly integrating with the landscape. What ensues is a significant redesign of the network of cities created in the previous decades: the network intensifies, cities increase in number, and the dots on the map become atolls in an urbanised expanse.

Fig. 28. View of Zhengbian New District, 2009.

No Space Left Behind. The Urbanisation of Rural Areas

While regional planning activities and urban agglomeration policies are reshaping the territory based on a top-down approach, several initiatives have been undertaken at lower levels. Even though the construction of new towns continues, other forms of grassroots urbanisation are gaining momentum. Among these, the most important are occurring in rural areas. These are driven by national and local policies that wish to mitigate the rural–urban divide, one of the major concerns of the administrative cadres since the late 1990s. In fact, the gap between the salaries of urban and rural workers has consistently increased and in 2005, urban incomes were 3.2 times higher than rural ones (China National Bureau of Statistics, 2020). Furthermore, the lack of medical and educational services in the countryside exacerbated social inequality (Hong, 2021; Y. Li & Hu, 2015; Rozelle & Hell, 2020; Ye, 2009). These problems compounded the "three rural issues": decline in agricultural output, deterioration of rural villages, and impoverishment of peasants (DuBois & Li, 2016). For these reasons, "the widening gap between urban and rural areas is no longer just an economic issue, but has become a politically charged matter as well" (Su, 2009, p. 133).

To address this situation, the Chinese administration has undertaken several initiatives since 2003. For instance, a guaranteed minimum procurement price for agricultural products has been established, most agricultural taxes have been abolished, and numerous subsidies have been financed.[16] Coupled with these economic measures, the Building a New Socialist Countryside (BNSC) programme was launched in 2006 (Ahlers, 2014; Su, 2009; Ye, 2009), focusing on providing rural services, conserving agricultural land, securing food supply, boosting domestic consumption, and reversing migration from the country to the cities. Based on Wen Jiabao's conviction (2006) that "in order to build a new socialist countryside, we must accelerate development of rural infrastructure", water systems, road networks, electrical power grids, and housing estates in rural areas have been improved.[17] Even though these initiatives have been promoted at the national level, their implementation has been the task of local governments.[18]

Fig. 29. View of Zhengbian New District, 2009.

Consequently, each village is in charge of drafting a long-term plan (20 years) that, in line with the strategic regional plan, determines land use, functional zoning, infrastructure provision, and environmental protection (Bray, 2013).

These long-term plans, which are generally drawn up by the design institutes of major municipalities, implement two approaches (Ahlers, 2014; Bray, 2013; Lee, 2016). One foresees renovating the existing villages by improving sanitation, sewers, and energy infrastructure, as well as by integrating cultural educational facilities and cultural and economic amenities (such as markets and entertainment halls). The other consists of demolishing several settlements and relocating the villagers to new agricultural towns. Both approaches aim to reduce land consumption. While the first strategy promotes the densification of existing settlements by replacing part of the housing stock with high-rise buildings, the second attempts to substitute several villages with a single denser agricultural town. Thus, municipalities collect "land quotas" that can be redistributed to other locations.[19] At that point, the system of strategic plans at provincial and higher levels is called upon to manage the reallocation of the quotas. Hence, these planning activities can be considered as the lower tiers of the large-scale urban projects (F. Wu, 2015).

Due to this practice, the BNSC programme is criticised for being nothing more than an alibi for the cannibalisation of rural areas for further urban development (Smith, 2021; F. Wu, 2006). While this may be true, such a comprehensive approach is also leading to a "townisation" process that overrides the formal distinction between city and country (Rowe & Kan, 2016; Shepard, 2015; Yang, 2014). In fact, rural areas are now equipped with new services and infrastructures and integrated into the economic system of urban agglomerations to such an extent that it is possible to view the "countryside as a city" (Lee, 2016, p. 210). This condition can be clearly seen in the renderings produced by design institutes to promote the new agricultural towns, showing villagers driving luxury cars to reach their suburban-style villas, or "new peasants" dressed in fine clothes while shopping in supermarkets branded by famous international firms. Even if these images do not fit the current reality, they demonstrate the attempt to rethink the urbanisation of rural China: an effort to leave no one and no space behind.

Fig. 30. View of Tushan New Agricultural Town, 2013.

Fig. 31. View of Tushan New Agricultural Town, 2013.

Zhengbian New District. Spreading the Urbanisation

Since 2005, Zhengzhou has become crucial in its role as the capital of the Central Plains urban agglomeration: a "regional level agglomeration" (also known as Zhongyuan City Group) made up of nine prefecture-level cities (Zhengzhou, Luoyang, Kaifeng, Xinxiang, Jiaozuo, Xuchang, Pingdingshan, Luohe, and Jiyuan), 23 cities, and 413 townships. This 58,400-square-kilometre area accounts for 3.06 percent of China's GDP, and is home to 45.5 million inhabitants, of which 13.7 million (30 percent) are considered "urban population" (Henan Province Bureau of Statistics, 2020). This increasing importance has led the provincial government and its municipalities to adopt a new strategy based on two objectives: the creation of the biggest logistics hub in central China and the implementation of a coordinated development plan between industrialisation, urbanisation, and agricultural production (Fang & Yu, 2016; X. Wang & Tomaney, 2019).

As part of this strategy, since the mid-2000s, Zhengzhou municipality has engaged in numerous planning activities to promote the Zhengzhou Integrated Transportation Hub (which includes a new high-speed railway station, new railway lines, and a highway logistics hub), the Zhengzhou Airport Economic Zone, and the Zhengzhou–Kaifeng Industrial Belt (K. Li et al., 2010a). In 2006, these initiatives were amalgamated into a comprehensive project promoted by the government of Henan province and the Central Plains urban agglomeration: Zhengbian New District. This new urbanisation extends over a 2,100-square-kilometre area between Zhengzhou and Kaifeng, which is currently populated by 4.5 million inhabitants. In 2008, the new district was included in the *Henan Province Urban System Planning*, and, in the following year, an international competition was launched for its design (X. Wang et al., 2013). This was won by the London-based firm Arup with a project titled *Planning for Low-Carbon Urban Systems: the Zhengbian New District Plan*, which was awarded a prize by the International Society of Cities and Regional Planners (ISOCARP) in 2010. The same year, the project was included in the *Regional Strategic Plan of the Central China Economic Region*, in turn, part of the *National Main Functional Area Plan* published by the NDRC in 2010 (F. Wu, 2015).

The design adopted for Zhengbian New District is radically different from that of Zhengdong. Zhengbian is a series of smaller projects coordinated over a much wider area. Arup planned to develop 500 square kilometres (24 percent of the total area), while the remaining 1,600 square kilometres would be devoted to agriculture, nature reserves, and leisure activities. Half of the urbanised area is designated for residential use (230 square kilometres), while the remainder is home to several functions, such as industry (72 square kilometres) and logistics infrastructures (50 square kilometres) (Zhengzhou Municipality, 2009). The plan organises the territory along two axes (Arup Engineering Consulting Company et al., 2009, 2010). The east–west axis is an 80-kilometre-long linear city connecting Zhengzhou and Kaifeng; it includes: Zhengdong New District, Kaifeng New Area, and four new clusters. Each has industrial zones located in the southern part and commercial, administrative, and cultural activities at the centre. The entire development is connected by an infrastructure corridor made up

Fig. 32. Masterplan for Zhengbian New District, 2009.

N
0 1 2 5 10km

Fig. 33. View of Zhengbian New District, 2009.

of two highways and three railway lines, and is situated between two ecological areas. The northern one serves as an environmental buffer along the Yellow River, which is used for leisure activities, luxury compounds, and agricultural parks. The southern one is the New Agricultural Zone, which will be home to new agricultural towns and food-processing industries. The north-south axis is mainly for industrial activities. By developing along this infrastructural corridor on the western border of Zhengbian, Zhengdong New District will eventually merge with Zhengzhou Airport City.[20]

At first, the north-south axis was considered a secondary project to the urban corridor linking Zhengzhou and Kaifeng, but it has now become increasingly important. In 2014, Henan province drafted the *Zhengzhou Airport Economic Comprehensive Experimental Zone Development Plan (2014-2040)*, which was approved by the State Council in 2016 (X. Wang et al., 2013; X. Wang & Tomaney, 2019). In the same year, Zhengzhou Airport City was the first to be included in the national development strategy. As the thirteenth FYP (2016-2020) explicitly pointed out, this was essential to "accelerate the development of the Zhengzhou Airport Economic Zone [...] [in order to] support the development of an open, inland economy [leading to] the rise of the central region" (Central Committee of the Communist Party of China, 2016, p. 106). As a result, while the original plan foresaw Zhengzhou Airport City covering an area of 100 square kilometres, the development now exceeds 400 square kilometres (Kasarda, 2018; Zhengzhou Municipal Bureau of Urban and Rural Planning, 2018). The urban layout of Zhengzhou Airport City is a grid pattern centred on the airport and extending east. The plan organises the area in three parts: the High-End Manufacturing Area (south), the Henan Free Trade Zone (centre), and the Urban Comprehensive Services Area (north). These

Fig. 34. Arata Isozaki's interpretation of Zhengbian New District as Solaris, 2012.

not only include infrastructure and services, but such a wide variety of functions that it can be regarded as an "aerotropolis" (Kasarda, 2019, p. 74). In light of this, Zhengbian New District and its Airport City are now considered the means of integrating not only Zhengzhou and Kaifeng but also Xuchang (the fourth largest economy in Henan), forming "the growth triangle of the Central Plains" (X. Wang et al., 2013; X. Wang & Tomaney, 2019).

While planning activities continue, new developments are gradually taking shape. The infrastructural corridor between Zhengzhou and Kaifeng is now complete, as well as the infrastructural grids of the clusters along the east-west axis. Furthermore, between 2013 and 2015, a second terminal was added to the international airport, and it is now expected to handle 70 million passengers and 5 million tons of cargo per year (i.e., more than London Heathrow airport) (*The Economist*, 2015; Williams, 2017). In the meantime, numerous factories have been set up in the industrial clusters, and the logistic hubs are expanding to the east and north. Along with these major transformations, a multitude of minor projects are also currently underway. In the last five years, more than 300 villages have been demolished, and more than 100 new agricultural towns are under construction. In addition to these settlements, the farmland is also being reshaped by the establishment of experimental zones, new agricultural parks, and leisure areas. Finally, a widespread infrastructural network made up of parks, canals, open spaces, scenic sites, and facilities has permeated the entire area.

In conclusion, due to the multiple urban projects and radical territorial transformations currently underway in the area, Zhengbian New District offers a unique opportunity to investigate the urbanisation processes affecting the Central Plains of China. However, Zhengbian is not unique. The provincial government has been the main promoter of a strategy to spread urbanisation based on the construction of new districts all over Henan. In just three years, from 2010 to 2013, 14 new provincial districts were established, bringing the total to 16 districts on 4,902 square kilometres.[21] This highlights the shift from "centripetal urbanisation" to "centrifugal urbanisation" brought about by the gradual regionalisation of forms of economic competition (X. Wang, 2007). Thus, Zhengbian New District is the result of new policies which endeavour to redesign more malleable and pervasive spaces, instead of investing in the creation of strong polarities. A plethora of plans emphasise this shift: the new order they envisage is capable of containing industrial districts and eco-cities, CBDs and agricultural towns, large stretches of countryside, and huge logistics areas. Within this loose and formable space, the programme does not function in terms of morphological construction, and the spatial layout is transformed into a dynamic surface that changes according to demand and opportunity. This has been noted by Isozaki (2012), who compared the urbanisation occurring in Zhengbian with the planet described by Stanisław Lem in his novel *Solaris* (1970): a sentient being in the form of a liquid surface that generates complex and impermanent structures. The relationships that new rhizomatic and polymorphic urbanisation will establish with cities, villages, new towns, infrastructures, and other environmental elements are vital to determining the new configuration of the Central Plains.

Fig. 35. View of Zhengzhou Airport Economic Zone, 2014.

1 The administrative definition of cities in the Chinese context has changed over time, since "city" is primarily a status designated by the government. For more details on this topic, see Richard J. R. Kirkby (1985), L. Zhang and Simon X.B. Zhao (1998), and Laurence J.C. Ma (2005). **2** The *hukou* system is a household registration system dividing the population into urban and rural segments. This was first adopted during the Mao era "to divide and organise people, to manage and allocate resources, including labour, and to enable political and social control" (F.-L. Wang, 2005, pp. 5–6). Although *hukou* is still in force, it has been progressively relaxed. **3** The TVEs replaced the People's Communes of the socialist period, which were progressively dismantled with the establishment of the Household Responsibility System in 1979 (Ren, 2013). **4** Zhengzhou was founded 3,600 years ago as an imperial city during the Shang dynasty and was the capital city of China from 1600 to 1046 BC. The city declined soon after the Han dynasty (*c.* 200 BC), and was just a minor administrative centre until the beginning of the twentieth century (Y. Liu et al., 2008; Zhu, 2012). **5** The cotton came into Zhengzhou from western China and was then sorted for the major coastal cities (especially Shanghai, Tianjin, and Quingdao). **6** Zhengzhou was one of the 156 key construction projects promoted by the central government for the industrialisation campaign undertaken in the 1950s (Hsu, 1996). **7** The first textile factory was operational in 1953 and two more came to fruition the following year. In 1956, with the construction of two more plants, the land surface occupied by the textile industry totalled 2,227,400 square metres west of the railway lines. Furthermore, in the same period, the government invested in constructing over 60 large and medium-sized enterprises, and in the early 1960s another 47 heavy industries were built in Zhengzhou (Cai et al., 2012). **8** Another relevant law of that period was the Provisional Measures for the Administration of Foreign Investors to Develop and Operate Plots of Land (1990). This allowed foreign investors to acquire land use rights for idle land from municipalities, and then develop it at a later stage (Yeh & Wu, 1996). Considering that in the first half of the 1990s approximately 90 percent of all foreign investments were absorbed by the land market, this law made a substantial contribution to the great urban transformation of that period (Q. He, 2000). **9** As reported by George C.S. Lin and Samuel P.S. Ho (2005), "of the land use rights distributed by conveyance during 1995–2002, 86 percent of the cases were done through closed-door negotiations (*xieyi*), and only 14 percent were transacted through public tender (*zhaobiao*) and auction (*paimai*)" (p. 426). **10** As reported by George C.S. Lin and Samuel P.S. Ho (2005), between 1995 and 2002 "a total of 945,213 cases of illegal land occupation, conversion, and transaction were uncovered, a number not far from the cases of land conveyance (964,868 cases). These illegal activities involved a total land area of 189,792 hectares, or 42 percent of the land obtained through legal conveyance" (p. 428). For an in-depth study on the mechanisms of illegal land transactions see Qinglian He (2000). **11** As reported by Laurence J.C. Ma (2005), "by the end of 1999, 97 percent of the cities at and above the prefecture-level had subordinate counties under their jurisdiction" (p. 487). **12** Kurokawa's proposal was based on previous architectural and urban studies already applied in projects such as *Hawaii Dreamland* (1966), the *Housing Plan* in Al-Sarir, Libya (1979–1984), *Hishino New Town Plan* (1967), *Shonan Life Town* in Fujisawa (1967), and, in particular, the *New Tokyo Plan 2025* (1987) (Kurokawa, 1991, 2005; Xue et al., 2011). **13** Most of the competitions' documents and projects either completed or still underway are illustrated in the series of five books edited by Li Keqiang, the Administrative Committee of Zhengdong New District, and the Zhengzhou Urban Planning Bureau (2010e, 2010b, 2010d, 2010c, 2010a) titled *Urban Planning and Architectural Design of Zhengdong New District in Zhengzhou City (2001–2009)*, published by the China Construction Industry Press. **14** See for instance the report *China Real Estate Bubble* (2013) by the CBC programme *60 Minutes* and the article by Gus Lubin (2011). **15** Jiang Xu and Anthony Yeh (2009) identify six main factors that drive re-hierarchisation and recentralisation of statehood in land governance. Three are directly related to the administrative body: the disobedience of local cadres, the emerging of powerful public–private partnerships (PPPs) and "growth coalitions", and the competitive strategies of some institutions. The others concern the management of real estate capital, the problems caused by increasing social stratification, and excessive spatial fragmentation. **16** Due to these policies, farming income across the country increased by more than 50 billion CNY, and direct benefits for farmers rose from 45.1 to 126 billion CNY. Furthermore, the central government invested 339.7 billion CNY in rural areas, and local governments also increased expenditures by an average of 20 percent (Su, 2009; Ye, 2009). **17** Since 1998, the central government financed the construction and improvement of rural power grids with 288.5 billion CNY. Between 2003 and 2007, 1.3 million kilometres of new roads were constructed, and from 2006 to 2008, investments in the Rural Drinking Water Safety Plan rose from 4 billion CNY to 7 billion CNY (China National Bureau of Statistics, 2020). **18** In 2008, the City and Country Planning Act extended the planning practices already applied by the municipal institutions in urban areas to the countryside. **19** In 2008, the MLR introduced a strict policy of farmland protection based on quotas. According to Fulong Wu (2015): "the policy was invented to maintain the nationwide stock of agricultural land at 1.8 billion mu (15 mu = 1 hectare)" (p. 58). However, since these quotas are just numbers without any established geographical position, they can be easily relocated from one place to another. **20** Within this general framework, several detailed plans have been developed for each area since 2006. Besides the *Zhengzhou City General Plan (2008–2020)*, the *Kaifeng City General Plan (2008–2020)* and other planning activities for Zhengdong New District and Kaifeng New Areas; under the guidelines of Arup's comprehensive plan several national and international experts were involved in drafting the *Zhengzhou Logistic and*

Technical Development Zone General Plan (2006–2020), the *Zhengbian Industrial Belt General Plan (2006–2020)*, the *Zhongmu County General Plan (2008–2020)*, and the *Zhengzhou Airport General Plan (2008–2035)* (Zhengzhou Municipality, 2009). **21** The Henan province hosts over 40 percent of Chinese provincial new districts. These involved the following municipalities: Zhengzhou – 1,840 square kilometres, Luoyang – 518 square kilometres, Kaifeng – 287 square kilometres, Anyang – 226 square kilometres, Shangqiu – 198 square kilometres, Nanyang – 190 square kilometres, Puyang – 189 square kilometres, Xinxiang – 188 square kilometres, Sanmenxia – 187 square kilometres, Jiaozuo – 180 square kilometres, Xuchang – 180 square kilometres, Luohe – 148 square kilometres, Pingdingshan – 148 square kilometres, Zhumadian – 148 square kilometres, Zhoukou – 145 square kilometres, and Hebi – 130 square kilometres (Fang & Yu, 2016; Henan Province Bureau of Statistics, 2020).

Artefacts and Structures

Cycling along County Road 006, one crosses the vast agricultural plain between Zhengzhou and Kaifeng. Until 2005, this concrete strip was the main route to most of the small rural settlements in Zhongmu County. Today, it is intersected by new highways, canals, and parks which have taken over the land between the traditional villages and farms. About four kilometres outside of the main town, the road abruptly vanishes into a grid of four-lane roads running alongside blocks of high-rise compounds. This is the edge of one of the many high-tech eco-cities currently under construction. Travelling along this new motorway, the sound of music captures one's attention. Suddenly, the street is fully occupied: a makeshift stage stands in the middle, surrounded by a large crowd of people enjoying the show, sitting on stools and rickshaws and eating instant noodles. Scenes like this are commonplace everywhere in the Central Plains. Here, the great socio-economic and political transformations are giving rise to a combination of new and old artefacts and practices that temporarily coexist and mix in unexpected ways. This shifting landscape is explored on the following pages by looking at ten sample territories in an area of 60 × 60 kilometres. These samples shed light on three phenomena: the overlaying of infrastructures, the juxtaposition of settlements, and the assembling of functions.

Assembling Functions

three samples

Juxtaposing Settlements

four samples

Overlaying Infrastructures

three samples

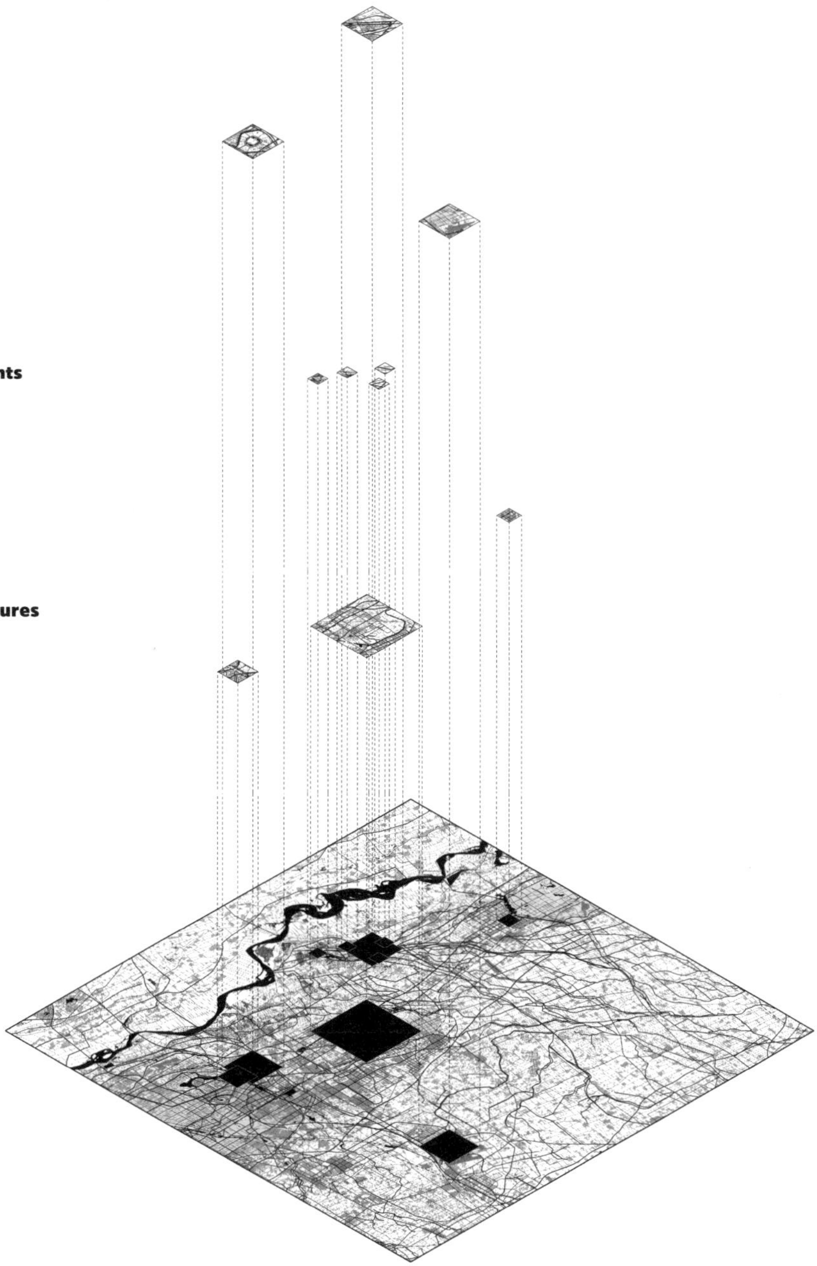

Fig. 1. Zhengbian New District.

Sampling the Field

Overlaying Infrastructures

In the last few decades, the infrastructural network in the Central Plains has been greatly improved. In Zhengzhou municipality alone, total roadways built per year have increased from 230 kilometres in 1978 to 2,101 kilometres in 2018; consequently, the overall paved area for infrastructural use has risen from 2,300 to 58,210 thousand square metres. Over the same time period, the water supply system has also been expanded from 306 to 4,420 kilometres (Zhengzhou Municipal Statistics Bureau, 2018). These are just a few examples of infrastructural improvement. However, this transformation has occurred in stages. Before 2010, most of the major changes involved the construction of long-distance connections and rapid mobility systems, whereas most of the infrastructure currently under construction involves grids devoted to homogenising the infrastructure across the entire territory. However, the pre-existing infrastructure networks are still being used, allowing those areas that have not yet been reached to continue functioning.

As a result, the territory of the Central Plains of China is organised around a precarious overlaying of superimposed infrastructures. On the following pages, we will seek to understand how these elements interact. To do so, we will describe the transformations that have occurred over the last two decades in three sample areas: Sample 1.A (9 × 9 kilometres) illustrates the changing relationship between the historic and modern systems of mobility; Sample 1.B (3 × 3 kilometres) demonstrates the impact of rapid, long-distance mobility systems; and finally, Sample 1.C (3 × 3 kilometres) clarifies how infrastructural grids are now used to organise future urban development.

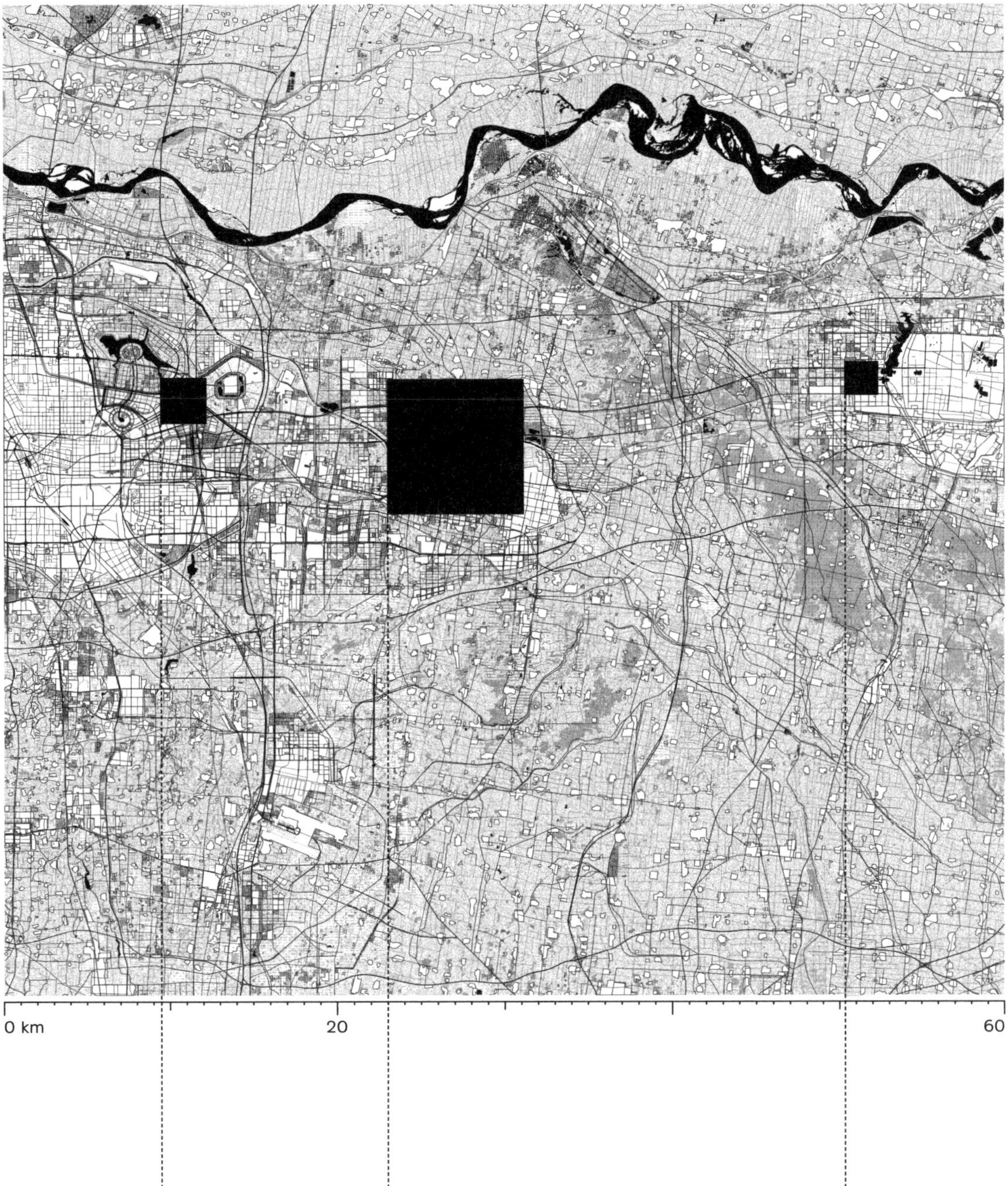

Sample 1.B.

Xiong'er River

Highways, Railways, and Rivers

[3 × 3 km]

Sample 1.A.

County Road 006

Paths, Concrete Roads, and Small Canals

[9 × 9 km]

Sample 1.C.

Kaifeng New Area

Grids

[2 × 2 km]

Fig. 2. Zhengbian New District.

Overlaying Infrastructure, Three Samples

May 2nd, 2019
Moving Inside the Kaifeng Grid

From the top of the monumental bridge leading to Kaifeng New Area, the enormous expanse of water and trees that is West Lake Park dominates the landscape. What was a fertile agricultural landscape until 2014 is now a recreational area as big as Central Park in Manhattan. I am in a bus entering the main strip of Kaifeng New Area: a ten-lane boulevard lined by greenbelts and towered over by skyscrapers, shopping malls, museums, and many other facilities. Crowds of shoppers fill the plazas, white-collar workers enter offices, and tourists head for parks and monuments. However, only a few plots down the road, this lively city fades: buildings gradually thin out, until construction sites give way to empty plots and fields. When I finally get off the bus, I am on a monumental square in the middle of nowhere. Only a few people and families are present in the vast expanse, exercising to the sound of traditional music and playing with kites. I approach a man and ask for information. "This is the centre of the new town," he explains. Then, pointing with his finger to construction on the opposite side of the square, he adds: "That's Kaifeng Museum! Go see it, it's amazing!"

The Kaifeng Museum looks like an ancient castle with large stone ramparts, towers at every corner, and surrounded by a moat. Everything is carefully designed to glorify the ancestral role of Kaifeng in shaping Chinese culture and its importance as a trading post along the Silk Road. However, the Kaifeng municipality's exhibition hall is also here. Passing from one side to the other, visitors are suddenly propelled from a bucolic past into an exciting future. This ends in Zhengbian New District: the ultimate megalopolis merging Kaifeng and Zhengzhou into a massive urban area full of ecological zones, international airports, logistic centres, industrial areas, and cultural facilities. This is illustrated with views, plans and official documents, and the most illuminating presentations are two short 4D movies. The first exalts the magnificent legacies of the past: imperial palaces, parks, lakes, and ancient pagodas. These are incorporated into the future city centre of Kaifeng, a complete reconstruction of the ancient city, replete with artisan workshops and traditional houses. The second is a virtual tour of the urbanisation newly under construction. Viewers soar high above the new town, passing by skyscrapers, through high-speed railway stations and university campuses, to finally enjoy a fireworks display in front of a huge lake. Together, these two movies provide a clear vision for the future of Kaifeng: while the city centre will be a simulacrum of the glorious past, the New Area will be a pleasant futuristic city.

After the show, I exit the building and I find myself thrown back into reality. So far, the new town is still in a suspended state, awaiting the great urban transformation. Since I have decided to explore this future dreamland further, I rent a bike and cycle south. Alongside the four-lane road, cleared fields alternate with recently completed high-rise apartments and low-rise compounds. The infrastructure grid is predictable, after about half a kilometre I intersect with another motorway. This is topped by a suspended railway: a new infrastructure connecting the entire Zhengbian New District, allowing commuters to travel between Zhengzhou and Kaifeng in less than 30 minutes at a cost of only 12.5 CNY. Under the bridge is a traditional agricultural village. Inside, life carries on as if nothing was out of the ordinary: chickens roam freely on dirt paths and people hang out their washing. I ask a woman about the massive concrete structure hanging over the villagers' heads and she exclaims: "It's our new sky!"

After crossing several intersections with troops of traffic lights controlling a non-existent flow of vehicles, I finally reach the southern part of the new town. Here, the big boxes of the production plants appear behind the greenway vegetation, and trucks transporting goods and raw materials in and out of warehouses and factories populate the streets. However, moving west along Yongcheng Road, building sites give way to farmland, and small warehouses and low-rise industrial sheds alternate with cropland growing poplar, grain, and vegetables. Finally, it is just agricultural fields. The grid of four-lane roads continues in the middle of farmlands, and, in the end, stops at the edge of a rural village. I decide to have a closer look and immediately notice several piles of rubble just outside the settlement. Although still inhabited, this will not be the village that stops the expansion of the infrastructural network. In fact, a small excavator is already digging a canal: it is just a matter of time before the grid continues its westward march.

Moving north along the western edge of the new town, the area seems progressively more attractive for real estate companies, and I am soon surrounded by the skeletons of high-rise buildings under construction. Wandering around in this anonymous and unpopulated landscape, my attention is suddenly caught by a group of young people walking carefree in the middle of the street with food in their hands. Since midday has just passed, I decide to ask them if there is a place nearby to eat something. Following their directions, I turn the corner and I am surprised to find a crowd of people gathering around several food stands. Here it is, the new town canteen! Soon, I am sitting on a stool, eating noodles from a plastic bag. Several people stare at me, a foreigner: eventually, a construction worker comes forward and asks something in Chinese. Since I cannot understand, he starts laughing, but a girl in her twenties eating nearby with a friend explains to me: "He wants to know where you are from!" After a short chat, I discover that the entrance of a huge university campus is just in front of these kiosks, and there are many more campuses along the road. The stands had set up here to serve the students and workers. When I ask her if she enjoys living in a place so far from the city centre, she answers: "I like the campus, all the facilities I need for study and sport activities are inside. There are several shopping malls in the new town, and there are plenty of buses to reach the city centre. Furthermore, the university is not far from the railway station, so I can easily visit my hometown in Sanmenxia."

After lunch, I keep travelling until I reach the north-west edge of the new town. Here, next to a four-lane road under construction, a nonstop stream of motorcycles, cars, and small trucks moves along a small dirt track. This arouses my curiosity, and leaving my rented bike behind I decide to follow the flow, asking a woman for a ride on the back of a three-wheeler. The road crosses the high-speed railway first, then a highway. When it finally emerges from the tangle of infrastructural lines, I am in a rural landscape: lines of trees run parallel to the concrete road, passing fishponds and cultivated fields. But what surprises me most is the congestion caused by vehicles and people compared with the emptiness of the new town's grid. At the end of the day, this old road is still the most used street between Kaifeng and the villages south of the Yellow River.

Back in the new town, I finally arrive at Kaifeng North railway station. As everywhere in China, it seems to be impossible to promote a new urban area without building a great infrastructural hub. The main railway station is now about nine kilometres from the city centre, in the middle of an expanse of empty plots still to be occupied. Like the museum, the design of the Kaifeng terminal is a nod to the historical legacy of the city. The low building is covered by a roof reminiscent of traditional Chinese palaces. A huge eight-lane boulevard ends a half-kilometre before the station, culminating in a huge plaza. There are no people, but the station is operating in full swing: trains move in and out, voices announce the latest information, and an endless line of taxis waits just outside the building. I ask one for a ride back to the city centre. While the taxi drives along the huge boulevards, a high-speed train flies right past me; if the new towns are a great promise of a world yet to come, one thing is already clear: the promise is backed by a solid infrastructural network.

Fig. 3. New embankments and parks along the Jailu River, Zhongmu County, 2017.

Fig. 4. Wentong Road under construction, Zhongmu County, 2019.

Sample 1.A is a 9 × 9-kilometre area located north-west of Zhongmu County in the heart of Zhengbian New District. In 2003, this place was still an agrarian landscape characterised by a capillary network of unpaved roads and footpaths. This dense and porous mobility system linked as many as 53 traditional agricultural villages and established relationships of proximity with farmland, small public spaces, and commercial activities. Of all the transport routes, the most important was County Road 006: a two-lane road paved with concrete, connecting fifteen villages.

From the mid-2000s to 2014, a first stage of infrastructural development led to the construction of rapid mobility corridors linking the major urban centres of the Central Plains. Until that time, the only highway from Zhengzhou to Kaifeng was the G30, built in the early 1990s in the northern area of Zhongmu County. In 2005, to tackle traffic congestion, Zhengkai Avenue was realised: a ten-lane road with 30 metres of greenway on either side, for a total width of 100 metres. Four years later, the Zihuan Road was also completed: a six-lane road (25 metres wide) with a greenway on each side (each 20 metres wide) crossing the area along the north–south axis. Major changes occurred between 2009 and 2014 due to the development of the infrastructural backbone of Zhengbian New District. First, the Zhengbian Logistics Passageway was built: an eight-lane expressway (40 metres wide), with 40 metres of greenway on each side, running a mere 1.5 kilometres south of Zhengkai Avenue. Second, the Zhengkai Intercity Railway was completed: a 50-kilometre-long high-speed intercity track that connects the new towns of Zhengzhou and Kaifeng in 35 minutes, with trains reaching a maximum speed of 200 km/h. The line was opened in 2015 and eleven stations serving the entire new district are under construction. Parallel to the building of rapid transit connections, greater attention was also given to the establishment of ecological corridors. Most greenways and riverbanks were turned into parks with bike paths, canals, and minor avenues of transit. Furthermore, several sites were converted into recreation areas, such as the China Green Expo completed in 2010 at the centre of Sample 1.A: a 2-square-kilometre garden exhibition encompassing a 150,000-square-metre artificial lake. Despite these great transformations, the previous pattern of small infrastructures was still in use in most of the area. Moreover, several pre-existing infrastructures, such as County Road 006, were integrated into the new system of mobility and open spaces entirely. Consequently, the overall network was upgraded while maintaining the porosity of the historic system.

These conditions started to change in 2014, when a second wave of infrastructure development got underway in preparation for the forthcoming urbanisation. Indeed, as envisaged in the plans for Zhengbian New District, Sample 1.A is expected to be one of the main residential nuclei of the new urban expansion. Consequently, 31 traditional villages have been demolished and the land redeveloped. Eighty-five new compounds, mostly high-rise buildings, have been built in their place, and 28 more sites are under construction. These settlements are organised according to a new infrastructural layout composed of two main elements. First, grids of four-lane roads divide the area into mega-plots that range from 500 × 500 to 1,000 × 1,000 metres. Second, there is a new

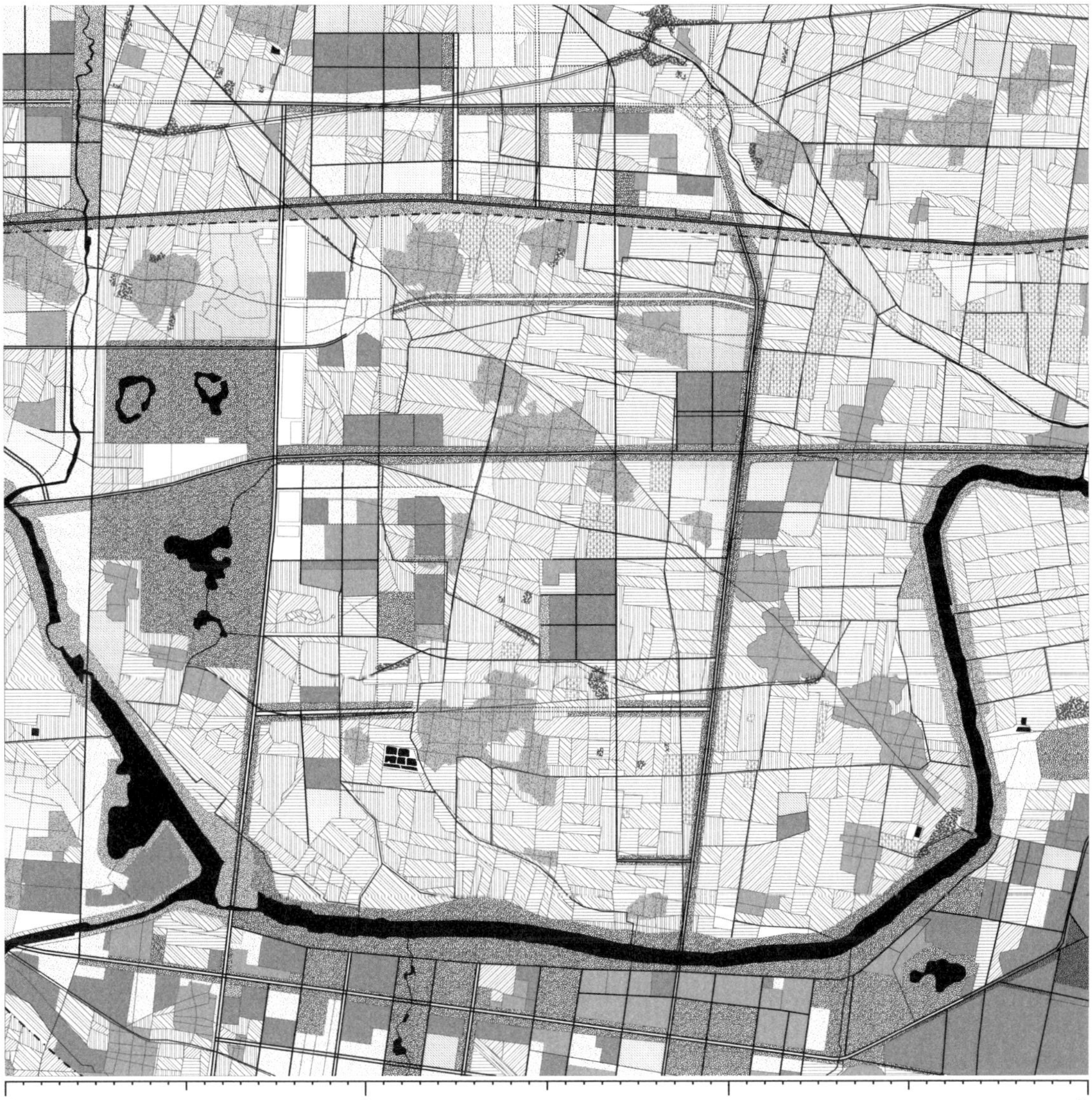

Fig. 5. Sample 1.A.

County Road 006

Legend

- railways
- roads
- built-up areas
- water
- parks and parks under construction
- crops, arable land, and greenhouses
- demolished areas
- non-permeable surfaces

ecological system made up of parks, large canals, and recreation areas. Indeed, greenways have been realised along all the main streets, and canals and riverbanks have been transformed into linear parks. Moreover, a total area of 5 square kilometres has been converted for recreational activities and includes the China Green Expo, the Zhengzhou Fantawild Dreamland (1.2 square kilometres), and a new "historical park", under construction on an over 500,000-square-metre area south of the intercity railway station. As a result, during the last five years, 175 kilometres of new roads and 12.5 square kilometres of new parks have been built in Sample 1.A. These massive infrastructures are radically altering the pre-existing network: they are not just additions, rather they progressively assimilate and ultimately replace the previous configuration. However, during the latency which precedes a complete substitution, the ancient network of infrastructure continues to function. County Road 006 is a perfect example of this: while the western part has recently been dismantled, the eastern section remains one of the busiest roads to the centre of Zhongmu County. This highlights the complexity of today's infrastructure system in the Central Plains of China: a mix of incongruous elements precariously sharing the same space, allowing it to work in unexpected ways.

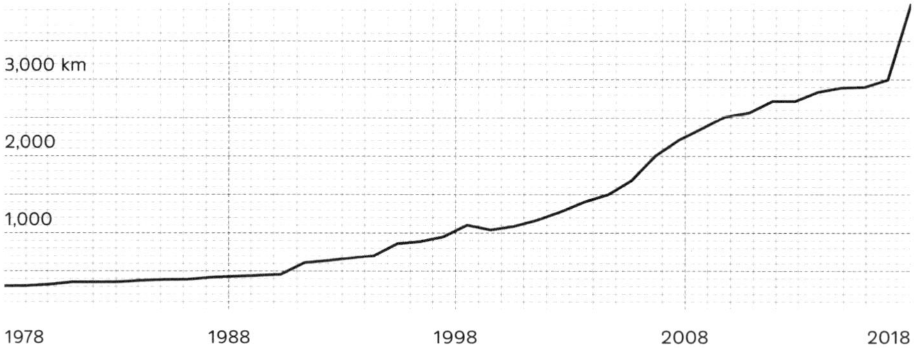

Fig. 6. Water supply system in Zhengzhou municipality, 2019.

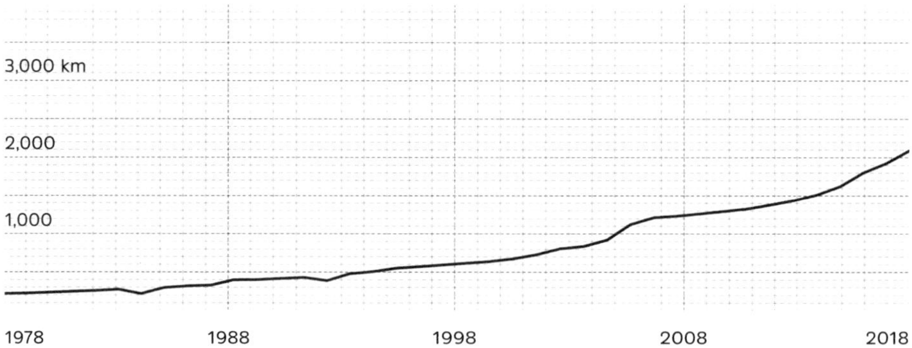

Fig. 7. Road network in Zhengzhou municipality, 2019.

2003

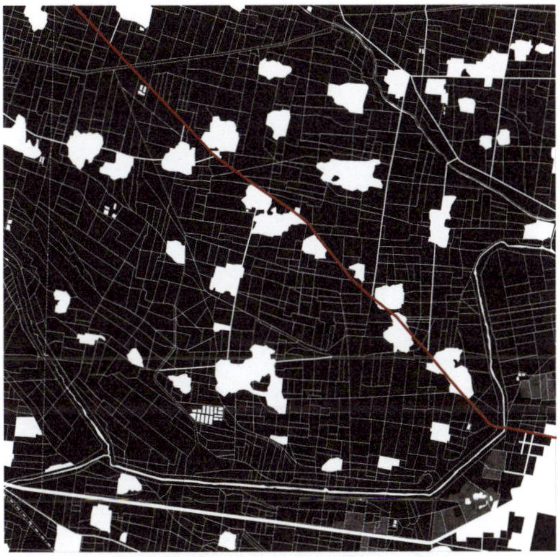

2011

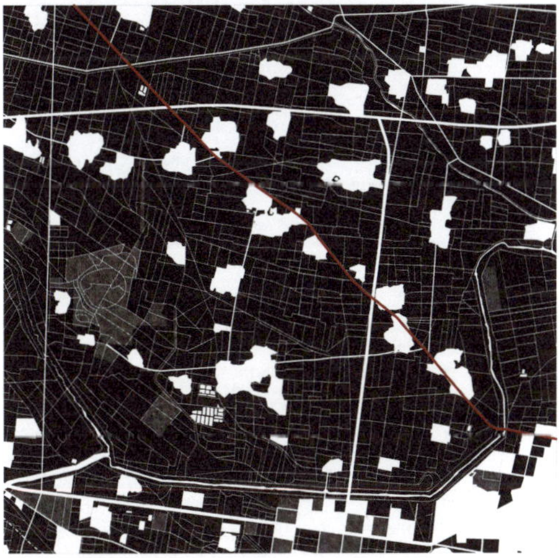

2019

Figs. 8–9–10. Sample 1.A over time.

County Road 006

Legend

County Road 006

areas under construction

built-up areas

permeable surfaces

Fig. 11. Track north of Qinggudui Village, Zhongmu County, 2019.

Fig. 12. Road in Gangtouqiao Village, Zhongmu County, 2019.

Sample 1.B is a 3 × 3-kilometre area located north of Zhengdong railway station, between Zhengdong CBDs and the university town. Since it is at the physical intersection of three main infrastructure networks, this site is representative of how new major rapid transit infrastructures have changed the landscape and the allocation of natural resources in relation to new land use.

As for Sample 1.A, the diachronic description of the transformations reveals the same shift from a dense network of minor roads to a rapid transport system made up of highspeed railway lines and motorways (above all, the third ring road of Zhengzhou and the major axes of Zhengdong New District). This has led to an increase from 720,000 square metres of non-permeable surfaces in 2003 to 2,900,000 square metres at present. Paved roads accounted for two-thirds of this growth. The new mobility layout uses two kinds of roads to section the land: four-lane roads creating blocks, and two-lane roads providing access. This dual network separates the rapid and slow traffic systems and rigidly divides the land into sections. This changes the relationships between different urban artefacts: if they were once based on proximity, as was the case for the traditional villages where the spaces for different functions intermingled; the new system of mobility now allows fast connections between distant elements while subdividing clearly defined functional areas such as public parks, schools, or residential compounds.

In parallel with this process, the water system was also subject to radical restructuring. Since Sample 1.B is crossed by the most important waterways in Zhengbian New District (the Jialu and the Xiong'er Rivers, and the Dongfeng Canal), there has always been a plentiful supply of water. This lowland has thus been modelled over time for fish farming: a productive landscape made up of a network of small canals ensured the functioning of more than 500 fishponds on 207,500 square metres. All this began to change with the construction of Zhengdong New District in 2004. In order to support the network of navigable canals and major lakes envisaged in Kurokawa's plan, the entire water system needed to be reinforced and rationalised. Consequently, between 2004 and 2009, the artificial riverbeds of the Xiong'er River and the Dongfeng Canal were both widened to 95 metres, and a system of dams was built to retain water. With urban growth reaching the southern part of Sample 1.B, the network of irrigation canals was progressively dispensed with, and many fishponds in the northern part were drained. In 2016, the reorganisation of the water system was completed by widening the Jialu riverbed from 10 to 60 metres and building a new waterway to connect the Dongfeng Canal directly to Longhu Lake. In the meantime, drainage works continued, and, apart from a few small lakes inside the university campuses, all water is now collected in the main canals. The result is a new system made up of great waterways to maintain the multitude of parks created along the main infrastructural corridors. This demonstrates a radical shift in water use, which is now no longer chiefly devoted to agrarian production, but landscape beautification.

Fig. 13. Sample 1.B.

Xiong'er River

Legend

- railways
- roads
- built-up areas
- water
- parks and parks under construction
- construction sites
- trees and vegetation
- non-permeable surfaces

Indeed, the creation of a "green infrastructure", that is, a network of parks, is the third major change. This has been occurring together with the construction of new roads and waterways: the riverbanks of the main canals have been progressively transformed into river parks with a width ranging between 50 and 150 metres, and greenways that commonly reach 15 metres have been realised alongside main traffic routes. Furthermore, as was envisaged in the plan for the new town, a series of new parks have been realised. A shining example is the Zhengzhou High Speed Rail Park: a 700-metre-wide ecological corridor running along the railway line for more than 10 kilometres. As a result, in Sample 1.B, parks account for a total area of 2,840,000 square metres, and a further 650,000 square metres are still being implemented. In contrast, all the agricultural land has been converted, with a total loss of about 5,000,000 square metres of arable land. As for the transformations affecting the water system, the network of parks evidences the shift from a landscape suited to production activities to an environment that promotes an image of health and wellbeing.

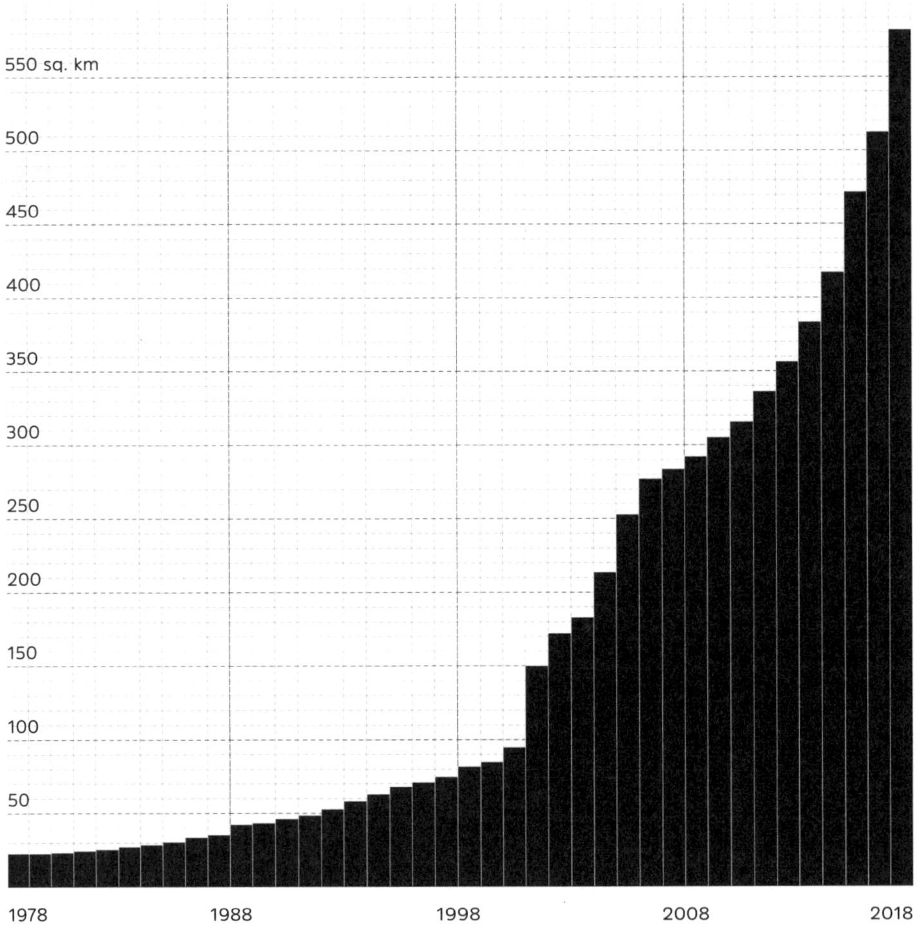

Fig. 14. Paved roads in Zhengzhou municipality, 2019.

2003

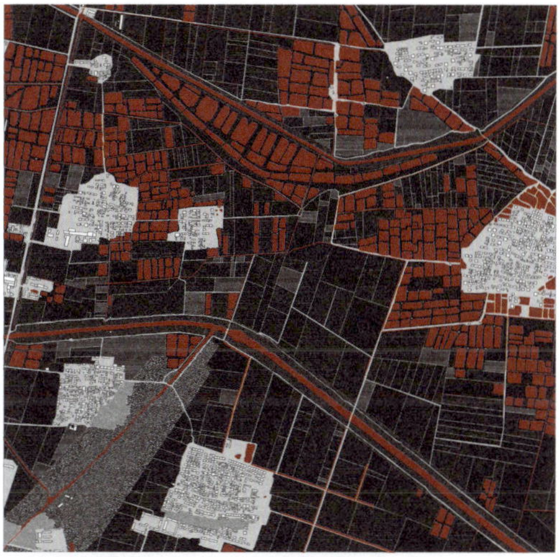

2011

2019

Figs. 15–16–17. Sample 1.B over time.

Xiong'er River

Legend

water

areas under construction

built-up areas

permeable surfaces

Fig. 18. Zhengdong High Speed Rail Park, Zhengdong New District, 2019.

Fig. 19. Qili River, Zhengdong New District, 2019.

Fig. 20. Xiong'er River, Zhengdong New District, 2019.

Sample 1.C is a 2 × 2-kilometre site located in the Kaifeng New Area, the eastern part of Zhengbian New District. In the last twenty years, this place has been progressively equipped with infrastructure based on a grid layout which hybridises programmes and uses. Indeed, in 2003, this area was still only used for agriculture, with just a few shops and amenities located inside the two villages of Yanzhai and Maozhai. As with samples 1.A and 1.B, this site was also once characterised by a dense network of small infrastructure systems mainly composed of dirt roads and irrigation canals. In 2005, work began on the infrastructure for promoting the Kaifeng Free Trade Zone, an industrial cluster to be developed on 15 square kilometres near the existing railway line. However, only minor changes occurred, mostly due to a lack of industries setting up in the southern portion of Sample 1.C. One of these changes was a six-lane road (Songcheng Road) built in 2005 to connect the area to Kaifeng city centre by demolishing the southern part of Maozhai Village. Between 2007 and 2008, the Zhengkai Avenue was also realised, crossing the northern part of the site to connect Kaifeng to Zhengzhou.

The infrastructural developments in Sample 1.C have gained momentum since 2009 as part of the promotion of the Zhengbian New District. As the new plan envisaged doubling Kaifeng in size by urbanising 40 square kilometres north of the Free Trade Zone, an orthogonal layout was set to parcel the land out into 500 × 500-metre mega-plots. This layout is made up of 100-metre-wide strips composed of three types of infrastructure. First, four-lane or more roads, ranging in width from 25 to 40 metres. Second, greenbelts separating the interior areas of each mega-plot from the rapid mobility system, designed as urban parks containing minor transit networks such as bike paths, pedestrian avenues, and main waterways. Finally, an infrastructure network made up of pipes, cables, sewers, heat, and energy running both overhead via power lines and below ground. This combination of infrastructures aims to equip each mega-plot the same way, allowing it to support all programmes. Indeed, Kaifeng New Area is now a mix of different uses and morphologies, all side by side. The new infrastructural grid hosts more than forty residential compounds, nine major factories, and two of the main shopping malls in the city. Seven university campuses have been established, together with other public facilities, such as museums, monumental squares, and theatres. Moreover, pre-existing elements and programmes have been retained within the infrastructural grid: eleven agricultural villages are still inhabited, and plots that have not yet been developed are still used for farming. As a result, this infrastructural grid, like many others under construction in the Central Plains, is a means of homogeneously equipping the whole area, shaping a vast, open landscape to assure the correct functioning of programmes and morphologies that are radically different from one another.

Fig. 21. Sample 1.C.

Kaifeng New Area

Legend

- railways
- roads
- built-up areas
- water
- parks and parks under construction
- construction sites
- crops and arable land
- non-permeable surfaces

Fig. 22. Grid and villages, Kaifeng New Area, 2019.

2003

2007

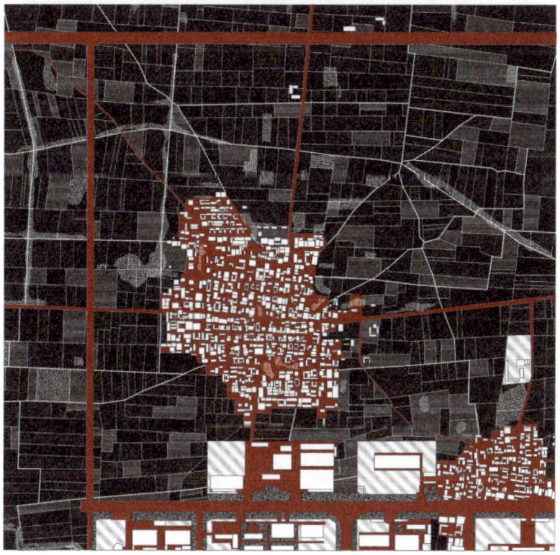

2019

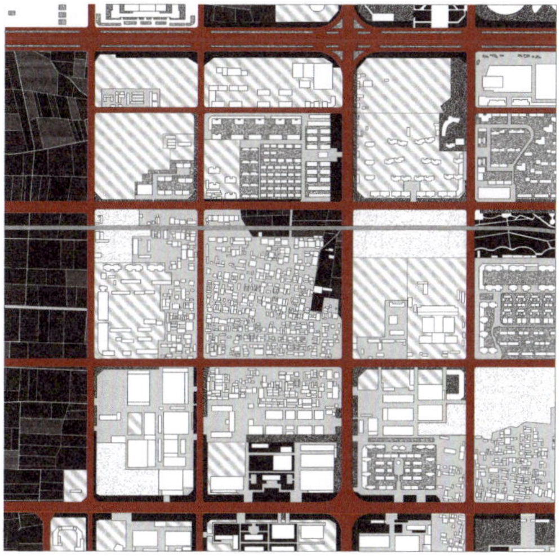

Figs. 23–24–25. Sample 1.C over time.

Kaifeng New Area

Legend

roads

areas under construction

built-up areas

permeable surfaces

Fig. 26. Songcheng Road, inside the grid of Kaifeng New Area, 2019.

Fig. 27. Jinyao Road, inside the grid of Kaifeng New Area, 2019.

Juxtaposing Settlements

Over the last 25 years, real estate investments in the Henan province have grown from 5 to 709 billion CNY (Henan Province Bureau of Statistics, 2020). Consequently, the total floorspace of new buildings realised per year has increased dramatically from 15,335,500 to 207,363,300 square metres, and revenue has grown from 1.6 to 713 billion CNY. In 2017, residential construction accounted for 88 percent of total transactions, and investment in residential buildings amounted to 533 billion CNY, generating a total revenue of 590 billion CNY (Henan Province Bureau of Statistics, 2020). This enormous property boom, which is characteristic of all municipalities in the Henan province, is completely transforming the Central Plains territory. While major changes occurred mainly in urban fringes and new towns until 2010, over the last decade these have affected the entire territory, progressively transforming ways of life and perceptions not just in urban areas, but also remote places. This is evident when considering the mix of housing that is found throughout Zhengbian New District. Here, in addition to the well-known high-rise apartments that epitomise the rapid urbanisation of China, four types of settlements can be identified: traditional agricultural villages, modern agricultural villages, new agricultural towns, and real estate compounds.

A perfect example of this incredible mix of settlements is Yanming Lake Town, in Zhongmu County, an area located 15 kilometres north of Zhongmu Town, 35 kilometres east of the Zhengdong New District, and 15 kilometres west of Kaifeng New Area. At present, Yanming Lake Town comprises 21 administrative villages, of which two are new agricultural towns, with a total resident population of 28,000 inhabitants, whose average income is 1,300 CNY per month. According to the plans for the Zhengbian New District, the site is part of the ecological corridor south of the Yellow River and is therefore designated to become an "agricultural park" based on recreational activities and efficient agricultural production (Arup Engineering Consulting Company et al., 2010). To accomplish this, the plan provides for the development of new settlements and the conversion of the existing villages. In light of these transformations, the following pages present the spatial features of the four different types of settlement in Yanming Lake Town: the traditional village of Yuezhuang (Sample 2.A), the modern agricultural village of Weigang (Sample 2.B), the Zhugu New Agricultural Town (Sample 2.C), and the Chang Jiyun Compound developed by the real estate company Vanke (Sample 2.D). These cases highlight a progressive shift in dwelling typologies, manifesting how rural zones are increasingly being integrated into the urban dynamics, to the point that the distinction between urban and rural areas is being progressively blurred.

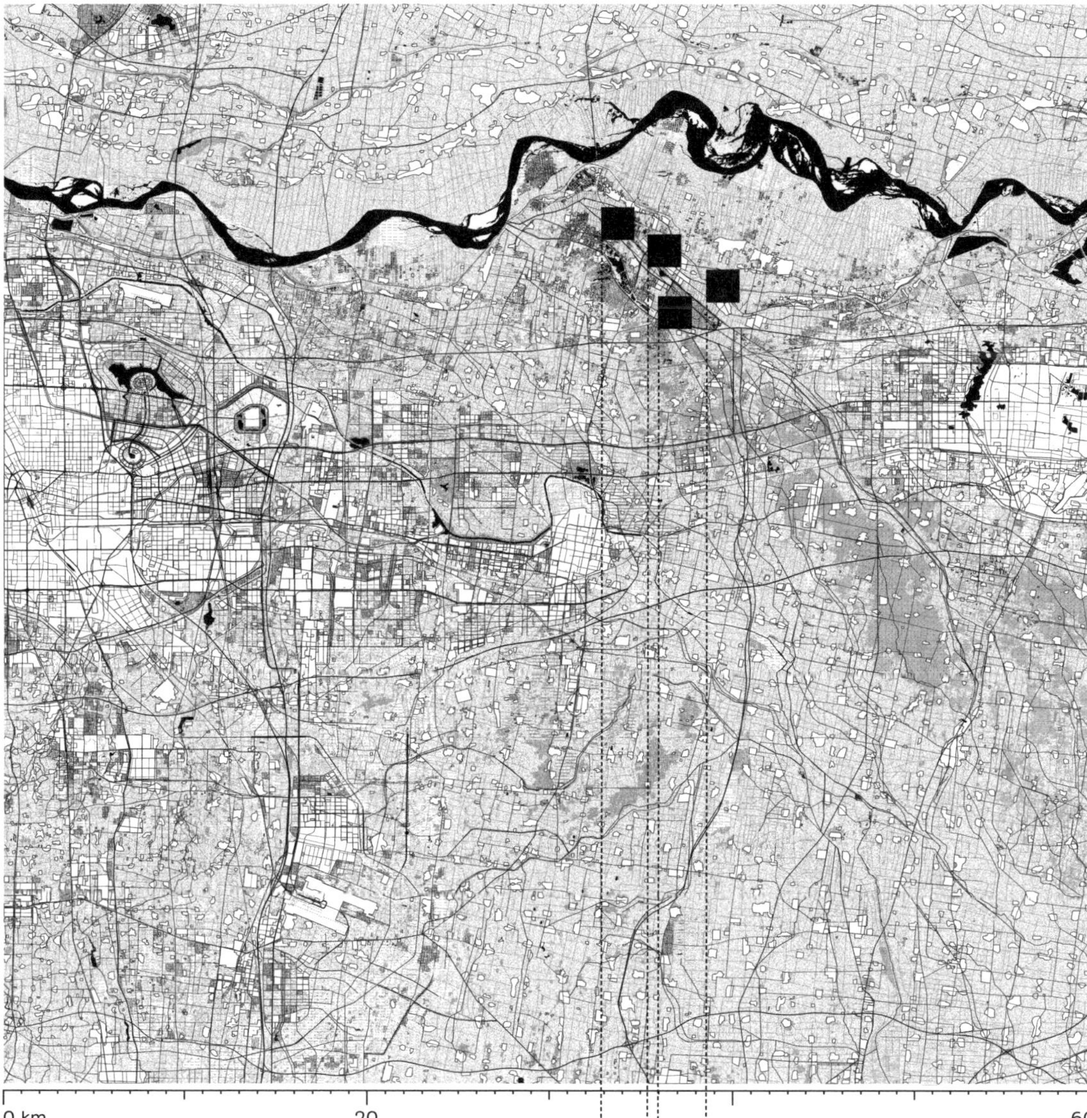

Sample 2.A
Yuezhuang Village
Traditional Agricultural Villages
[1.5 × 1.5 km]

Sample 2.D
Chang Jiyun Compound
Real Estate Compounds
[1.5 × 1.5 km]

Sample 2.B
Weigang Village
Modern Agricultural Villages
[1.5 × 1.5 km]

Sample 2.C
Zhugu New Agricultural Town
New Agricultural Towns
[1.5 × 1.5 km]

Fig. 28. Zhengbian New District.
Juxtaposing Settlements, Four Samples

October 14th, 2017

Life at the Edge of the New District

Most books and articles depict Chinese new towns as sorry imitations of European cities, full of empty skyscrapers and abandoned shopping malls. These mainstream descriptions illustrate one side of the coin, but what about the other side? What does it mean to inhabit the fringes of a new town? In search of answers, I convinced my travel companion, photographer Samuele Pellecchia, to visit Yanming Lake Town and explore this lesser known "life at the outskirts". Despite the name, Yanming Lake Town is not a proper city; it is not even a single settlement, but an administrative area located in the northern part of Zhongmu County, south of the Yellow River.

After breakfast at our hotel in Zhongmu, a taxi drives us towards the Yellow River. Soon, after passing Zhengkai Avenue, we find ourselves in a peaceful countryside with no signs of the ongoing urbanisation process. We decide to continue the search for visible signs of development and I ask the driver to take a side road. After a while, we stop in a village. The dense settlement is made up of a hodgepodge of dwelling styles. While some are reminiscent of stereotypical traditional Chinese buildings, the scene is much less bucolic since the majority have recently been "improved" by the addition of three or more storeys of steel frames and prefabricated concrete walls. The increased height of the new constructions turn the streets into narrow alleyways between five- or even six-storey buildings. These muddy lanes are filled with a motley assortment of cars, small tractors, agricultural tools, and wastebins; hammocks hang from trees and tables are scattered all along the main street. Presumably, most of the villagers are at work at the moment, and we just hear voices coming from the houses.

After passing through a similar settlement, our attention is caught by a row of identical houses in the distance: featureless three-storey concrete boxes with an enclosed yard in front, forming unbroken lines of semi-detached homes. Entering the village gate, we come to the centre: a large square with a Chinese flag flying in the middle. Some kids are playing, but most of the space is taken up by bushels of corn left out to dry. All around are public buildings, such as the school and the town hall. At first sight, the village seems to be an attempt at creating a space of socialist monumentality in a rural area: an updated version of the agrarian commune based on an egalitarian system that reflects a clear political ideal. This, together with the poor condition of the structures, makes us think the settlement must have been built in the late 1970s but, surprisingly, this is not the case. Walking around, we see a date painted in red on a gate: 2013! We ask a young girl passing by and she confirms our hypothesis, the village was built just five years ago, with the aim of improving the living conditions of people in rural areas. Using the translation app on our phone, we manage to ask the girl if she is happy living in the new village, and she says she is. However, just beyond the last houses is a young mother with a baby on her back, kneeling to pick vegetables. And she is not alone, the entire field is full of peasants tilling the land using hand tools.

This scene underscores the glaring contradictions of the rural areas: in the villages, brand-new cars are parked all around, here, one sees only a few small tractors and simple farm machines. Paradoxically, in this emerging industrialised country, where train speeds exceed 300 km/h, people still work the land using primitive methods.

While Samuele is taking pictures, I turn and find what I am looking for. Within this agrarian landscape, a construction crane stands as a beacon of urbanisation in a sea of agrarian fields: something is happening there! We approach the spot, the small road we are on turning into an expressway with greenways and gardens; we finally arrive in the central area of Yanming Lake Town, where various plots of land have recently been cleared, numerous sites are under construction, and several high-rise buildings are going up. We stop in a parking lot where a man dressed in a smart uniform guards a gate. We approach him and ask whether it is possible to visit the site under construction: a luxury housing complex promoted by the Vanke real estate company. He pulls out his phone and tells us to wait. In a few minutes, a young woman appears dressed in business clothes. In simple English, she asks if we want to have a tour inside the compound. As soon as we enter the gate, we find ourselves in a place completely detached from its surroundings. A path through a bamboo grove ends on a green lawn running down to a large artificial lake surrounded by lush vegetation. In this peaceful landscape, there is almost no noise but the sounds of nature. This scenic effect is even more astonishing when the paved path goes a metre below the level of the lake, and we unexpectedly find ourselves walking like Moses through the water. Around us, children are trying to catch little fish just below the calm surface of the lake, and their parents are saying goodbye to the staff. The exhibition centre is about two hundred metres away: a huge building in the style of an exclusive country club, with great windows looking out onto the beautiful scenery. Entering the building, we pass through a series of bright, carefully designed, and beautifully furnished rooms: a lobby, a lounge area, a library filled with books about architecture and design, and a playroom with billiards and games for children. Finally, our guide stops in front of a huge model that displays the layout of the urban area and tells us that the majority of the apartments have already been sold, although a few houses are still available, and begins to meticulously describe the different housing typologies currently under construction. Another woman brings us a cup of tea, and someone else gives us several brochures with plans and images illustrating the wide variety of available dwellings. When the woman concludes her presentation, we move to another room, where several stands display the high-quality building materials and fixtures used for construction. Here pipes, building insulation, bathroom fixtures, and security doors are exhibited to celebrate the progress of technology in the construction industry.

When we are about to leave, our guide asks us if we would be interested in visiting the showhouses. She explains to us that although the site is still under construction, a building of each housing type has been completed so that buyers can experience first-hand what life in Vanke's compound is like. The tour inside the full-size models is astonishing. The houses look as if they are currently inhabited, their owners kindly letting us visit their private realms. Not only have the dwellings been stylishly furnished with expensive ceilings lights, luxury rugs, and fancy tables, there are even fake personal objects to create atmosphere, pictures hanging on walls, clothes inside the wardrobes, and laptops propped open on the desks. Even the fridge is full of plastic food. Of course, everything is Westernised: not chopsticks, but cutlery; not Chinese food, but baguettes and croissants; not Chinese books, but English ones. There is a clear message here: living in this compound means being part of a more-than-bourgeois elite of international businesspeople. This mood is emphasised by the luxury conveniences: each dwelling has a private lift, on each rooftop is a gazebo with a jacuzzi, not to mention the walk-in closets decorated with replicas of Rolex watches.

After our visit to the real estate compound, a nearby development draws our attention. As we enter, we immediately understand that the socialist-style agricultural village we had just visited is now out of date. This is a new agricultural town, radically different not only in building construction and urban layout, but also in the imaginary promoted. Here, the housing type is similar to suburban villas: two- or three-storey buildings with composite tiled roofs, bow windows, garages, and private gardens. However, the housing density is much higher than in any non-Chinese suburban developments we have ever seen, and the monotonous rows of semi-detached houses seem to stretch for miles. The taxi moves on and we arrive at the centre, a big square surrounded by administrative buildings and facilities such as the school, medical centres, and shopping areas. The latter have probably been built recently and are, for now, mostly still empty. A canal crosses the town, dividing it into two sections. At present, it is just a small trickle of water with wasteland along the banks, but a poster shows that it will soon become a public park with trees and gardens all around. After crossing the waterway, the road becomes a dirt path, and we decide to continue on foot. The rows of houses are seemingly endless. Although some are yet to be finished and the streets are yet to be paved, the majority are already inhabited. Most of the front yards are used to dry crops and corn, some of them have vegetable gardens, others are used to store tools for farming or construction. Several people are walking along the street. They look puzzled and a little taken aback to see us, but after we wave and greet them, their expressions turn friendly and smiling. A group of young kids is particularly intrigued by our presence. Three of them are riding a small motocross bike and another follows on a bicycle. They start to circle us, asking something in Chinese and laughing. We say hello and finally, the bravest gets off his bicycle and asks to get a photo of us all together. Just after taking the picture, a woman comes out of her house. Dressed in light teal pyjamas and light teal sneakers she approaches us smiling: "Hello! Do you need help?" Seeing our surprise at her perfect English, she immediately explains that she is an English teacher at the middle school in the village. After introductions, we take the opportunity to have a chat and ask her about the new settlements. She tells her story: "It is about a year since I moved in with my family. The new house is spacious, and there are many conveniences compared with our previous place. Before this, we lived in the ancient Zhugu Village, just at the end of the road." When we ask her whether they were given the choice to remain in the previous village or move to the new one, she looks at us in surprise and says: "Of course not! But, anyway, why? Who would want to live there? Nowadays, there are just a few families left, but they will probably move soon."

The teacher was right, crossing the last line of houses we suddenly see a large expanse of ruins: the old Zhugu Village. We decide to look around the scene of devastation, where only a few walls stand as survivors in a landscape of ash and dust. In the middle of this no-man's land, a house surrounded by rubble piled as high as its rooftop catches our attention. This quaint, ancient building looks like it is still inhabited. We approach the construction site and I peep inside the courtyard gate. Plastic basins and small tables are scattered around the patio, wooden tools lean against the walls, and wet laundry is hanging from the window. Sitting on a stool is an old man working. As soon as he sees us, he waves and turns to call to someone inside. Suddenly, an old woman dressed in a blue jacket with a scarf over her head walks out of the house and comes forward until she stands less than a metre away. We stare at each other. Her face, furrowed with deep lines, hints first at doubt, and then her expression turns to surprise. She says something to us in Chinese and points to the camera. Samuele uses gestures to ask her if he can take a picture and she starts smiling and laughing. We take some pictures while the woman continues to speak to us in Chinese and touch our face and our hands: we had become friends. After a while we say goodbye and conclude our journey.

On the way back to Zhongmu, the taxi crosses a mixture of scenery: agricultural fields, factories, huge building sites, villages, and fields again. Our journey has been crucial to understanding the transformations that come with the construction of new settlements in rural areas. It seems obvious that we are witnessing a great process of urbanisation that is radically affecting the entire area in many different ways, but the main questions still remain: what is the purpose of this great process? What kind of city is ultimately expected to come out of all this?

Fig. 29. Yanzhang New Agricultural Town, Zhongmu County, 2019.

Traditional Agricultural Villages

Many settlements in the Central Plains of China are still agricultural villages developed in olden times, almost unchanged in the last century. Like Yuezhuang, described in Sample 2.A, these traditional agricultural villages are generally compact settlements occupying 120,000 to 250,000 square metres. Their fringes are marked by vegetation, small artificial ponds, and minor public spaces. Communal spaces for agricultural production, barns, and sites for waste collection are found on the outskirts of such settlements. The main public services, such as the town hall and the school, are generally situated at the centre of the village in small buildings near the main crossroads. Commercial activities, small warehouses, and restaurants are integrated into the dwellings, which are courtyard houses situated side by side and oriented north–south, with narrow lanes running between. There are normally between 350 and 450 of these buildings, housing a total population of 1,000–1,500 inhabitants.

Most of the oldest houses in these traditional agricultural villages are one of two types that share similar features. Both are courtyard houses with a total footprint of 200 to 250 square metres. The house is a rectangular one- or two-storey structure located on the north side of the court, with the entrance and the windows facing south. The floor plan consists of about 95 square metres divided into six rooms, organised as follows: at the centre is the living room (about 18 square metres), which is connected to three smaller spaces, commonly used as the kitchen (about 9 square metres), and two bedrooms (about 14 square metres each). The buildings on the western and eastern sides of the courtyard are smaller structures not directly connected to the main block. The interior is divided into small rooms used as workspaces, storage areas, henhouses, or small barns. Finally, the southern side of the courtyard is enclosed by walls with a gated entrance. Each block of the courtyard house is made of brick with wooden trusses supporting a pitched tiled gable roof. Apart from decorations on the roof ridge and the courtyard gate, the form of the complex is simple and linear.

Although these traditional typologies are still dominant in traditional agricultural villages, the New Socialist Countryside programme has been replacing them with modern buildings since the mid-2000s. Still greater changes have occurred since 2010, when owners were allowed to add steel structures clad in prefabricated concrete or corrugated steel to their buildings. Such structures often completely cover the entire courtyard, adding up to six or seven storeys to the existing dwelling. As a result, some villages are now composed of rows of massive compact buildings (20 × 15 metres) separated by dark narrow lanes.

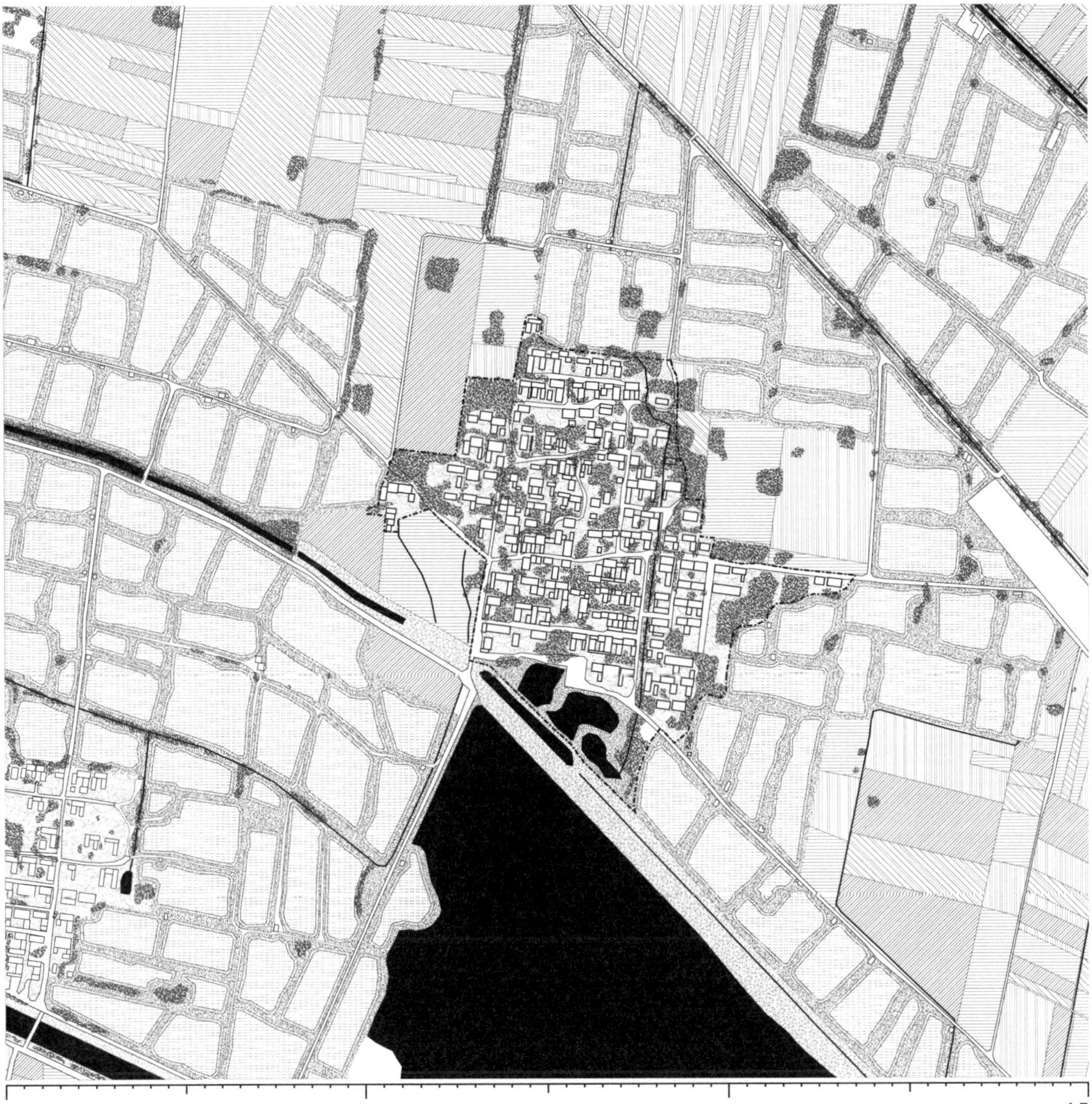

0 km 0.5 1.5

Fig. 30. Sample 2.A.

Yuezhuang Village

Inhabitants: about 900 people

Construction period: NA

Total area: 180,000 sq. m

Total housing units: about 250

Legend

- fishponds
- roads
- built-up areas
- water
- trees and vegetation
- bare land
- crops and arable land
- non-permeable surfaces

Fig. 31. Housing types in Sample 2.A.

Yuezhuang Village

Type A

House area: 200 sq. m

Number of houses: about 500 units

Type B

House area: 250 sq. m

Number of houses: about 300 units

20 m

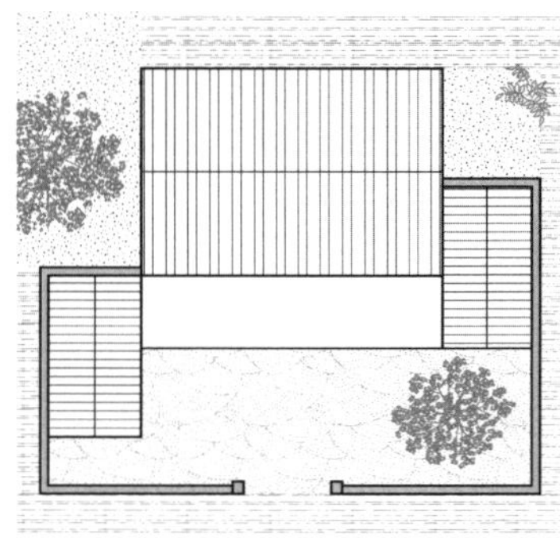

TOP

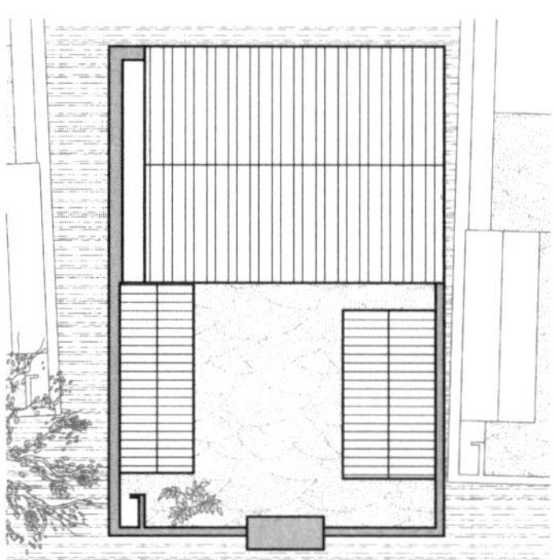

TOP

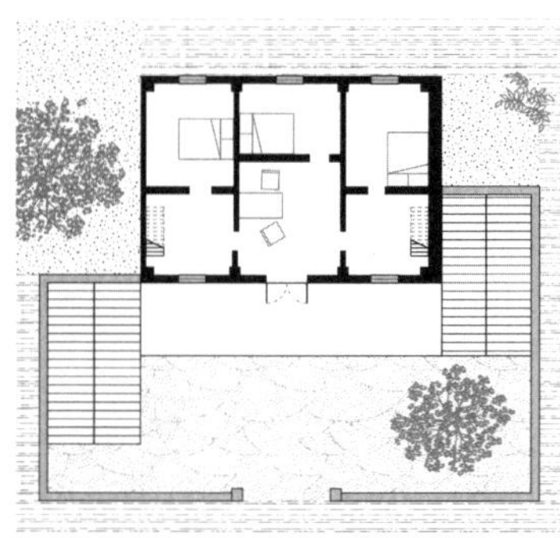

1F

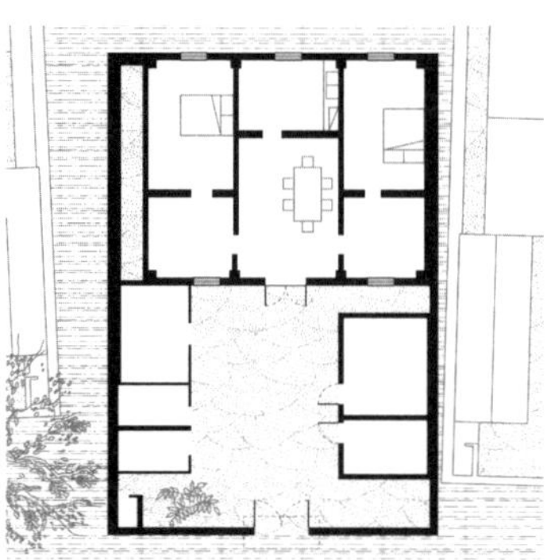

GF

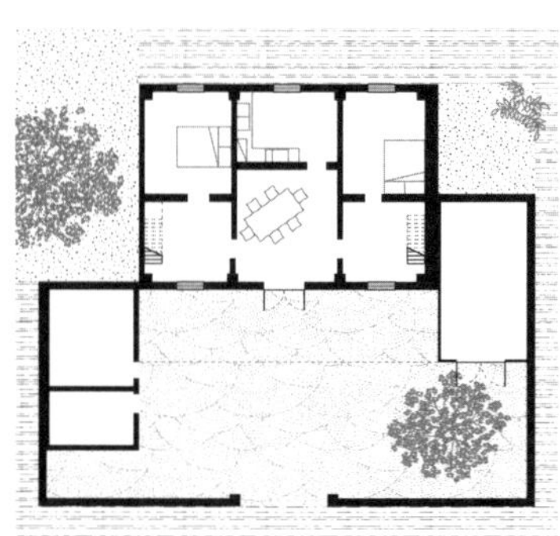

GF

Type A

Type B

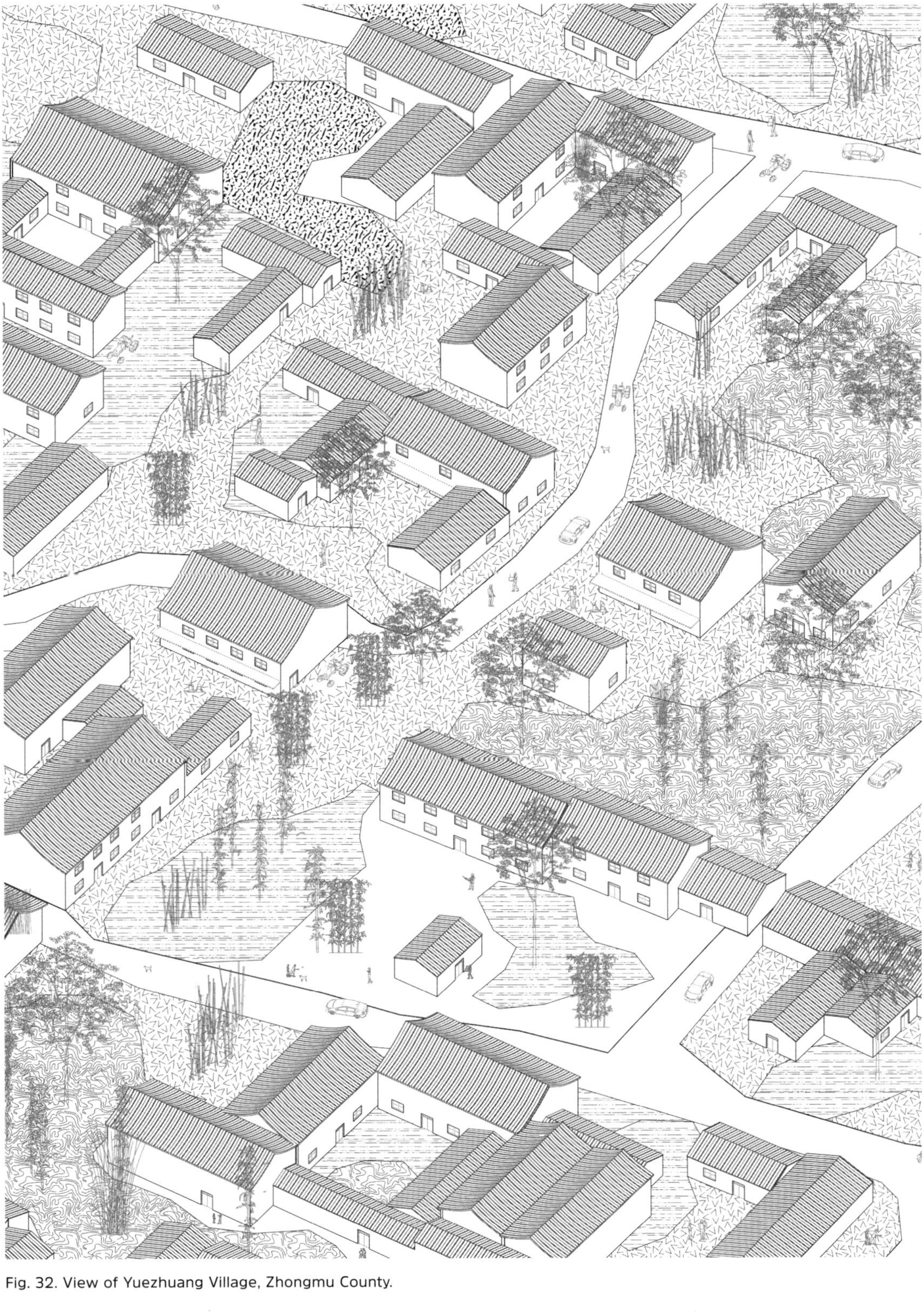

Fig. 32. View of Yuezhuang Village, Zhongmu County.

Fig. 33. Lizhuang Village, Zhongmu County, 2019.

Fig. 34. Yuezhuang Village, Zhongmu County, 2019.

Modern Agricultural Villages

As a consequence of the New Socialist Countryside programme, the construction of modern agricultural villages began in the mid-2000s and reached its peak between 2010 and 2013. The construction of modern villages is in response to the need for new housing in rural areas to improve the living conditions of the population. As in the case of Weigang Village in Sample 2.B, these modern settlements are usually composed of 250 to 300 houses accommodating 800–1,000 persons. Unlike the spontaneous organisation of the traditional settlements, the modern villages have a clear and well-defined urban layout, each consisting of a compact north–south rectangular nucleus, generally covering a footprint of about 800,000 square metres. A town square (200–250 square metres) is located at the centre of the settlement, surrounded by most of the public services: town hall, administrative offices, medical centre, primary school, and public toilets. In some cases, education and sports facilities are sited at the outer corners of the settlement; while ancestral halls can be found in the countryside near the village. Other amenities such as shops, markets, and restaurants are carved out of the family home by the business owner. Therefore, apart from the main public facilities, the village consists of semi-detached rows of family houses.

The dwelling typologies adopted in the modern villages are an updated version of the traditional courtyard houses. Each housing unit occupies a total area of 165 square metres and with a built surface of between 175 and 255 square metres. The main building is a two- or three-storey structure on the northern side of the courtyard. Its interior floor plan consists of a living room (25 square metres) located at the entrance that is the centre of the home, connecting all other rooms on the ground floor, which are commonly used for storage or as a kitchen (10.5 plus 5 square metres each). Behind the main rooms, a corridor and stairs are on the northern side. The upper floor is divided into rectangular rooms facing south, each opening directly onto the main hallway (10.5 square metres each). In addition to the main building, a smaller single-storey structure (12.5 square metres) is located along one side of the courtyard. This structure, intended as a garage, opens both to the street and to the inner courtyard. In many cases, this room has been converted to use for farming activities or storage. Unlike the ancient dwellings, the modern courtyard houses are made of prefabricated concrete elements, and are usually flat-roofed. This austere composition generally has no decoration except for the main courtyard gate, which is usually red with a painted pediment. However, there are variations in the standard housing typology that include gabled roofs, stringcourses between floors, tiled walls, and terraces. Generally, houses in modern agricultural villages have not undergone the major alterations that have occurred in the ancient settlements since 2010. However, the owners of some buildings have added verandas, self-built structures above the garage, or terrace enclosures.

Fig. 35. Sample 2.B.

Weigang Village

Inhabitants: about 1,000 people

Construction period: 2013

Total area: 100,000 sq. m

Total housing units: 264

Legend

fishponds

roads

built-up areas

water

trees and vegetation

bare land

crops and arable land

non-permeable surfaces

Fig. 36. Housing types in Sample 2.B.

Weigang Village

Type A

House area: 175 sq. m

Number of houses: 174 units

Type B

House area: 90 sq. m

Number of houses: 941 units

20 m

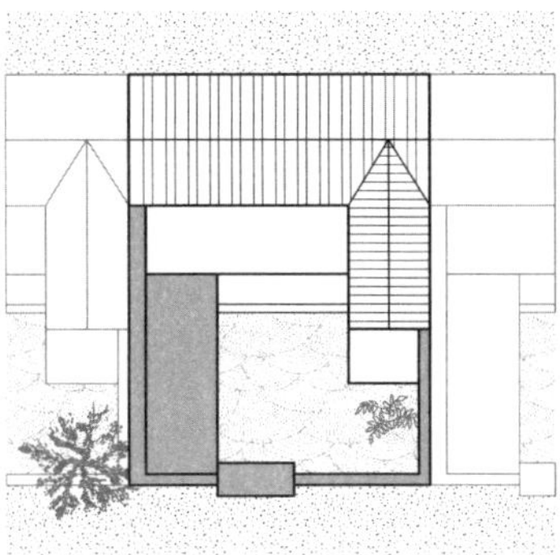

TOP

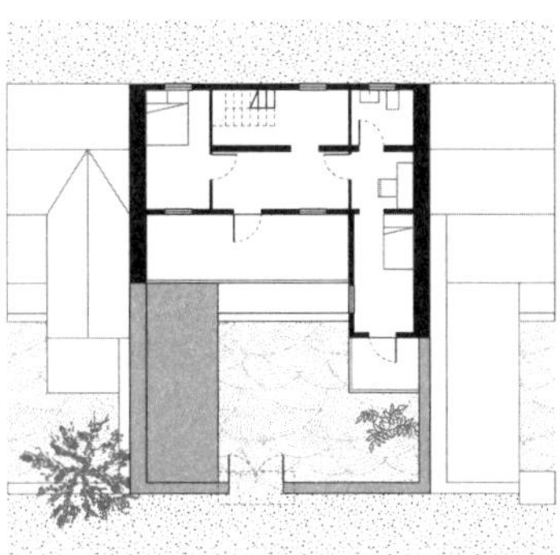

1F

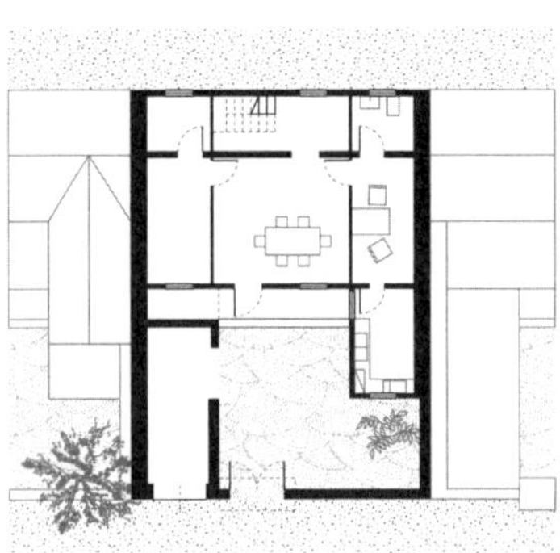

GF

Type A

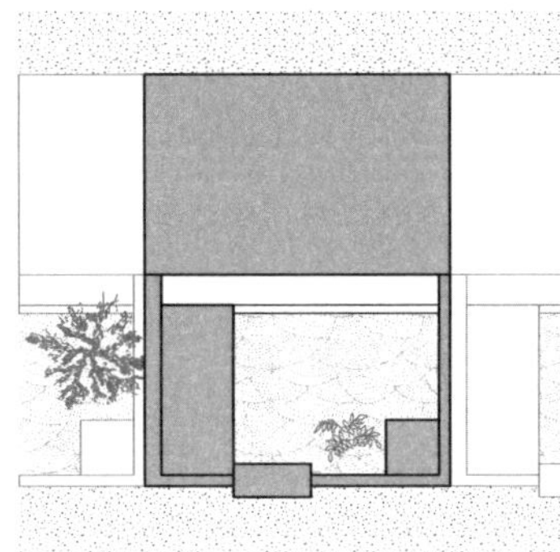

TOP

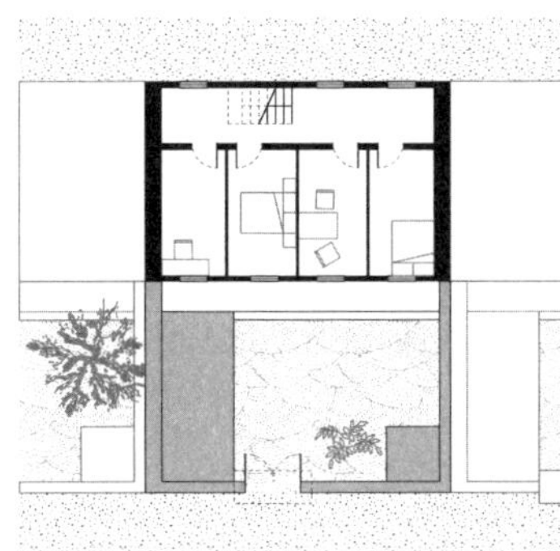

1F–2F

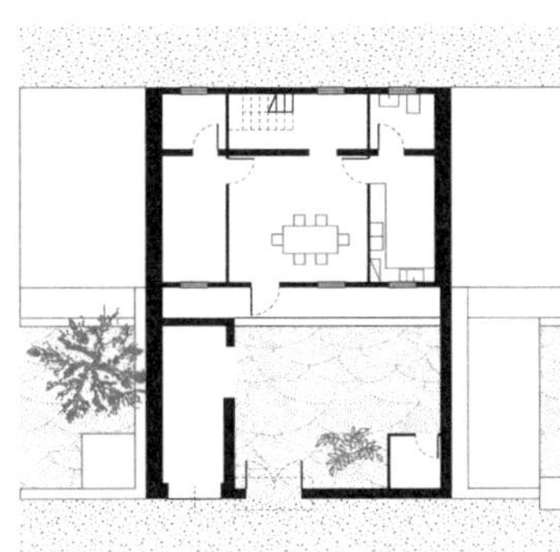

GF

Type B

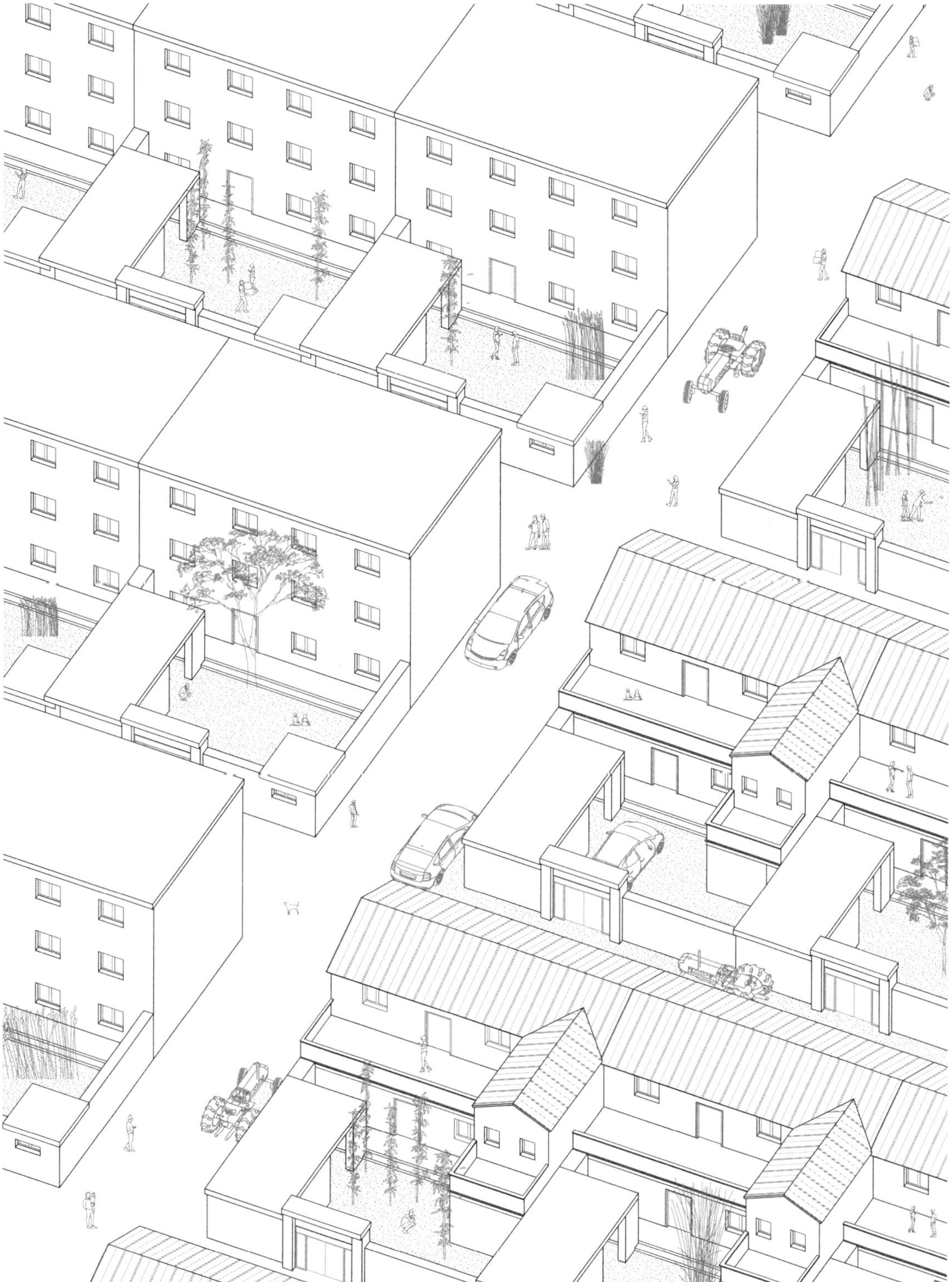

Fig. 37. View of Weigang Village, Zhongmu County.

Fig. 38. Wangjia'an Village, Zhongmu County, 2017.

Fig. 39. Weigang Village, Zhongmu County, 2019.

Following the implementation of the second stage of the New Socialist Countryside programme, the construction of new agricultural towns began in 2013 and is still ongoing. Unlike the modern agricultural villages, the new settlements aim not only to add housing to rural areas, but also to reclaim land by optimising its use, that is, by reducing the footprint of the built-up areas in the countryside. In order to achieve these objectives, the new agricultural towns are densely populated settlements built to relocate the inhabitants of three or more pre-existing villages. In Zhengbian New District alone, the process has led to the recent demolition of approximately 380 traditional villages, and the construction of more than 100 new agricultural towns. These are multi-phase projects planned by local governments and designed by the planning institutes of the major municipalities. Looking at Zhugu New Agricultural Town (Sample 2.C) as an example, after it was designed by a planning institute in Zhengzhou, in March 2015 the Yanming Lake Town administration launched an invitation to tender for the first phase of the project, with an estimated cost of 23 million CNY (Ministry of Finance of the People's Republic of China, 2015a). Then, in November 2018, another tender was launched for the second phase, with an estimated expenditure of 25 million CNY (Ministry of Finance of the People's Republic of China, 2017). Finally, all public amenities were developed by separate invitations to tender (Ministry of Finance of the People's Republic of China, 2018). After a construction process like this has been completed, the total footprint of a new settlement is generally about 800,000 square metres, with about 1,300 to 1,700 housing units accommodating 4,500 to 5,500 inhabitants.

New agricultural towns are commonly located alongside a newly built expressway directly connected to the regional infrastructure network. The new settlements have specific entrances which mediate between the town and the main infrastructure and in some cases are even gated. Like the modern agricultural villages, the new towns have a compact, regular urban layout marked by a tree-lined road along the external perimeter of the settlement. Inside, most new agricultural towns are laid out along two main axes. Commonly, the north-south axis is a linear park with canals, vegetation, and small lakes, while the east-west axis is a four-lane road with shops and commercial facilities. At the intersection of the two axes, a main square hosts most of the public services: town hall, public offices, schools, libraries, clinics, and medical and sports facilities. Other amenities are located in the public parks at the corners of the settlements. In addition to the two main axes, the towns are crisscrossed by orthogonal roads and public gardens with pedestrian footpaths. The remaining areas are organised by small and often dead-end roads lined with terraced houses. Since every agricultural town is planned by a different design institute, this general layout may also be more organic and less hierarchical. However, no new settlements have spaces dedicated to agriculture or other production activities.

The housing units of the new agricultural towns are completely different from those of the traditional and the modern agricultural villages: they consist of compact structures in the style of suburban houses. Even when the dwellings from different design

Fig. 40. Sample 2.C.

Zhugu New Agricultural Town

Inhabitants: about 5,500 people

Construction period: 2017–present

Total area: 725,000 sq. m

Total housing units: 1,682

Legend

demolished areas

roads

built-up areas

water

trees and vegetation

bare land

crops and arable land

non-permeable surfaces

institutes vary, all buildings have a supporting concrete frame, brick walls, and a pitched tiled roof. Three housing sizes have been adopted in all villages: 180, 240, and 280 square metres. As in Sample 2.C, the main entrance to the houses is located on the southern side, facing a private garden (65 square metres). This space is frequently planted with an orchard or paved and used to dry harvested crops or to store work tools and other materials. The ground floor of all typologies consists of a main living room with a bow window and a kitchen on the southern side (respectively 25 and 8–15 square metres); a garage (18 square metres), a restroom, and another room on the northern side (respectively 18, 5, and 15 square metres). Type A is a two-storey house (180 square metres total) with three rooms (13, 15, and 25 square metres) and a bathroom on the upper level. Types B and C are three-storey buildings (240 and 280 square metres). Type B has three bedrooms (13, 15 and 25 square metres), a north-facing terrace (16 square metres), and a restroom on the top floor; while Type C has the same layout with an extra room instead of a terrace. Finally, on the second floor of Type B, there is a room with an ensuite bathroom (20 and 3 square metres), and a terrace (45 square metres); while the upper level of Type C is a copy of the first floor. In the case of Zhugu New Agricultural Town, most houses are Type B; however, several owners have extended their property by enclosing the balcony on the first floor, or self-constructing structures that cover the terrace on the upper floor. Nowadays, the price of such a house (for 70 years of property rights) ranges from 700,000 to 1.6 million CNY, or 2,885 to 6,150 CNY per square metre.

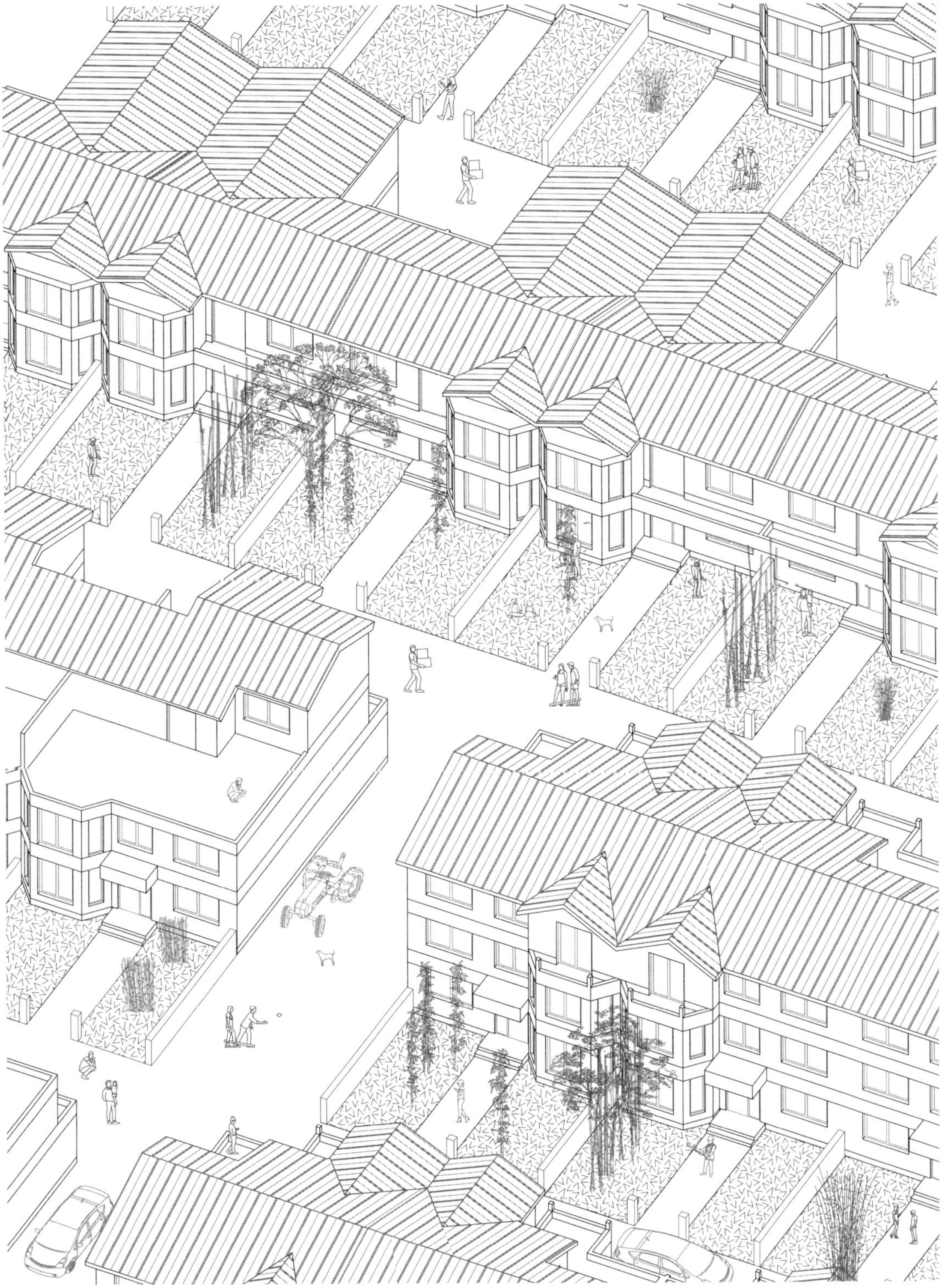

Fig. 41. View of Zhugu New Agricultural Town, Zhongmu County.

Fig. 42. Tushandian New Agricultural Town, Zhongmu County, 2019.

Fig. 43. Housing types in Sample 2.C.

Zhugu New Agricultural Town

Total housings: 1,682 units

Construction period: 2017–present

Average cost: 4,500 CNY/sq. m

Type A

House area: 180 sq. m

Number of houses: 349 units

Type B

House area: 240 sq. m

Number of houses: 941 units

Type C

House area: 280 sq. m

Number of houses: 392 units

20 m

Graphic Scale

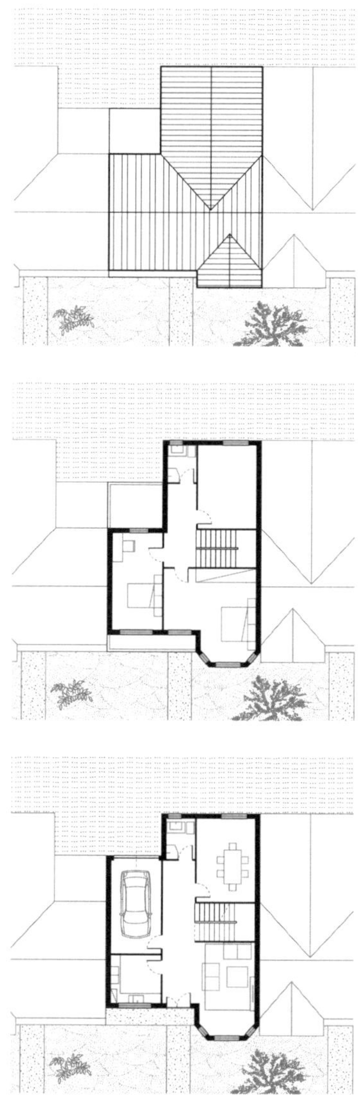

TOP

1F

GF

Type A

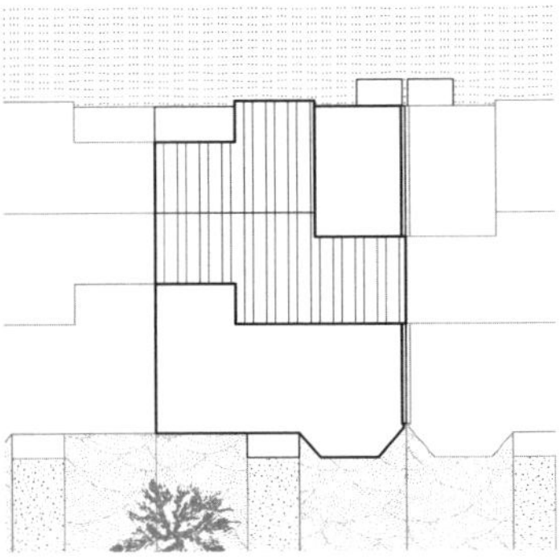

TOP

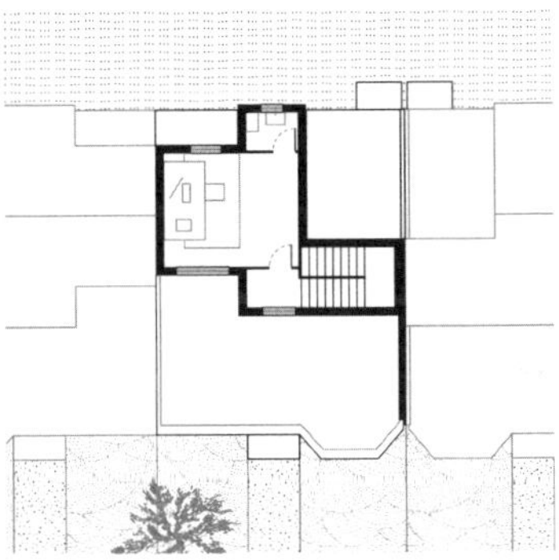

2F

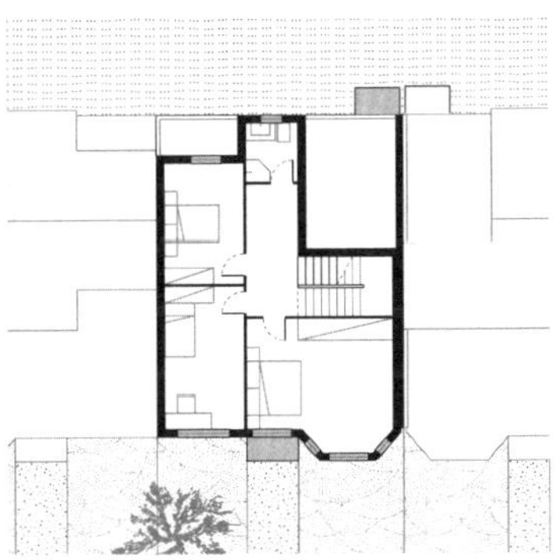

1F

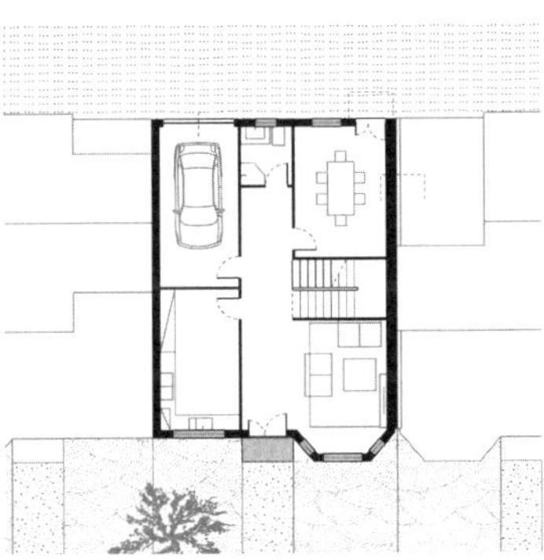

GF

Type B

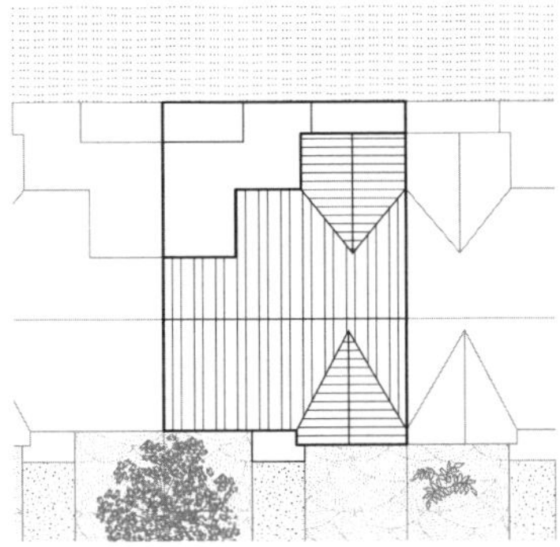

TOP

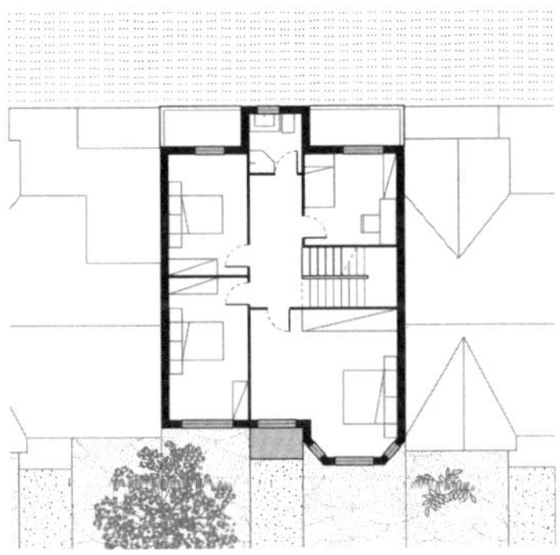

2F

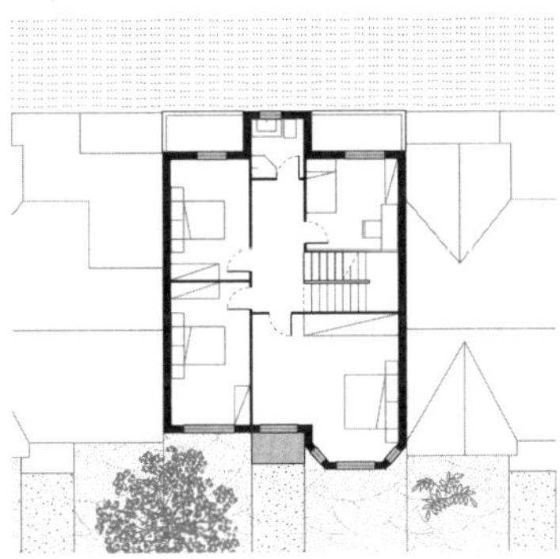

1F

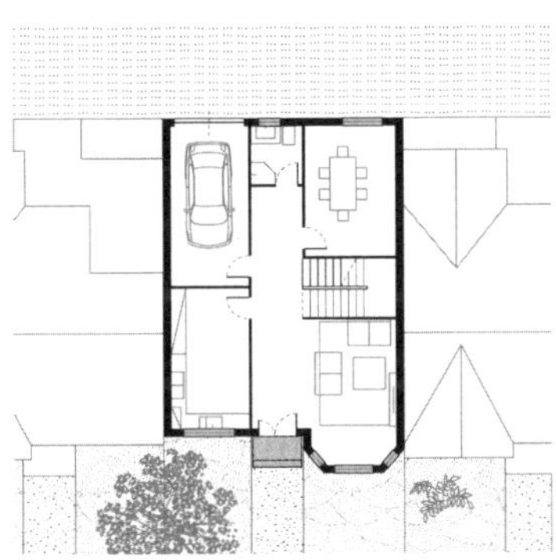

GF

Type C

Fig. 44. Taiqian New Agricultural Town, Zhongmu County, 2019.

Fig. 45. Zhugu New Agricultural Town, Zhongmu County, 2017.

Although there is a strict administrative separation between urban and rural areas, the ongoing process of urbanisation in the Central Plains is progressively blurring the distinction between city and countryside. The new residential areas under construction by real estate companies in the Zhengbian New District make this evident. While until ten years ago this phenomenon was mostly centred on the outskirts of major municipalities and in new towns such as the Zhengdong New District, nowadays, new compounds are being built everywhere. As a result, even those areas that claim to be ecological and agricultural parks such as Yanming Lake Town are filled with the construction sites of real estate companies promoting a luxury environment and guaranteeing wellbeing.

Real estate companies attempt to imbue each site with a unique atmosphere, varying housing typologies radically from one compound to another. Despite this, it is possible to identify some common features. The overall size of each compound usually ranges from 1.5 to 4 square kilometres. Similar to the new agricultural towns, sites are bounded by a tree-lined road marking the outer perimeter. Internally, the compounds have an organic urban layout that is not hierarchical: open spaces and the public gardens are uniformly distributed throughout the area and there is neither a main street nor a central square. Each compound has its own exhibition hall, a huge building located near the outer road, often surrounded by a large park. The exhibition hall is where the real estate offices selling the houses are located. After selling most of the houses, the real estate company puts on a celebration for the new owners, after which the exhibition hall is converted into shared private facilities such as swimming pools, gyms, kindergartens, libraries, and private schools for the compound's community.

Among all the compounds in Yanming Lake Town, only a few include high-rise buildings. The majority of new constructions are low-density dwellings with no more than six storeys. The prices vary greatly according to the different typologies: the average cost of an apartment is about 7,800 to 10,000 CNY per square metre while semi-detached houses and villas range between 15,000 and 28,000 CNY per square metre. The houses are sold "without decorations", that is, without flooring, bathroom fittings, or furniture, and buyers have 70 years of property rights. Apart from smaller apartments in the high-rise buildings, which have a minimum size of 80 square metres, the housing units normally range between 130 and 250 square metres. Every compound has a few luxury typologies that commonly range in size between 250 and 400 square metres, and the largest housing unit in Yanming Lake Town is a 600-square-metre villa.

Sample 2.D has one of the most exemplary compounds in Yanming Lake Town: the Chang Jiyun complex constructed by Vanke real estate company. Most common typologies are present in this compound. The smallest apartments (Type A) are duplexes in six-storey buildings with sizes ranging from 175 to 200 square metres. The first floor of the apartments hosts the main living room (35 square metres), the kitchen (9.5 square metres), a guest room (10.5 square metres), and a bathroom. On the upper level, there is a small bathroom and three bedrooms (9, 10.5, and 23 square metres), the

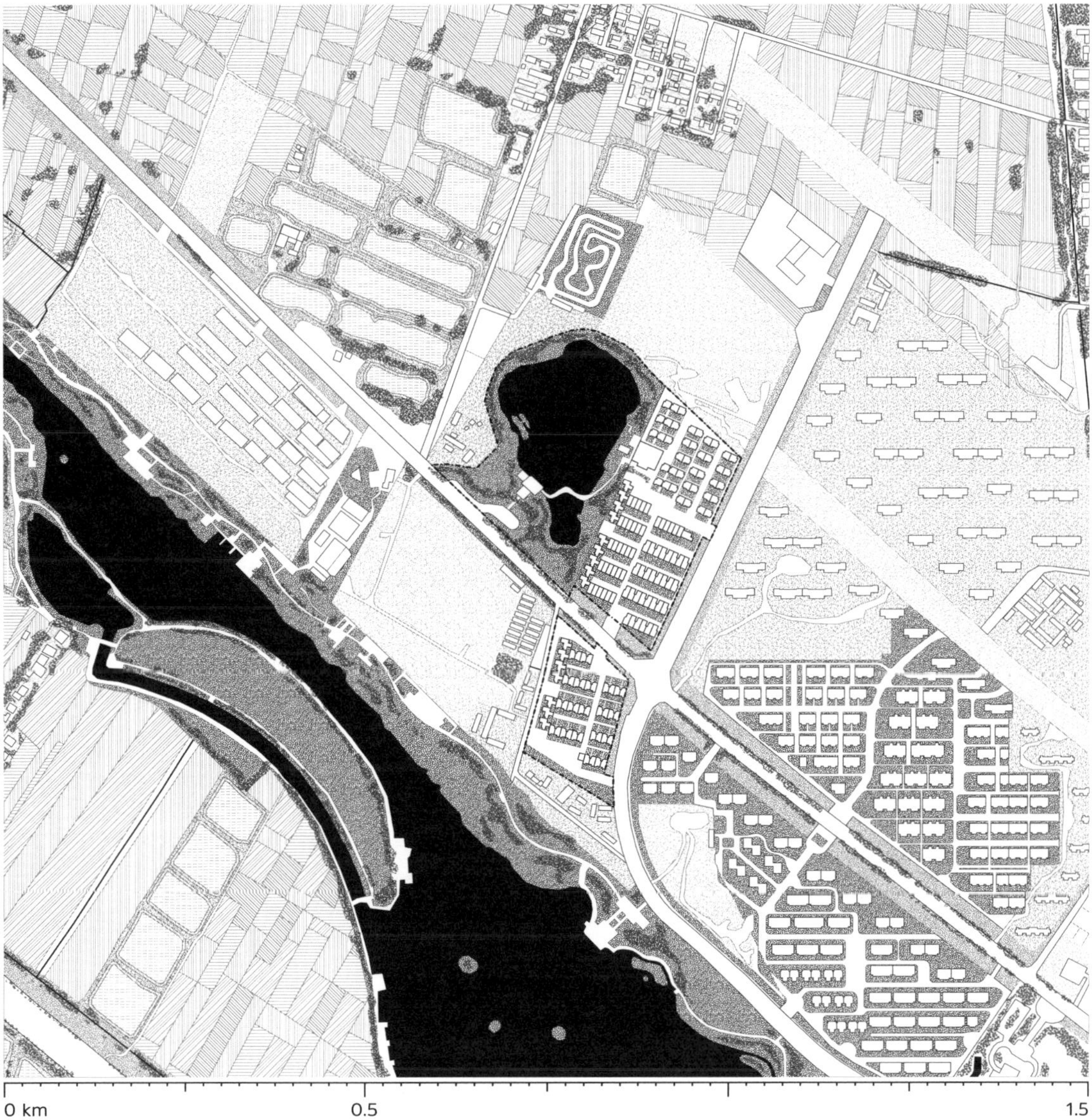

Fig. 46. Sample 2.D.

Chang Jiyun Compound

Inhabitants: about 600 people (projected)

Construction period: 2018–present

Total area: 125,000 sq. m

Total housing units: 200

Legend

- fishponds
- demolished areas
- built-up areas
- water
- trees and vegetation
- bare land
- crops and arable land
- non-permeable surfaces

larger of which has an ensuite bathroom (8 square metres). Each apartment has a garden, balcony, and/or terrace depending on its level. A similar layout is used for the 200-square-metre duplexes in the four-storey buildings (Type B). The only difference is a double-height living room on the first floor and thus the only two bedrooms upstairs. Type C, a semi-detached house, has a floor space of 200 and 220 square metres, and a private garden (100 square metres). The ground floor has the same layout as the duplexes, while the second floor is split into two parts: one side is a bedroom with an ensuite bathroom (25 and 4 square metres); the other has a bedroom (20 square metres), an ensuite bathroom, and a private study (9.5 square metres).

Although no villas were built in the Vanke compound, there are two types of four-storey luxury terraced houses. Type D is 260 square metres in size, with a hall, a double-height living room separated into two areas (30 and 13 square metres), small kitchen, and toilet on the ground floor. On the first upper floor is a bedroom (11 square metres) and a bathroom; and on the second, a bedroom with a walk-in closet (18 and 9 square metres), a study (9.5 square metres), a terrace (12 square metres), and a bathroom. Finally, the top floor holds a study/living room (20 square metres), a terrace (25 square metres), and a restroom. Each dwelling has its own private lift and its own gardens (70 square metres). Finally, Type E is the largest housing unit (360 square metres), organised as follows: on the ground floor is a hall, a double-height living room (45 square metres), a dining room (15 square metres), a kitchen (7.5 square metres), and a small toilet; the first upper floor has a study (20 square metres), a bedroom with its own bathroom (15 and 7 square metres), and another restroom; on the second upper floor are two bedrooms, each with a private bathroom (17 and 7.5 square metres), and a terrace (23 square metres); finally, the top floor consists of a study/living room (30 square metres), a terrace (35 square metres), and a toilet. In this typology, each dwelling also has its own private lift and private gardens (150 square metres).

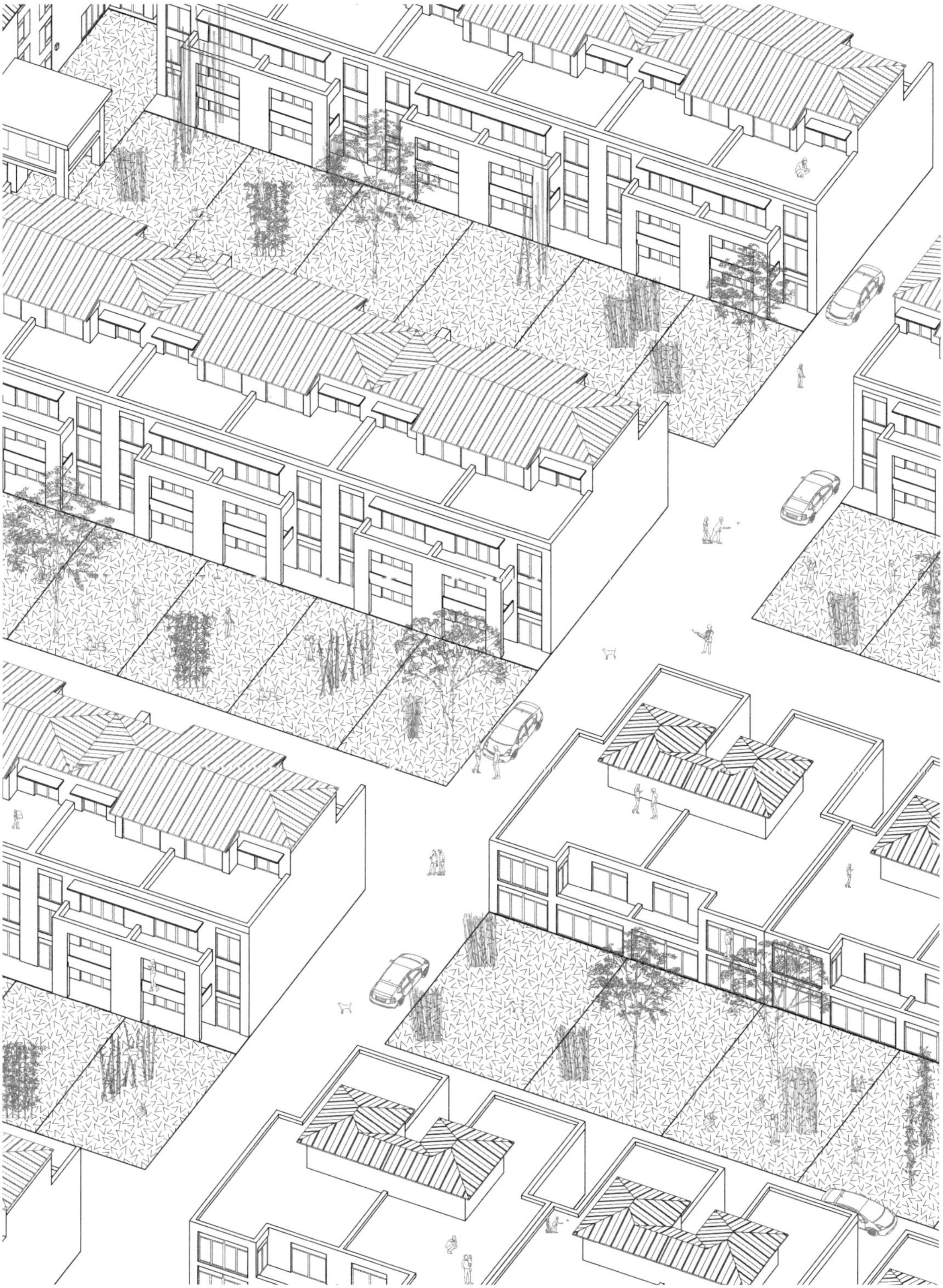

Fig. 47. View of Chang Jiyun Compound, Zhongmu County.

Fig. 48. Housing types in Sample 2.D.

Chang Jiyun Compound

Inhabitants: about 600 people (projected)

Construction period: 2018–present

Average cost: 15,000 CNY/sq. m

Type A

House area: 175 sq. m

Number of houses: 38 units

Type B

House area: 200 sq. m

Number of houses: 30 units

Type C

House area: 220 sq. m

Number of houses: 41 units

Type D

House area: 260 sq. m

Number of houses: 35 units

Type E

House area: 360 sq. m

Number of houses: 16 units

20 m

Graphic Scale

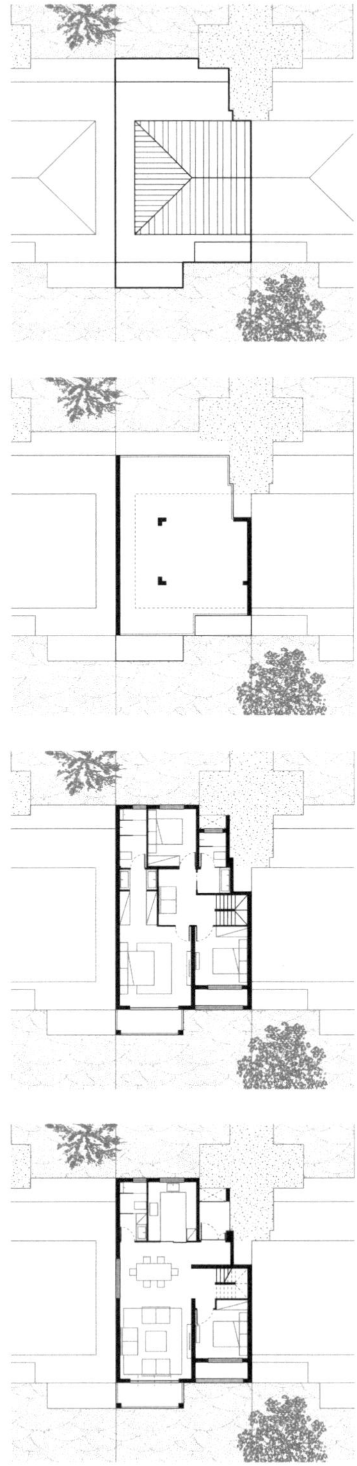

TOP

2F

1F

GF

Type A

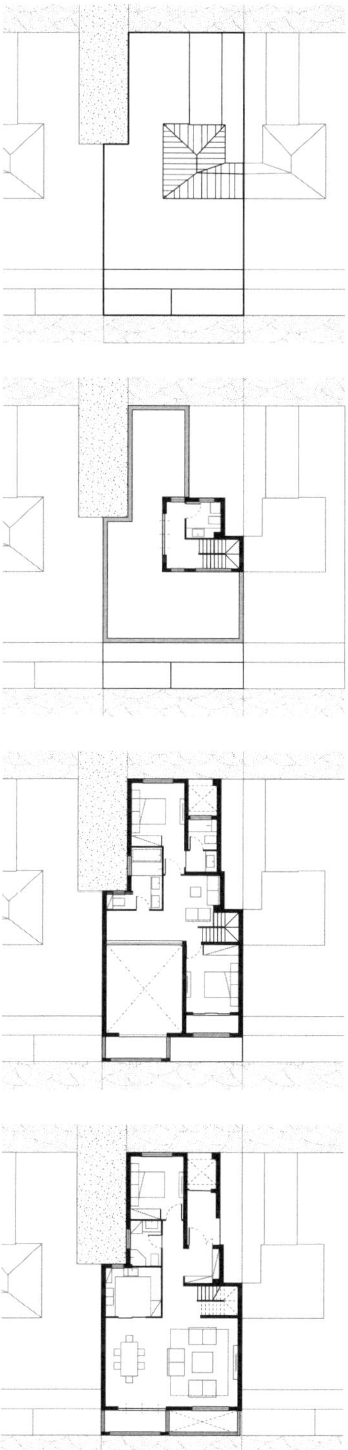

Type B

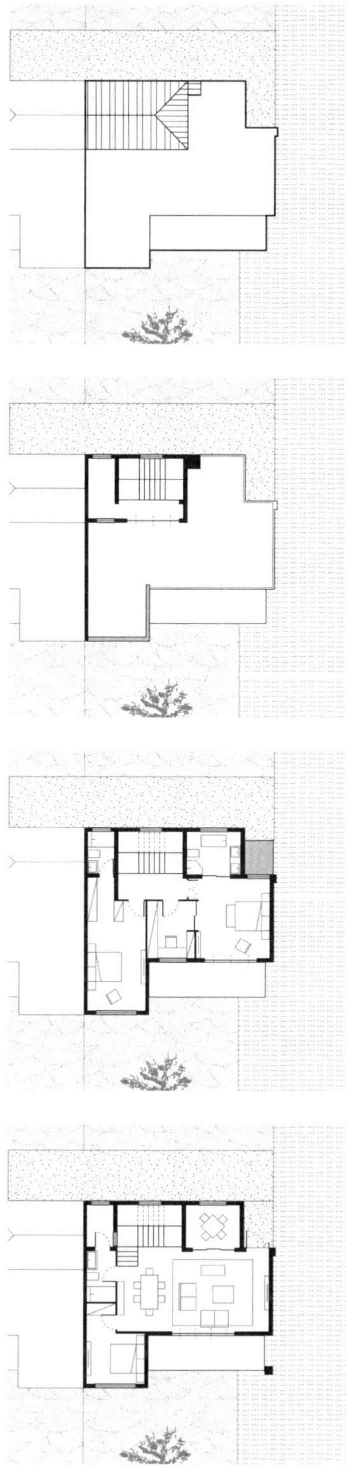

Type C

3F

2F

1F

GF

Type D

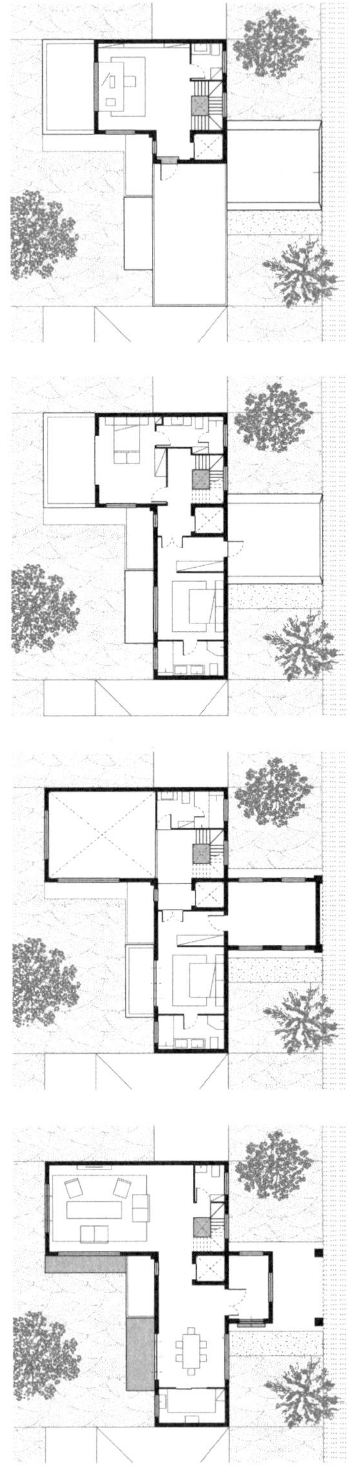

3F

2F

1F

GF

Type E

Fig. 49. Type E, Chang Jiyun Compound, Zhongmu County, 2019.

Fig. 50. Type A, Chang Jiyun Compound, Zhongmu County 2019.

Fig. 51. Chang Jiyun Compound, Zhongmu County, 2019.

Fig. 52. Swimming pool inside the Greentown Exhibition Hall, Zhongmu County, 2019.

Assembling Functions

In the past twenty years, the economy of Henan province has undergone great changes. From 2000 until the present, employees in the primary sector have decreased from 64 percent to 36 percent of the total labour force while workers in both the secondary and the tertiary sectors have increased from 18 percent to 32 percent (Henan Province Bureau of Statistics, 2020). In parallel, while in 2000 the primary sector still accounted for 23 percent of the GDP, it now only represents only 9 percent of GDP; and the tertiary sector has grown from 31 to 43 percent of the GDP, and the secondary sector has held steady at 45 percent (Henan Province Bureau of Statistics, 2020). This trend was even more pronounced in major municipalities such as Zhengzhou, where today the primary sector accounts for only 1.5 percent of the total workforce and produces only 1.5 percent of the GDP, while the secondary and tertiary sectors employ 44 and 54.5 percent of the labour force respectively and produce 43.5 and 55 percent of the GDP (Zhengzhou Municipal Statistics Bureau, 2018).

The changes in the economic structure of the area have also affected the ways in which production space is designed and constructed, as well as the relationships between the production system and the city itself. The following pages illustrate the spatial organisation and artefacts that compose these new production zones, how the spaces work, and what kind of imaginaries they promote. We will examine three samples of 5 × 5 kilometres: the Zhongmu National Agricultural Park in the ecological corridor south of the Yellow River (Sample 3.A), the Foxconn Science Park in Zhengzhou Airport City (Sample 3.B), and the university town in the Zhengdong New District (Sample 3.C).

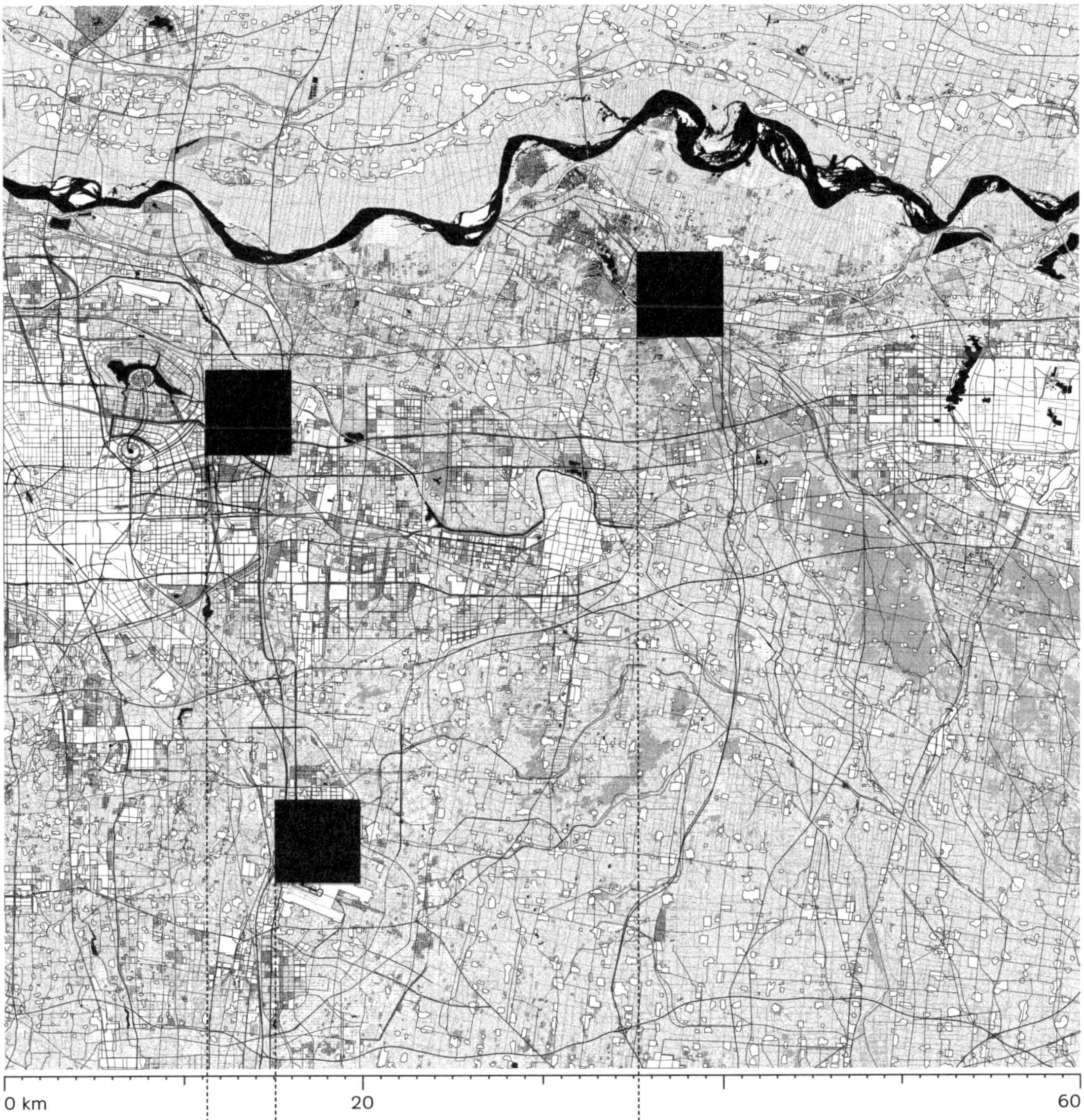

Sample 3.C
Zhengdong University Town
University Towns
and Research Clusters
[5 × 5 km]

Sample 3.B
Foxconn Science Park
Technological
and Industrial Parks
[5 × 5 km]

Sample 3.A
Zhongmu National Agricultural Park
Agricultural Parks
and Touristic Areas
[5 × 5 km]

Fig. 53. Zhengbian New District.
Assembling Functions, Three Samples

April 26th, 2019
Experiencing the New Town

Getting to Zhengzhou Airport from the city centre means voyaging deep into the earth. One must take Metro Line 1, change to Line 2 halfway through, and ride to the end of the line. The journey takes about an hour-and-a-half and nothing is visible for most of the trip. All that can be heard is the noise of the engine as it brakes and speeds up again. After 20 kilometres, the subway stops at the outer fringes of urban Zhengzhou, and passengers are asked to get out and wait. Another train soon arrives and takes one the rest of the way. Fortunately, the new line is suspended, and it is finally possible to see the light again. Despite this terrible journey, a silent army of workers fills the subway cars. People stand, glued to their phones: sending messages, playing games, watching TV series. When possible, they squat or occupy a vacant seat. As the subway approaches the Airport City, the area turns into one giant construction site: an expanse of skeletons waiting to be fleshed out. I decide to get off the subway four stops before the airport to walk around the new town and the industrial zone. As I emerge from the station, I am surrounded by hundreds of high-rise apartment buildings crammed into an area of about a dozen city blocks. Most of them are under construction and the plots are full of shacks, machinery, and piles of building materials. Apart from the workers, no one is around: the parks and the houses are deserted, as are the main facilities and shopping areas. The new town is just too new to be inhabited. Nearer the airport, the houses disappear, and industrial sheds and warehouses dominate the scene. This is one of Henan province's major industrial zones: smoke is billowing out of the chimneys and the sound of engines and machines can be heard in the distance. The manufacturing plants are surrounded by greenery and enclosed by walls. When I finally reach the entrance of one, the Henan Logistics Centre, I see an industrial area with a large yard inside where several people are unloading goods from trucks. I try to enter but the guard does not let me, so I take a taxi and head south. Finally, I arrive at Zhengzhou Xinzheng International Airport: a huge infrastructural hub with a futuristic design. I have to go through several checkpoints to get in. The scene inside is like any airport: people waiting to check in for their flights, and others meeting someone in arrivals. I look at the timetable and I notice that even though it claims to be international, there are few non-Chinese destinations. Probably, as the website states, most international routes are for airfreight, not passengers. I walk around inside the immense structure, and then return to Zhengzhou. Certainly, the Airport City is one of the most important gateways to inland China, a great logistics centre where people and materials flow in and out; but it is also a giant factory where goods are produced; the entire space is an immense urban worksite.

After visiting the Airport City, I tour the Zhengdong University Town. It is at the very last subway stop to the east and the ride is even longer than the outward journey. One should not be surprised by the great distances here. It is well known that the city not only reaches upward to the sky with its towers, but also burrows deep into the earth, digging tunnels like a tree spreading its roots. Indeed, even though the metropolis of Zhengzhou has only two subway lines today, the municipality already plans to build 20 more lines, with one set to open next week. When I finally see daylight again, the landscape seems no different from where I left about two hours ago. I am again in a great construction site, but at least the sun has come out now. There are several three-wheelers parked near the subway station, and a woman immediately approaches me asking if I need a ride to one of the universities. Like most university towns in China, the one in the Zhengdong New District also covers a huge area in which more than ten campuses are located next to each other. It is not easy for students to reach their dormitories from the subway station: the distance is sometimes more than two kilometres. Since I have no specific destination, I decline the ride and start to walk. The subway stops in the central zone, a site planned as a "research cluster"; that is, a place where private and public companies set up their headquarters, offices, and research centres. Though some towers and futuristic structures have already been built, most of the facilities are still under construction. Moving south, I reach a monumental plaza opening onto the great lake, with a perfect view of the several campuses located on the other bank. Some of them are clearly recognisable from the iconic shapes mimicking the Western neoclassical architecture typical of Anglo-Saxon universities: domes topped with a great lantern, giant Ionic colonnades and neogothic towers. High-rise apartments filled with dormitories and buildings for sports facilities can be seen in the distance. All the buildings are surrounded by peaceful and flourishing vegetation, perfectly maintained by the constant work of troops of gardeners. As a result, the overall scene looks like a peaceful oasis of nature and calm. Inside the park, there are many students from the different faculties. Some are running, paddling, or doing other physical activities, some are fishing or flying kites, others just lie on the grass and enjoy the sun, and a few kissing couples retreat to more secluded places. After my walk, I go inside one of the campuses. Like most of the main entrances to the universities, the gate opens onto a monumental boulevard that connects the public road to the main offices and common facilities. The remaining buildings are in a great park with small lakes and rolling hills. Students are walking quickly along the main paths and several food delivery guys are cycling along the main streets. Observing them, one thing is clear: distances are great in such monumental campuses. Since it is almost lunch time, I decide to go to the canteen. The mess hall is a noisy room inside a big building close to the dormitories. The tables are full of young people: some are talking loudly, some are eating alone reading a book, others are sleeping with their head on the table. Following the directions some students give me, I manage to get food; however, as soon as they notice me, I suddenly become the centre of attention. Several curious guys approach me asking for information: Where do I come from? Why am I at the university? What is my WeChat account? And so on. I am getting too much attention, so I decide to leave as soon as I finish my lunch; my tour of the university town is over. However, it is clear to me that even if this space claims to be characterised by a clear function, it is also a city in itself: a place where thousands of people not only work and study but live their daily lives.

There is still time, and I decide to spend the afternoon in the Yellow River Scenic Area of Zhengzhou. It is a long bus ride to get there, but the bus finally stops in front of a ticket office. A small group of tourists and I are soon entering the park gate, maps and brochures in hand, ready for a visit. The Scenic Area is famous for its giant sculpture of emperors Yan and Huang, two legendary heroes. The monument was inspired by Mount Rushmore; however, unlike the American memorial, the faces are not carved from the rock, but built on top of a hill. According to the brochure, construction took 20 years, more than 7,000 cubic metres of concrete, more than 1,500 tons of steel, and more than 6,000 cubic metres of granite to complete the statue. The monument faces an immense plaza with a central pyramid made of three square terraces, like many traditional Chinese "temples of earth". The monument has a curious spatial solution to compensate for the fact that the great square makes it look smaller: the base of the hill has been planted with small pine trees to balance the proportions. As I walk up the hill, a young girl asks me for a picture in front of the monument, and we soon become acquainted. Her name is Qing Mu and she comes from a village near Kunming, in Yunnan. She shows me a photo of her hometown, a picturesque settlement set in a wonderful landscape of terraced mountains and rice paddies. She is now travelling around China on a one-year vacation, and her dream is to go to Tibet. We decide to explore the park together. The Scenic Area extends across several hills in addition to the main monument and has many attractions: pagodas, suspended glass bridges across small chasms, cable cars, boats, and so on. After visiting a few of them, we arrive at a place surrounded by walls. Mu stops and tells me she will wait for me outside. I don't understand why at first, but entering the gate brings me into a great monumental cemetery. It is peaceful, secluded in the midst of the hills and surrounded by woods; there are lines of gravestones and a few pagodas. Most of the memorials are adorned with flowers or coloured ribbons and a few of them have pictures of the departed. When I come out, Mu is waiting for me with eggs and ears of corn she bought at a nearby kiosk. After eating the snack, we rent a three-wheeler and drive to the highest mountain of the park, on the western side of the Scenic Area. There is a wonderful panoramic viewpoint here from where one can admire the Yellow River, a great waterway flowing peacefully eastwards, crossed by many bridges. There are two to the east: the older one, built for the old railway, and next to it a new steel bridge for the high-speed transit line. To the west, there is another bridge, for one of the main highways connecting northern and southern China. Beyond the river, cultivated plains extend to the north. After admiring the landscape, where the forces of nature meet the will of mankind, we conclude our tour.

On the return to Zhengzhou, the bus again crosses the anonymous landscape that is most Chinese cities: endless masses of monotonous, featureless buildings, alternating with a few commercial facilities at best. After visiting the Airport City, the University Town, and the Scenic Area, it seems to me that the new towns herald a different kind of urbanisation: an urbanisation with clear suggestions of function and characterisation of spaces.

Fig. 54. Vegetable gardens and new constructions in Zhengzhou Airport City, 2019.

Fig. 55. Western square of Zhengdong Railway Station, 2019.

绿地中心
小吃集

One of the main objectives of the Central Plains urban agglomeration is to create an area demonstrating the coordinated development between industrialisation, urbanisation, and agricultural modernisation (Fang & Yu, 2016). This aims to address the great disparities between the inhabitants of urban and rural areas, as well as those within rural areas. In Zhongmu County, for example, the average income of an urban household is about 2,350 CNY per month, while a rural resident earns only 1,500 CNY per month (Henan Province Bureau of Statistics, 2020). Furthermore, a villager employed in the secondary sector receives about 2,100 CNY per month, whereas the average income for a farmer is just 600 CNY per month (Lee, 2016). To address this, several initiatives have been undertaken by local administrations to foster agricultural modernisation and to promote the tourist sector, two issues that have been the focus of numerous plans for the Zhengbian New District and the *Zhongmu County Urban and Rural Master Plan (2016–2030)*. All these documents envisage the creation of ecological corridors devoted to agricultural, recreational, and cultural activities. One of these areas is along the southern bank of the Yellow River, which also includes Yanming Lake Town in the north-east sector of Zhongmu County. This location was chosen in 2008 as the site of a new golf club and a luxury resort. Since then, the administration has decided to implement a two-fold strategy: first, to stimulate wellness and tourist activities; and second, to promote the creation of a high-tech and high-quality agricultural zone.

With these goals in mind, in March 2011, the China Agricultural University and the China Tourism Design Institute were appointed by the Zhongmu County administration to draft a plan for the Zhongmu National Agricultural Park (Sample 3.A). The park was to be built on 5.3 square kilometres with a total investment of 3.5 billion CNY. The plan organised the site into six functional areas: a management services zone, aquaculture, agricultural facilities, fruit tree cultivation, horticulture, floriculture, and a "cultural creativity area for agriculture". These areas together encompass 550,000 square metres of multi-span greenhouses, 194 solar greenhouses, 550,000 square metres of modern fishponds, and eight demonstration pavilions. Another 8.3 kilometres of artificial navigable canals, with an average width of 30 metres, were planned to enclose the park on three sides. Work began in 2012 and, two years later, the definitive infrastructural layout was ready, most of the agricultural facilities were built, and the remaining parts were under construction. All the buildings were said to be high-tech and high-quality, and the pavilions were given names such as The Future Agricultural Museum or The Agricultural Science Museum. In April 2014, the park was opened to visitors for the Agricultural Carnival, an annual festival repeated for the following two years. However, despite these events, the work to complete the park stopped in 2017 and no other events have taken place at the site. At present, although the administration of Zhongmu County states that the National Agricultural Park is still under construction, it appears to have been abandoned: construction work on the unfinished buildings has come to a standstill, and the greenhouses and structures that hosted the previous events are neglected or, at best, used as farmland.

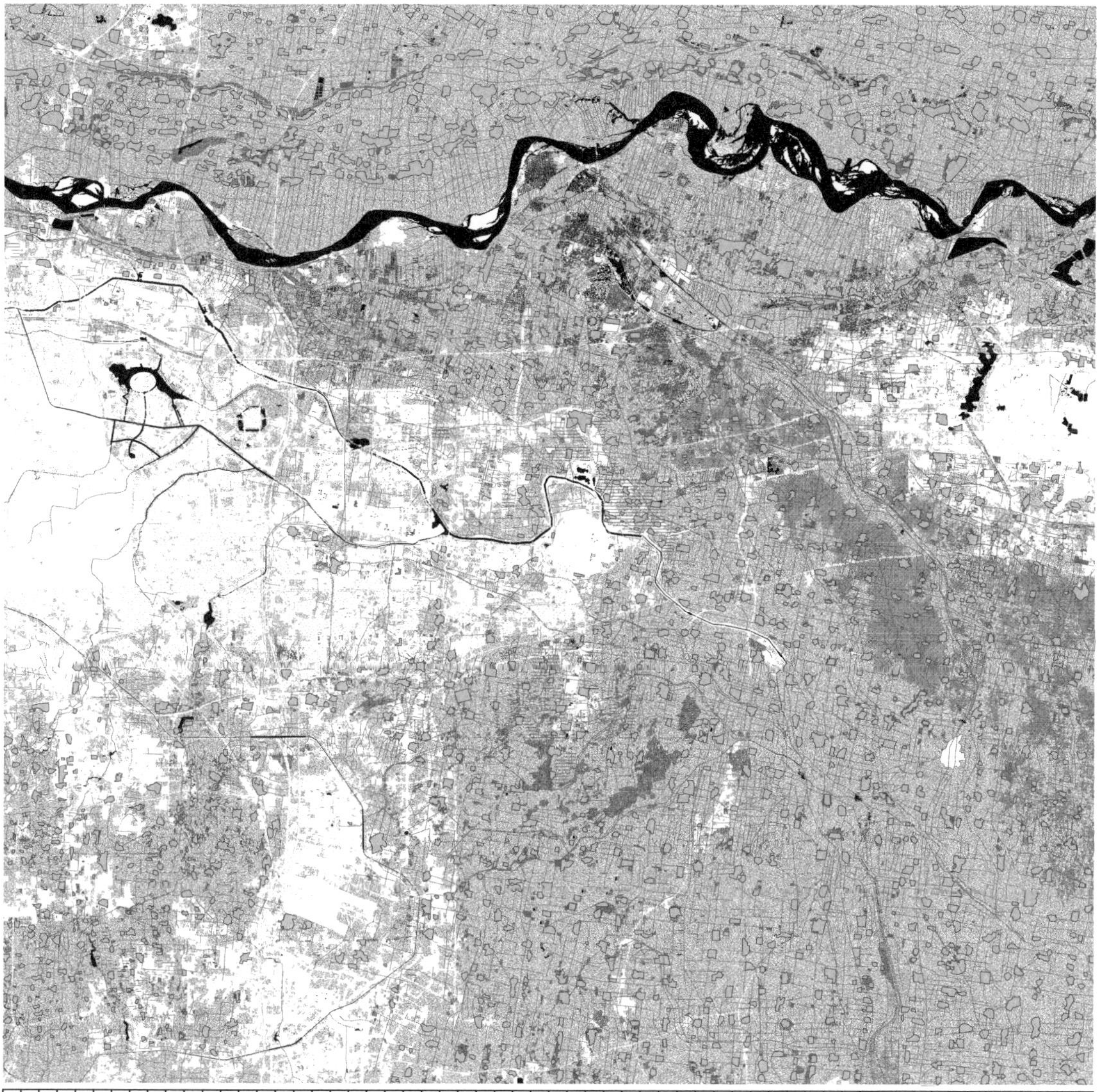

0 km 20 60

Fig. 56. Zhengbian New District.

Agricultural Parks and Tourist Areas

Legend

minor roads and waterways

main rivers and lakes

agricultural fields and crop areas

agricultural villages

woods and forests

built-up areas

Although the Zhongmu National Agricultural Park might be considered a failure at first glance, this is not the case. In fact, the park has driven several initiatives undertaken in the area. In 2015, the Yanming Lake Town administration invested 25.63 million CNY in constructing agricultural infrastructure projects. The majority were for improving the irrigation system, while 1.8 million CNY was used to reclaim 15.4 square kilometres of land. Additionally, 1.2 square kilometres were reforested and a total area of 162,000 square metres was converted to greenways and parks. Such initiatives, together with other promotional activities, drew more than 390,000 tourists to the area during the eleventh Golden Week, generating an income of 74.1 million CNY (an increase of 40 percent over the previous year). Of this, 58.5 million CNY came from catering and accommodation, and more than 7.8 million CNY from the sale of agricultural products (Bai, 2016).

In light of this success, in May 2015 the administration of Zhongmu County launched a competition for *The Leisure Agricultural Master Plan of Yanming Lake Town* (Ministry of Finance of the People's Republic of China, 2015b). The participants were asked to design an "urban ecological agricultural area" on 49.6 square kilometres, 20 of which were to be redeveloped into "farming demonstration parks" over the next 15 years. Moreover, they were to propose a branding strategy for the promotion of locally processed agricultural products. The Shanghai Weimei Landscape Design Engineering Company, in collaboration with the Beijing Oasis Environmental Garden Design, won the competition (Henan Tengfei Engineering Cost Consulting Co., Ltd., 2015). The new proposal sees the entire territory of Yanming Lake Town as a park composed of a mix of new urbanised areas, spaces for agricultural production, and recreational activities. Within this general framework, the settlements of Yanming Lake Town, Wantan Town, and Langchenggang Town are designated as main residential areas to attract new inhabitants, and more than 10 square kilometres of land are reclaimed for agricultural production by relocating the local population into the new agricultural towns. Nine sites are planned as tourist attractions consisting of parks, ecological resorts, and health clubs. While some of these already exist, most are now under construction.

In line with several other initiatives promoted by national and local governments in recent years, this project, like many others in Zhongmu County, demonstrates the effort to promote a new image of rural areas as healthy places of wellbeing and clean environment. At present, it is not possible to predict their success or future viability; perhaps they will be progressively abandoned like the Zhongmu National Agricultural Park. However, many places have already experienced the advantages of being a "scenic area" and an "environmental park". For instance, not only have tourism and real estate development boomed in Yanming Lake Town, but many agricultural products, like Yanming Lake hairy crabs, Zhugu radishes, pollution-free apples, or Yellow River carp have also reaped the benefits of having a local brand. In this way, the construction of agricultural parks, environmental areas, and tourist facilities also enhances agricultural production, thus leading to improvements in the standard of living in rural areas.

Fig. 57. Sample 3.A.

Zhongmu National Agricultural Park

People employed: NA

Construction period: 2013–2015

Legend

- Zhongmu National Agricultural Park
- buildings
- built-up areas
- water
- trees and vegetation
- bare land
- crops and arable land
- non-permeable surfaces

Fig. 58. Farmers market, Kaifeng New Area, 2019.

Fig. 59. Zhongmu National Agricultural Park, Zhongmu County, 2019.

Fig. 60. St. Andrews Golf Club, Zhongmu County, 2019.

Fig. 61. Farmers in Zhongmu County, 2019.

Since the mid-1990s, the major municipalities of the Central Plains of China have been fostering the development of the secondary sector by establishing satellite industrial zones and ETDZs. As a result, 180 technological and industrial parks are currently operating in Henan province, each employing 25,000 people, investing 30.4 billion CNY in fixed assets, and generating 12 billion CNY in revenue. Four are located in Zhengbian New District: the Zhengzhou Economic and Technological Industrial Parks, the Zhengzhou Airport Industrial Cluster, the Zhongmu Automobile Industry Cluster, and the Kaifeng Western Industrial Cluster (Henan Province Bureau of Statistics, 2020). In 2017, these industrial parks employed 439,911 people, invested 150 billion CNY in fixed assets, and generated 461.74 billion CNY in revenue from the principal businesses (Henan Province Bureau of Statistics, 2020). These above-average values are due to the Zhengzhou Airport Industrial Cluster, the major industrial area in the Central Plains. This cluster alone has 315,414 workers, 68.2 billion CNY of investments in fixed assets, and generates an income of 29.91 billion CNY (Henan Province Bureau of Statistics, 2020). Most of these results are from the presence of the Foxconn Science Park, one of the company's largest plants worldwide.

The Foxconn corporation has three subsidiaries in Zhengzhou, of which the largest production plant is the Hongfujin Precision Electronics Company located in the Zhengzhou Airport Economic Zone (Sample 3.B). Three-hundred-thousand people work and live in the factory, producing 500,000 mobile phones a day at a rate of 350 phones a minute. The plant is also known as "iPhone City" since it is the source of half of all iPhones sold in the world (Barnett, 2012; Jacobs, 2018). The Foxconn Science Park was founded by Bo Xue in 2010 and construction was completed by the end of the following year (National People's Congress, 2010). The production plant occupies a total area of 5.5 square kilometres, of which 1.25 square kilometres is currently under construction (Henan Province People's Government, 2012). Zhenggang 4th Street crosses the area north–south, dividing the industrial site into two equal parts connected by underground roads. The interior area of the factory complex is based on a grid layout of four-lane roads that divide it into 13 sectors (280,000 square metres each), labelled from A to M. Sectors B, D, E, F, K, and L are "work units" with an identical spatial organisation: each is divided into four equal parts, three of which host the productive nuclei, and the remaining section holds a 75 × 110-metre block facing a 50,000-square-metre outdoor sports and green area. The productive nuclei are composed of two four-storey blocks measuring 60 × 150 metres, each with a total footprint of 9,000 square metres, plus a smaller four-storey block (25 × 150 metres) located in between, with a total footprint of 3,750 square metres. Suspended and covered bridges connect all blocks and work units.

Since Foxconn Science Park is intended to be more than a factory, the company provides several facilities for employees living inside the corporate estate. As described in a report by China Labour Watch (2019), workers' accommodation is organised in dormitories that cost 150 CNY per month. The rooms are 25 square metres with bunkbeds accommodating 8–10 people, with a shared bathroom and a small balcony to hang

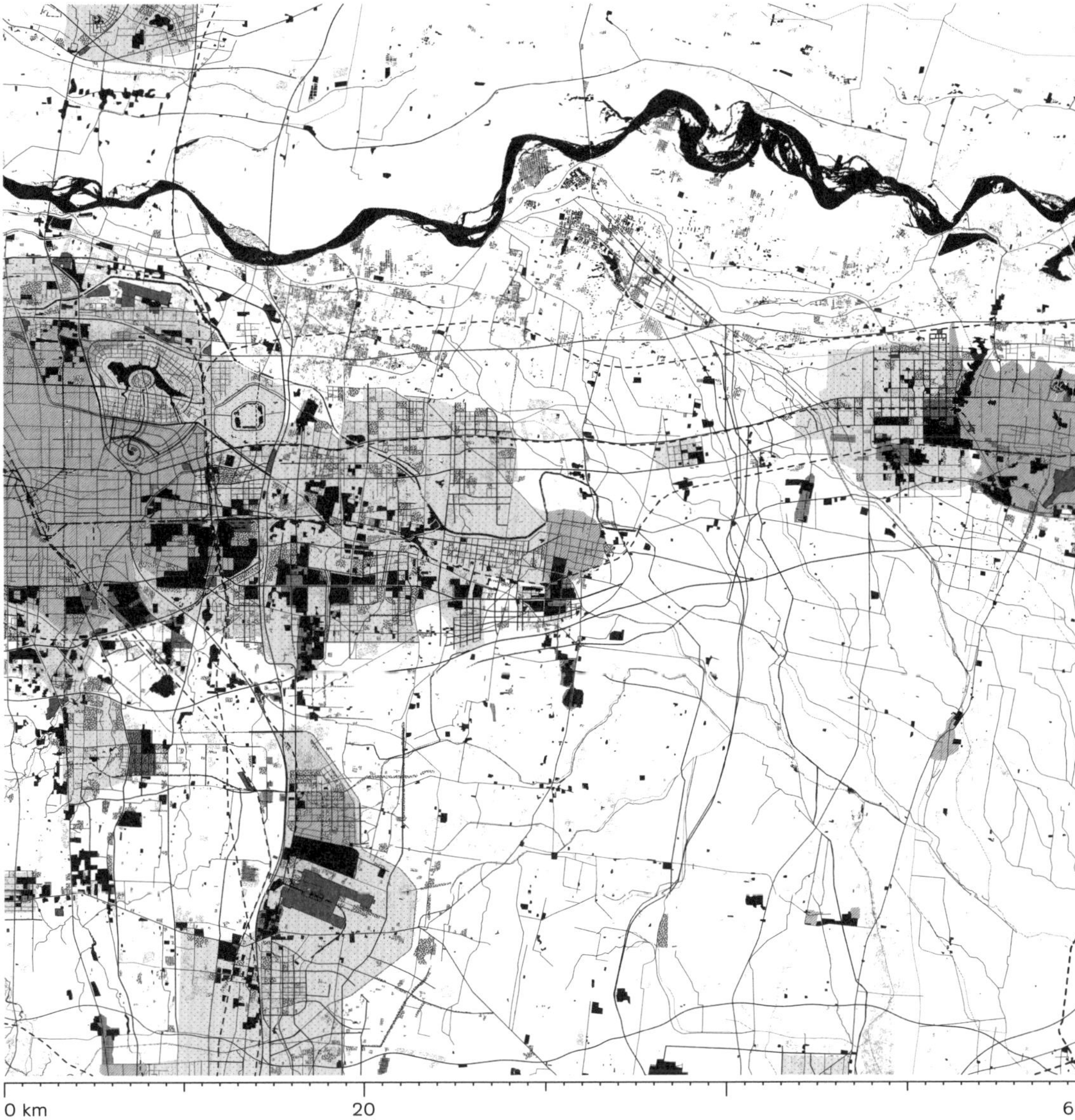

Fig. 62. Zhengbian New District.

Technological and Industrial Parks

Legend

- railways
- main roads and waterways
- main rivers and lakes
- areas under construction
- built-up areas
- ecological corridors
- logistic centres
- technological and industrial parks

washing. The dorms located in six-storey buildings use solar power for supplying hot water, while the ones in taller buildings have electric water heaters. Each dorm is equipped with air conditioning controlled by the property management department. The dining halls and canteens are three-storey buildings able to seat up to 2,000 people. The Foxconn Science Park also includes recreational facilities such as sports fields, basketball courts, table tennis rooms, billiard halls, gyms, libraries, and reading rooms; and the company organises several cultural and sports events. Finally, a system of shuttles and free buses connect different parts of the area so that the employees can commute to and from work. Although the company usually encourages workers to live inside the Foxconn Science Park, this policy is reversed during the peak season when the dormitories are full. During these periods, the company introduces a bonus payment of 1,000 CNY to workers who move out for three months.

According to the China Labour Watch report (2019), during peak season (August–November), the factory hires over 300,000 workers in a four-step recruitment procedure. First, applicants provide personal details to register, via the official website, WeChat or other devices. A subsequent interview at the recruitment centre includes a physical examination. After that, a one- to two-day company training course must be completed and accommodation in the dormitories is assigned. Finally, after a three-month probation period, the worker is called in to sign a labour contract and become a formal employee. Workers are given 400 CNY per month to spend at the canteen, and 20 CNY a day for meals. The company provides them with a uniform, and laundry, which was free until 2018, is now a paid service. The base salary for the probation period is 1,900 CNY per month; increasing to 2,100 CNY per month for full employees. There are incentive bonuses during production peaks that can bring pay up to as high as 3,200 to 5,000 CNY per month. Employees are expected to work five days a week, 8 hours per day, for a total of 40 hours per week; they are entitled to 11 days of vacation per year, and are covered by social insurance. Despite these conditions, the study conducted by China Labour Watch (2019) reveals that the employees are given production quotas that must be met, with the factory punishing those who do not reach the quota by taking away overtime hours. The study also reports several human rights violations, such as the over-recruitment of dispatch workers (i.e., temporary workers), who now make up 50 percent or more of the total workforce. During the peak season, students from vocational high schools are also hired to work at the factory as interns, under the same conditions as regular workers.

The Zhengzhou Foxconn Science Park is an exemplary case of well-known and documented manufacturing zones located on the outskirts of the major Chinese cities. As for the agricultural parks, it is not possible to foresee whether these sites of industrial production and their logistic platforms will become something more than sweatshops exploiting their workers. However, even now, these corporate estates are promoting global images based on the rhetoric of modern technological development, thus establishing rather weak connections between places that until a few years ago were considered "off the map" and outside the global production system.

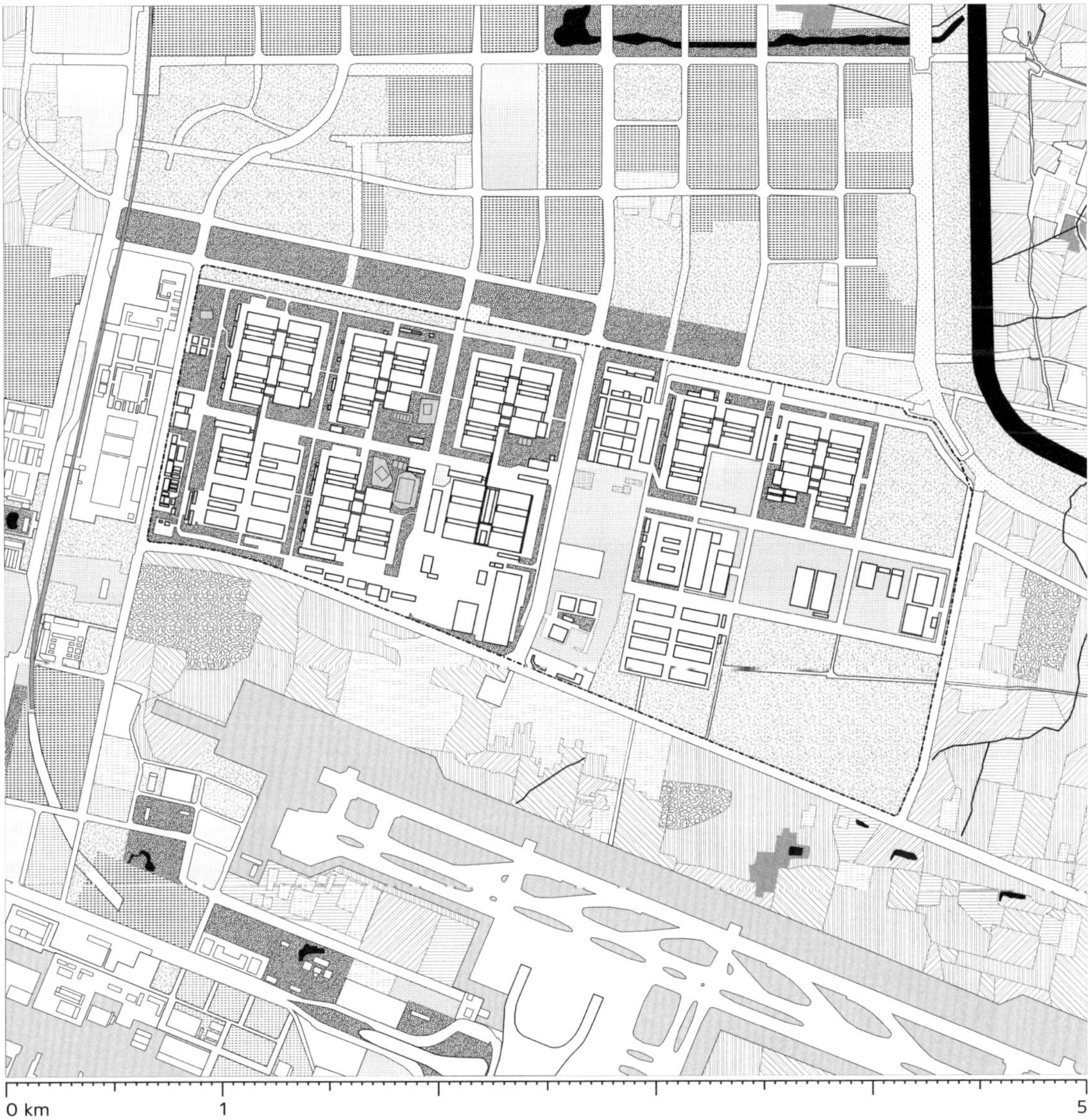

Fig. 63. Sample 3.B.

Foxconn Science Park

People employed: about 350,000

Construction period: 2011–present

Legend

- Foxconn Science Park
- buildings
- high-rise and low-rise compounds
- water
- trees and vegetation
- bare land
- crops and arable land
- non-permeable surfaces

Fig. 64. Zhengdong Building Material Centre, Zhengdong New District, 2019.

Fig. 65. Bathroom fixtures shop in Zhengdong Building Material Centre, Zhengdong New District, 2019.

In parallel with the initiatives to improve living conditions in rural areas and support industrial development, central and local governments have also fostered the development of cultural enterprises in recent years. According to the Henan Province Bureau of Statistics (2020), in the Zhengzhou municipality alone, there are 556 enterprises in culture and related industries, with a total of 80,910 employees. The total asset value of these activities is 88.2 billion CNY, and their revenues reach 69 billion CNY. The success of cultural industries is closely related to universities and cultural institutions, which have multiplied in recent years to more than 350, including 24 cultural centres, 38 museums, 17 public libraries, and 16 artistic performance groups (Zhengzhou Municipal Statistics Bureau, 2018). Zhengzhou municipality is also home to 58 university colleges (almost half of the universities in the Henan province), with 64,500 educational personnel for 935,332 enrolled students (Henan Province Bureau of Statistics, 2020).

Most educational personnel and students work and live in Longzihu Area, the university town of Zhengdong. The 28-square-kilometre site was first slated as a residential area in Kurokawa's plan, with a "sports city cluster" located in the north and a "research city cluster" to the south (K. Li et al., 2010b). However, while developing the project, Longzihu Area was entered for another planning competition, and subsequently redesigned by the Zhengzhou Research Institute of Urban Planning and Design (K. Li et al., 2010b). The final plan envisages a "research and university cluster" on 13.5 square kilometres north of Zhengdong railway station and east of the CBDs (Sample 3.C). This area is located between four infrastructure corridors: the northern and southern boundaries are the Jialu River and the Dongfeng Canal, respectively, while the eastern border is the G4 highway, and the western is the G107 expressway. A metro line connects this area to Zhengzhou city centre while another one is yet to be built (Busquets & Yang, 2019). Inside the area, 8.5 square kilometres are occupied by eleven university campuses located in a circle around a central artificial lake of 2.3 square kilometres. Finally, a "creative cluster" is situated on a 1.3-square-kilometre island in the middle of the lake and hosts research centres, hotels, banks, malls, and many other facilities. Today, it is reasonable to estimate that at least 250,000 persons live here, including around 150,000 full-time students and 15,000 faculty members.

Even if the campuses have different spatial layouts from one another, they do share some common features. While two of the faculties are small, the remaining campuses occupy portions of land ranging from 750,000 to 1,000,000 square metres, of which 160,000 to 540,000 square metres is built-up, or 20 to 50 percent of the total surface area (K. Li et al., 2010d). Each university provides accommodation facilities for 13,000 to 20,000 students and faculty members. Each complex has a main entrance with a 70-metre-wide ceremonial boulevard that links the external street to the central area of the campus, where the main library, the auditorium, the administrative offices, and all the representative buildings are located. These structures often have monumental and iconic shapes and are surrounded by vast open spaces, or parks with small lakes. This core zone is usually enclosed by a street that organises the layout and divides the site into different functional areas. Generally, a quarter of the campus is occupied by

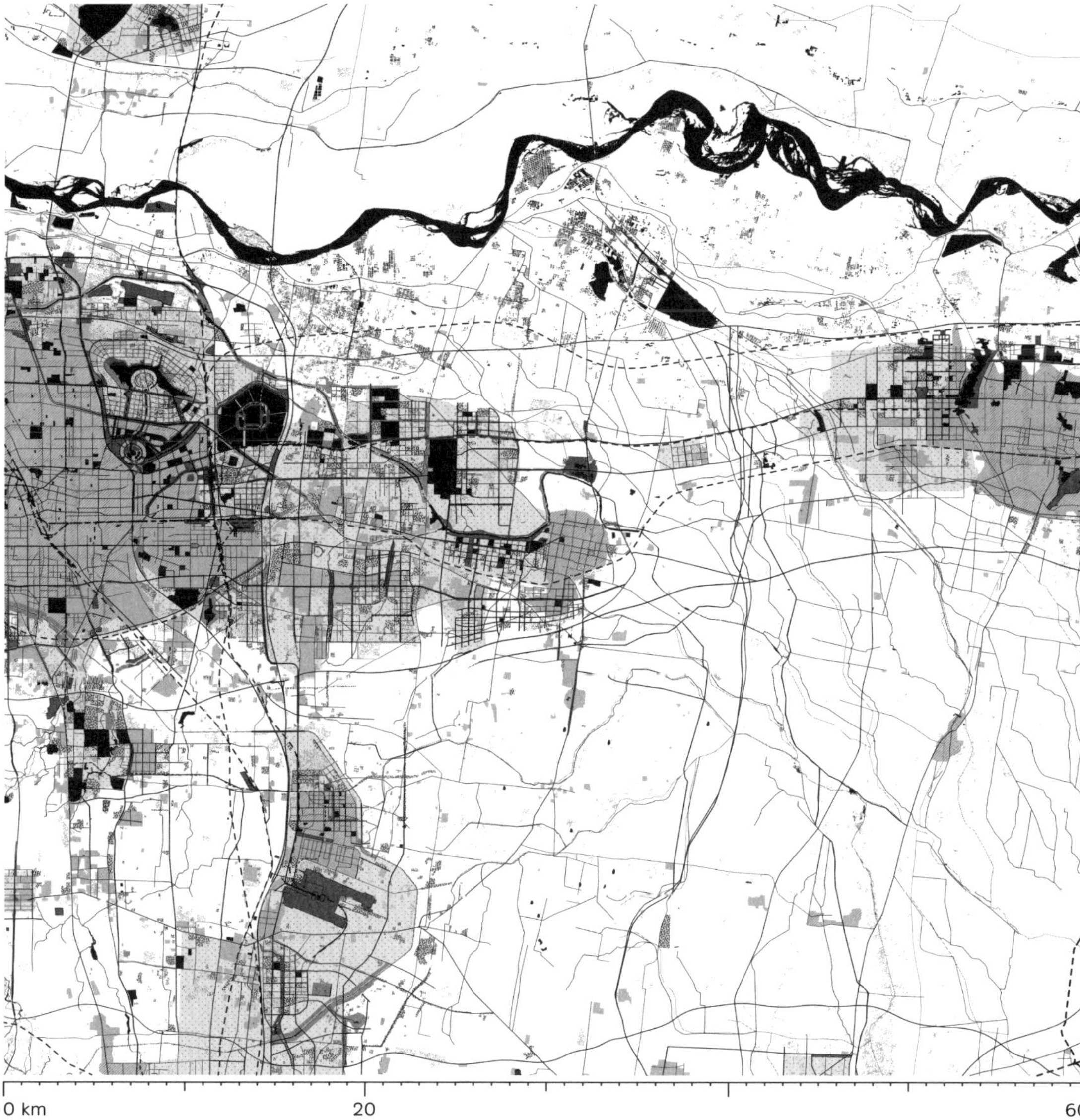

Fig. 66. Zhengbian New District.

Universities and Research Clusters

Legend

- railways
- main roads and waterways
- main rivers and lakes
- areas under construction
- built-up areas
- ecological corridors
- airports
- universities and research clusters

the dormitories, which are generally six-storey buildings oriented north-south. Inside the dorms, the students' accommodation is normally 28 square metres plus a small balcony, with either a shared bathroom or ensuite (K. Li et al., 2010d). The dorms also include a laundry room and small meeting rooms, while most of the main communal services, such as canteens and study rooms, are generally located in one or more buildings nearby. The remaining parts of the campuses are usually lecture halls and laboratories. Finally, each university has its own sports area that often includes a football field, a covered swimming pool, and 5 to 10 tennis and basketball courts.

Longzihu Area is part of a wider process of university town construction that has been underway throughout China since the early 2000s. Its urban layout recalls the emblematic case of the Guangzhou University Town built in 2002 to accommodate ten faculties on a circular island of 15 square kilometres (Liang, 2014). However, this is not an isolated case in the Central Plains. Six new campuses are located in the northern part of Kaifeng New Area, and all major cities are building additional university towns. While this trend has been criticised by scholars for being the result of a top-down bureaucratic process that turns hundreds of thousands of students and government employees into pioneers to populate new urban areas (Liang, 2014; Ren, 2013; Shepard, 2015), it also demonstrates the effort to promote cultural industries, that are not only able to raise educational levels, but to change the narrative of spaces located on the fringes of main cities.

Fig. 67. Sample 3.C.

University Town of Zhengdong New District

People employed: about 150,000

Construction period: 2005–present

Legend

- - - - - -	Zhengdong University Town		trees and vegetation
	buildings		bare land
	high-rise and low-rise housing		crops and arable land
	water		non-permeable surfaces

	Number of Campuses	Total Area (sq. km)	Enrolled Students (persons)	Faculty Members (persons)	Enrolled Professors (persons)
North China University of Water Resources and Hydro-power	2	1.55	34,100	2,376	1,707
Zhengzhou Institute of Aeronautical Industry Management	1	1.25	28,000	1,822	527
Henan Vocational and Technical College	1	0.83	19,000	NA	375
Henan Economic and Trade Vocational College	3	0.55	21,000	NA	996
Henan Institute of Economy and Finance	2	1.00	20,000	1,200	NA
Henan Institute of Animal Husbandry and Economics	3	1.40	33,000	1,700	1,120
Henan Agricultural University	1	2.83	30,000	2,162	757
Henan Police Academy	1	1.12	5,537	NA	NA
Henan University of Economics and Law	3	1.33	30,000	2,000	NA
Henan Judicial Police Vocational College	3	0.33	NA	NA	229
Henan University of Chinese Medicine	3	1.03	20,000	1,399	1,175
Zhengzhou Institute of Technology	4	0.98	12,866	1,144	788

Fig. 68. The universities in the University Town of Zhengdong New District.

Fig. 69. Entrance of the International Convention Centre, Zhengdong New District, 2019.

Fig. 70. Conference hall in the International Convention Centre, Zhengdong New District, 2019.

Fig. 71. Henan Agricultural University, Zhengdong University Town, Zhengdong New District, 2019.

Fig. 72. Research centre in Zhengdong University Town, Zhengdong New District, 2019.

Fig. 73. Zhengdong New District, 2019.

Concluding Remarks

Setting an Interpretative Hypothesis

The wave of change washing over the Central Plains of China has completely reshaped infrastructural systems, housing, factories, cultural centres, and everything else in its path. The hypothesis presented here is that this transformation has certain specific features that can neither be regarded as being exclusively circumstantial, nor the result of solely local characteristics. Instead, what the Central Plains, and the Chinese context in general, provides is a privileged site for investigation: the urban transformations here are more dramatic and radical than in other contexts around the world; and, given their radicality, are more easily studied. Not only do they reveal a great deal about China, but also about urbanisation elsewhere. Interpreting the urbanisation processes here can be helpful in reflecting on other territories, landscapes, and cities, and on how they are designed, built, and inhabited. The category of *enrichment* is employed here to create a body of common features, traces, and tensions seen in many urban transformations. As defined by Luc Boltanski and Arnaud Esquerre (2020) in their book *Enrichment*,[1] the term describes a type of economic process: "based on an effort to *enrich* things that already exist, especially by associating them with narratives; [...] it draws upon trade in things that are intended above all for the wealthy and that thus also constitute a supplementary source of enrichment for the wealthy people who deal in them" (p. 2–3). In this process, the value of goods not only relies on performativity, but also on narratives. Consequently, a multitude of actors are required for this process of valuation: government organisations that ensure product quality and the veracity of the narratives; cultural institutions that legitimise the narratives in order to generate value; market forces that craft commodities and exploit imaginaries; and private individuals (consumers) that aspire to differentiate themselves from the masses (Boltanski & Esquerre, 2020). This definition of enrichment is based on an economic analysis of contemporary European settings, mainly France. In this work, enrichment is regarded as a much deeper process at the core of all transformation in China, including urbanisation. Hence, while it is impossible to draw direct comparisons between the Chinese context and those investigated by Boltanski and Esquerre, the underlying processes appear to somehow possess a set of similar traits. Thus, it is not a question of how different or similar China is, or even about the ways that it is different or similar. Instead, the objective of this book is to bring about collisions, shatter multiple and diverse contexts, and to thereby challenge established interpretative models and categories. In line with this approach, the Central Plains of China is interpreted as a great *bassin d'enrichissement*, where all material elements and every transformation are part of an attempt to base an economy on the symbolic value of material goods. The questions raised by this hypothesis are manifold. For a start, is it possible to regard the infrastructures of the Central Plains of China (roads, railways, parks, canals, and grids) as the main vectors for an immense process of *environmental enrichment*? Is it accurate to view the residential spaces as branded commodities that exploit global imaginaries and local history to generate an *enrichment of the everyday*? Similarly, can we look at production spaces as creative clusters that extol cultural and technological advances, arts, and spectacles to produce an *enrichment of the experience*? All these questions are relevant for the entire Central Plains area. Wherever the gaze falls, we observe this kind of growth, expansion, and exaltation of functions, spaces, and meanings. However performative and inclusive these transformations may seem, the resulting landscape is a complex ground that abounds in contradictions and conflicts. Thus, what does the design of the enriched field entail?

Enriching the Environment

The infrastructuralisation of the Central Plains of China has taken place in three phases. At the beginning of the 2000s, this space was made up of a dense and porous network of paths, unpaved roads, and canals. This capillary system established relations of proximity between housing, farmland, and small public spaces, regulating and mediating the transitions between contiguous environments. This was evident in the traditional houses, where the passage from private rooms to public street was through an inner courtyard. Similarly, the transition from the agrarian settlements to the expanse of fields was filtered by roads that skirted the village, surrounded by groves of trees and small ponds. Beyond the fields lay other villages and other houses, all organised according to the same logic, forming a harmonious, unified landscape. Thus, the Central Plains was a *continuous surface*, where infrastructures established reciprocal relationships of interdependency between different artefacts and environments. This familiar scene was redrawn in the early 2000s, when the construction of a long-distance high-speed transport system cast a net over the existing landscape. It was made up of highways, canals, and suspended railways: all linking major centres while bypassing other areas. Consequently, the Central Plains turned into a *hierarchical surface* on which the transit infrastructures fixed new relations of scale by polarising economies and designating spaces for development. Zhengdong New District was the most exemplary case of this: a node of the national high-speed railway system that was planned as a monumental hub for catalysing global flows.

However, all this has changed since 2014. Due to hypertrophic urban growth, the latest development plans for Zhengbian New District promote a new infrastructure grid targeted at equipping large areas of land with roads, water, energy, and greenspace. This system has been applied to every urbanisation project under development in the Central Plains. It parcels land into regular 500 × 500-metre mega-plots suitable for supporting diverse programmes ranging from residential compounds to major factories, university campuses, shopping malls, agricultural villages, and cropland. Unlike the previous infrastructure networks, the new model redefines topographical characteristics, pre-existing urban fabric, environmental specificities, and positional values. The Central Plains has thus become an *equipotential surface*: a space capable of supporting disparate functions and practices without determining congruity or incongruity, harmony or conflict.

This new type of infrastructure is radically different from the diffuse and continuous network that characterises European territories. In the Central Plains, infrastructures are neither in-between spaces subject to constant appropriation and modification, nor "rooms to manoeuvre" capable of hosting a wide variety of individual practices (Secchi, 2000; Sieverts, 2003). The new infrastructure system is also different from that of North America. Even though it has the same morphology, the grid of the Central Plains does not attempt to provide coherence and continuity, nor to create an organic unicum as in the North American middle landscape (Busquets et al., 2019; Corner & MacLean, 2000; Tunnard & Pushkarev, 1964). On the contrary, the new layout produces an expansion of non-contiguous, non-proximal fragments that remain so, even when placed next to each other. Just like contemporary logistics spaces, which spring up everywhere, colonising the land regardless of context (Easterling, 2014). This new network is the foundation of an environmental enrichment aimed at "irrigating territory with potential" while preserving everything within a "scale of undecidability".[2]

However, unlike logistics spaces, the infrastructure grid of the Central Plains is not merely a construction made to prepare the land for domestic and foreign investments. The infrastructure has an age-old touch of magnificence: it enriches the space not only in terms of performance, but also by adding poetry.[3] Through this composition of enormous greenways, huge parks, expanses of solar panels, large water canals, and efficient public transportation systems, the infrastructure network displays a wealth of (enriched) technology able to rebalance ecologies, create new ecosystems, and generate environmental wellbeing. Its materiality and symbolism are thus as far from modern monumentality extolling the virtues of the masses (Harvey, 1989; Liang, 2014; F. Wu, 2015), as they are from the romantic exaltation of landscapes, wilderness, and pastoralism (Machor, 1987; Mozingo, 2011). This cannot even be regarded as a means of laying the foundation for a globalised "Potemkin metropolis", like the Olympics grounds in Beijing and Pudong in Shanghai (Koolhaas et al., 1995; Ren, 2011; Sklair, 2006). In the Central Plains, the materiality of new infrastructures is brimming with the rhetoric of contemporary environmentalism, that is, an attempt to respond to the imperative of creating sustainable, resilient, and ecological cities, whatever new layouts and configurations this may take.

Enriching the Everyday

The enriched environment resulting from the infrastructure network of the Central Plains means that artefacts may be brought together regardless of their characteristics. Within the *equipotential surface*, residential compounds, industrial zones, parks, leisure facilities, and all artefacts that compose the landscape claim their singularity and specificity. Thus the process of "place creation" that has characterised new towns, CBDs, Transit Oriented Developments (TODs), and university towns is now affecting all material elements. As a result, the new artefacts not only provide all space with services, but also with narratives and imaginaries, in turn enriching everyday living experiences. This process is evident in residential estates, even those sited in marginal areas such as Zhongmu County. Here, design activities carefully select new narratives, which are then staged through the highly expressive aesthetic of each building.

The new agricultural towns epitomise this condition. They not only provide public services (such as schools, medical centres, commercial areas, and spaces for leisure), but also promote new rural imaginaries. In completely abandoning the formal and functional features of a traditional village, the new variegated aesthetics emphasise the individuality of each living space. This emerges in the new dwellings: three-storey terraced houses with spacious rooms, private sanitation, bow windows, fenced gardens, and garages. While appearing to have been built using a single blueprint, they are never quite identical, concealing endless small variations. This emphasis on the unique character of each space is even more evident if one observes the compounds recently built by real estate companies near the new rural settlements. Made up of large houses, they have private elevators, reception rooms, and terraces with a jacuzzi. Rich with amenities, these new compounds also have architecturally decorative elements and stylistic names such as Vancouver Village, Little Paris, or Italian Town and are branded by the real estate companies as exclusive, high-quality products.

This wide variety of aesthetics can be found, however, in every space and urban material, and is widely celebrated in the exhibition halls of local governments and real estate companies, which do their utmost to turn dwelling into a spectacle (Repellino, 2019). In these exhibitions, billboards, guided tours, maquettes, and videos emphasise the environmental character, luxury amenities, collective facilities, and private services of each compound. Furthermore, the construction conduits, sanitation, insulation systems, and building materials are showcased to display the high quality of construction. Alongside this, advertisements celebrate the successful history of the real estate companies: famous developments, prestigious architectural firms, achievements, public awards, and even the founders' personal lives are all on display for the public.[4] Hence, the enrichment of the everyday is derived from the ever-greater variety of new devices and facilities, the assortment of architectural forms, the accumulation of local and international brands, and, above all, by turning all artefacts into a spectacle.

The landscape that results from this enrichment is radically different from that of urban diffusion. The artefacts that compose the Central Plains do not affirm the individual. Even the private houses are turnkey projects supplied to the final user complete with all the necessary fixtures, including a fictional narrative. Consequently, the inhabitants have little range to appropriate these spaces, to the point that they do not make any changes at all unless due to a compelling practical need (such as in new agricultural towns where the lack of spaces for storing crops leads inhabitants to build improvised barns). Thus, the artefacts are not a means for displaying collective labour or individual entrepreneurialism; they are just market products to be used like any material goods.

Likewise, these spaces cannot be considered as merely the result of a global suburbanisation process (Clapson & Hutchison, 2010; Phelps & Wu, 2011). The Central Plains is a far cry from the anti-urban roots that characterised the American middle landscape (Marx, 1964; Rowe, 1991; Waldheim, 2016). In China, the new settlements, the corporate offices, and the retail estates are not "machines in the garden", they do not tame the land in order to establish a peaceful relationship between humans and nature. This is also because the pastoral conviction that superior moral values are inherent to the rural environment does not fit the Chinese context. Here, rurality recalls the recent past of hardships and shortages, something to move away from (Bolchover et al., 2013; Rozelle & Hell, 2020; X. Wang, 2020). Thus, even agricultural towns and agricultural parks claim to be urban: they are part of the new city, which is primarily a space for redemption (Oakes, 2019); a redemption mainly achieved through the cohesive representation of a collective enrichment conveyed by a large assortment of architectural forms, the accumulation of local and international aesthetics, and, above all, the celebration of the narratives and genealogies that brand each and every place.

Enriching the Experience

Thus, the enriched field is a space first equipped by an infrastructural system that spreads nature, wellbeing, and urbanity, and then colonised by artefacts that celebrate their own uniqueness. However, it would be a mistake to imagine the Central Plains as a crazy pavement of stones in random patterns without rules for positioning, a zone equipped and deregulated for speculators, "a quintessential apparatus of the neoliberal state" (Easterling, 2014, p. 66). The Central Plains of China are actually anything but "extra-statecraft". Here, administrative institutions and planning agencies go to great lengths to regulate and govern urban development. Not only through management policies, such as the land quota mechanism, but mainly through planning activities that aim to recompose the individual parts into a greater whole, such as the plans for Zhengbian New District.

These plans attempt to defuse the confrontation between parts through mutual understanding, by adopting a new language capable of alternating meanings and thus changing the way in which spaces are perceived and used: cropland becomes ecological areas, factories turn into science parks, and logistics spaces transmute into TODs. These changes in perception then affect the ways in which these spaces are designed and finally constructed. In particular, they are open to a mix of disparate functions. In Zhengbian New District, there is a wealth of examples; the most emblematic are the production spaces that, by improving efficiency and performance, also host new housing, new facilities, and new devices, all celebrating cultural advances and technological progress. The Foxconn factory has been rebranded as the "iPhone City", which comprises research centres, dormitories, restaurants, and sports fields. Similarly, the agricultural land of Yanming Lake Town has been rebaptised the Zhongmu Agricultural Park to include its greenhouses, fishponds, and croplands, as well as its research centres, resorts, shopping malls, and golf and aviation clubs. Within this never-ending process of rewriting, every inch of the landscape is continuously being altered, and consequently enhanced, in order to increase its performance and heighten the experience.

The effort to preserve overall coherence through the managed alteration of meanings and the densification of functions leads to the conception of the Central Plains as a *syntrophic space*. Syntropy (or negentropy) is the opposite of entropy: a process that gives rise to structures that are evermore ordered and internally differentiated. In the Central Plains, functions and spaces are evermore unified and ordered, while single components retain their diversity. This is unlike urban diffusion, where the location of functions may be freely chosen, leading to a *mixité* of uses and practices (Secchi, 2005; Sieverts, 2003). It is also different from the construction of the middle landscape, where the modern technical approach determines a rigid separation of uses such as living, working, playing, and shopping into clearly defined zones (to the point of everything being listed and categorised in books such as: Easterling, 2001; Mozingo, 2011; Rowe, 1991). Finally, this *syntrophic space* is far more complex than the spaces of infrastructure and logistics, where a purely extractive economy demands highly specialised zones that, while optimising production, divest any functions that are not strictly necessary (Brenner & Katsikis, 2020). In the Central Plains, the spaces, even those for production, are not functional enclaves detached from their surroundings, but spaces that strive to be inclusive in order to establish relationships of interdependence. These relationships are more symbolic than physical, and so the sequences are never linear, not even when the things are being organised along primary axes such as that in Zhengbian New District.

As a result, the Central Plains appears more as an ensemble of empowered clusters, vaguely reminiscent of past models of development. For instance, the cellular urbanism of the *danwei*, which were constituted not only as workspaces, but also as living spaces (Bonino & De Pieri, 2015; Liang, 2014). However, the anti-urban objective of these socialist projects is reversed in the contemporary spaces: the current transformations do not aim to dismember the city into independent cells; on the contrary, they have integrated highly specialised technical spaces traditionally considered not part of the city into everyday living environments Thus, every space of the Central Plains is “a little bit more city”, and, in turn, the combination of these parts turns the entire landscape into a sort of augmented reality, within which it is possible to experience everything that a modern city has to offer.

The Project of the Enriched Field

The project of the enriched field is based on a new infrastructure system that improves the performance of all spaces. This leads to an *equipotential surface* in which differences in positional values of the landscape are erased. Furthermore, the ensemble of roads, canals, pipelines, cables, and parks is also the vector for a new ecological comfort grounded in a globally recognised and ever more institutionalised ethical position. This recovers the ecumenical aspirations of modernist design, but at the cost of abandoning anthropocentric arguments (i.e., social justice based on redistribution or participation) in the name of environmental, ecological, and non-human justice (Drori et al., 2006; Morton, 2016; Schlosberg, 2009; Swyngedouw, 2017). Thus, the project of the *enriched field* shares little with the rational stance, which aspired to develop a city based on human intellectual and physical features, or the humanist viewpoint, celebrating the cultural characteristics of each space and its practices. This is evident in the configurations of infrastructures and open spaces, which no longer extol the virtues of the masses as in modernist design, nor stage the singularities of individuals as in post-modern urban design. On the contrary, greenways, huge water systems, new plantations, reforested areas, hydroponic horticulture, solar farms, and low-emission public transport networks are said to be spaces that work for the planet, rather than for humans, with humans nothing more than one of the many species inhabiting the planet. Within this framework, design has adopted a holistic approach that operates in a techno-scientific mode, as familiar from many modernist projects such as the *Ecumenopolis* by Constantinos Doxiadis and the *4D Time World* by Buckminster Fuller, and contemporary proposals such as OMA's *Roadmap 2050* (2010), Turenscape's *Chinese National Ecological Security Plan* (2007), and the many eco-cities, low-carbon cities, and sponge cities under construction. However, in adopting this non-anthropocentric, technocratically based ecological universalism, the project of the enriched field promotes a concept of rigidly coded collective wellbeing that is, at this point in time, the object of strong consensus and fierce criticism.

Market forces may act freely within this environment. They mould the land by siting new artefacts that create added value, which is not solely a use-value, but comprises new imaginaries and promises. The process produces local cultural singularities that constitute "monopoly revenues".[5] Thus, "place creation through à-la-carte aesthetics" results neither from the emergence of a capitalist class, nor from the repositioning of territorial elites, as has been argued in the literature that considers these spaces as transnational models or copies of global architectures (Bosker et al., 2013). Instead, paradoxically, this meets a demand for authenticity, that is, being part of a specific tale promoting a specific identity.[6] This contrived identity is obtained by spectacularising the living environment, by branding every material artefact, and by promoting new lifestyles. Consequently, living spaces are no longer perceived as standardised commodities for the masses, but as standard products with exclusive characteristics and a "collector effect". This is exemplified by the way in which public administrations and private developers operate to ensure that living in the *enriched field* is effectively living in the *brandscape*: a combination of "collectible spaces", each with an intrinsic performative and symbolic value.[7] Hence, the exceptional character of each place must be made explicit, recounted, legitimised, and celebrated through its spectacularisation. This approach not only reverses the standardisation of modern design; but is also an overturning of the post-modern design that sought legitimisation in the *genius loci*, the collective memory, and the historical identity of a specific space. In contrast, the project of the *enriched field* (re)invents discourses, narratives, and identities to meet the ever-changing needs of the inhabitants and to ensure constant surprise. In this sense, it finds its own archetypes in Prada's *24-Hour Museum* (2012): an immersive exhibition showing a sequence of rituals unfolding over 24 hours. Similarly, the project of the *enriched field* differentiates each place and celebrates its uniqueness by inventing specific narratives that aim primarily at seducing rather than convincing.

Narrative freedom is, however, not unlimited. Not everything can be said. The narrative must be coherent; thus, urban development must be controlled since it is one of the most important media through which the narrative is articulated. This does not imply censorship, rather the modulation of meaning by adding and mixing functions and practices into new configurations. Perfect examples of this are the creative districts and agricultural parks that, while improving productivity, also provide new housing, facilities, and devices to celebrate cultural advances and technological progress.[8] Thus, places (even those for agriculture, industry, financial, and cultural production) are not confined to a simple practical function, but must simultaneously provide an experience as edifying as possible. For this to occur, the project of the enriched field must rely not only on the power of symbols (Ren, 2011), but also on its inclusivity, and welcome uses, and spaces that had previously been set outside the city. This approach operates differently from the modernist zoning that divided spaces according to function (Sclar, 2019); and from that of landscape theory, which searched for relationships and unity based on proximity and interconnection (Waldheim, 2006, 2016).

The previous paragraphs present the most striking features of the enriched field. Its complexity reveals much about the issues, opportunities, and challenges of the contemporary city, something that projects, plans and policies cannot ignore. Above all, the transition to a non-anthropocentric universal ethic, the spectacularisation of the everyday, and the modulation of relationships between spaces and their uses. A final question hovers in the background of these focal points: what tension encompasses all three? I believe that the project of the enriched field acts to affirm an eternal present in which "nothing more can happen; [...] [in that it] is disconnected, positioned at a safe distance from danger and above all from conflicts" (Boltanski & Esquerre, 2020, p. 310). What are the multitude of plans drawn up by various agencies if not a way to internalise all possible future transformations in today's narrative? To what do we owe the constant relaunching of plans and projects before their completion, if not to the construction of a narrative which affirms that the future is not tomorrow but rather what we are experiencing now? This *presentification* implies the abandonment of the progressivist tension of modernity: the project of the enriched field is not a common ground for negotiating a long-term future. Moreover, it is also far from the recent attention paid to resilience, constant change, never-ending transformation, the instability of events, and lack of inertia (Corner, 2006; Mostafavi & Doherty, 2016; Waldheim, 2016). On the contrary, in the project of the enriched field, all possible transformations collapse into a continuous present which performs them on stage, rendering them visible and liveable.[9] This actualisation of both past and future changes aims to remove all tension between times (the weight of the past, the uncertainty of the future), producing a reassuring and tranquil stasis: there is nothing to fear from the transformations in progress since "the city has become the epitomised landscape of social stability" (Oakes, 2019, p. 404). However, it would be wrong to believe that change will fizzle out. It is evident in China, but this evidence also allows us to reflect upon the situation in other contexts. In fact, in enriched fields, it is not true to say that "the stronger the identity, the more it imprisons, the more it resists expansion, interpretation, renewal, contradiction" (Koolhaas et al., 1995, p. 1248). On the contrary, the stronger the identity, the more it undergoes a continual alteration of sense and meaning. These alterations may be small and imperceptible, like in the West, or great and dramatic, as in China. Within this picture, the task of design is to guide and assist these shifts by establishing a *narrative structure* able to select and actualise the most convincing discourses. This presumes that, in the end, any future is feasible since it is already (and has always been) implicit in the present; indeed, it has already become part of the past and, thus, will be here forever. Hence, it is commonly said that the Central Plains have been, and will forever be, prone to property speculation; the south of France has been, and will always be, a place for leisure, recreation, and wellbeing; Silicon Valley has been, and will always be, the home of technological innovation; London has been, and will always be, the global financial capital. In brief, the project of the enriched field, rather than exalting discontinuity, becomes an instrument through which conflict, friction, and tension are internalised and obliterated in a universal narrative able to perpetuate itself, unchangingly, through time.

---

1 This meaning is grounded in the long tradition of socio-economic studies investigating how socio-cultural aspects affect the trade of material goods. Particularly, the studies: *Distinction a Social Critique of the Judgement of Taste* (1979) by Pierre Bourdieu; *The System of Objects* (1968), *The Consumer Society* (1970), *Symbolic Exchange and Death* (1976) by Jean Baudrillard, and *The New Spirit of Capitalism* by Luc Boltanski and Eve Chiapello (2018 [2005]). In the field of urban studies, also relevant on this topic, among others, *The Cultures of Cities* (1996) by Sharon Zukin. **2** The terms respectively recall the problematisation elaborated in *Whatever Happened to Urbanism?* (1995) by Rem Koolhaas, and *Scales of Undecidability* (2002) by Anita Berrizbeitia. **3** I refer to the notion of poetics elaborated by Brian Larkin (2013): "Poetics is thus a rearranging of the hierarchy of what signification within the speech event is dominant at any moment. [...] In the case of infrastructures, the poetic mode means that form is loosened from technical function. Infrastructures are the means by which a state proffers these representations to its citizens and asks them to take those representations as social facts" (p. 335). **4** This phenomenon is analogous to the one observed by Luc Boltanski and Arnauld Esquerre (2020), who argue that the craft workshop in France is a "living museum in which what is on display is not only the object for sale but the activity of the person who made it" (p. 285). Richard Sennet (2018) indicates something similar referring to the international residential compounds in Shanghai: "All these imitations correspond to a tested brand; they arouse the feeling to live in a precise place and by association they exempt a peculiar aura, that of being deeply rooted" (p. 136). **5** Luc Boltanski and Arnaud Esquerre (2020) describe the "monopoly revenues" as a localised form of valuation, such as the sites of wine production in southern and southwestern France. According to them, these *terroirs* are "zones whose soil is defined not only by specific mineral properties and climatic conditions but also by reactivated or invented traditions [...], by the creation of labels, and by the use of historical references to famous people who purportedly lived in proximity to certain vineyards [...], and also by administrative measures intended to limit and regulate production" (p. 20). **6** As for the contemporary spaces of cultural tourism in China, where "identities may be consciously localised as strategy to engage structures of political economy which increasingly connect local actors with broader geographical frameworks and more distant sources of power" (Oakes, 1993, p. 48). **7** This condition somehow recalls the *brandscapes* described by Anna Klingmann (2007) and Orvar Löfgren (2014). **8** Similar transformations can be found in other contexts worldwide. For instance, the major ports of European cities such as Rotterdam, Genoa, and Marseilles have recently been redeveloped as touristic destinations with museums, entertainment areas, and discos; in Silicon Valley, most of the AI campuses are open to the public and contain fitness centres, auditoriums, and other facilities. **9** This trend is similar to the "heritage creation" that characterises European cities.

Afterword

by Francesca Governa and Angelo Sampieri

Doing Urban Research in China

In October 2016, Leonardo Ramondetti began his research on the urbanisation processes underway in the Central Plains of China. He continued until January 2020, when the onset of the pandemic prevented him from carrying on with his fieldwork. In addition to his own research, Ramondetti has also been involved in several related projects in which we have also had the opportunity to participate, some of which we coordinated: "Chinese New Towns: Negotiating Citizenship and Physical Form" (2016–2019), leading to the publication *The City after Chinese New Towns* (Birkhäuser 2019); "Rescaling the Belt and Road Initiative: Urbanization Processes, Innovation Patterns and Global Investments in Urban China" (2020–2023), funded by the Italian Ministry of Education, University and Research; the exhibition *China Goes Urban* (2020–2021) at the Museum of Oriental Art in Turin, and a number of design projects for specific locations in China that verified Ramondetti's hypotheses through applied research. *The Enriched Field: Urbanising the Central Plains of China* reaps the fruit of these research activities by building on a vast body of experience from the China Room research group at the Politecnico di Torino, and from many international universities, scholars, experts, and technicians. It is our belief that two main principles underpin the foci of all these research activities. The first is the fundamental requirement for fieldwork. The second is the importance of positioning the observed phenomena in loco within the broader body of urban issues. In other words, the need to look beyond circumstantial characteristics in order to understand the role and meaning of the observed phenomena within wider processes and transformations that supersede national constraints. Although these two principles may be regarded as common aspects of most urban research, they are practiced less when the research is conducted by Western scholars in China. The field presents an endless series of spaces, data, and documents, all of which are very difficult to access. Furthermore, local and national specificities constantly resist any attempt to decontextualise and reposition within the wider body of knowledge concerning urban processes.[1] Despite these challenges, we consider this research to be exemplary in the two principles above, integrating them into an investigative approach that is invariably rigorous in arriving at findings with particular significance and originality. Therefore, in this afterword, we would like to draw attention to these two points: on one hand, the investigative approach employed in the project, and on the other, the openings achieved.

The field of research defined by Leonardo Ramondetti has been constructed through a series of operations that required an extended period of fieldwork in the Central Plains of China to gather data and information from heterogeneous sources, document the socio-political and economic events in the region, interact extensively with local actors and residents, create photographic reports, maps, and surveys of sites at different scales—from smaller architectural elements to large sections of landscape. We can clearly see how the intent was to understand phenomena of differing significance and reach, without presuming to forge them into a cohesive and coherent narrative, nor produce a hierarchy of facts with greater or lesser importance. The resulting field resembles an open composition made up of insights to which great detail is devoted, and is also marked by respectful silences where the investigated object is particularly ineffable or undefinable. However, this does not imply arbitrariness. We can identify at least two filters that guided the selection of research materials. The first is the physical dimensions of the city as defined in the fields of environmental, geographical, urban, and landscape studies. These disciplines regard space as being the result of the actions that were performed there. History, politics, economics, and the entire gamut of social and cultural phenomena can all be observed through the traces of their spatialisation. Thus, it is possible to build representations that take their cue from the material, yet are not confined to this inert dimension. We see this as being evident in the rich iconographic apparatus of this book: the re-conception of the territory in original maps, the survey of places and architecture, the photographic reportage of inhabitants and landscapes; all these materials coalesce to give shape to a hypothesis of a world that it is possible to validate using the right technical instruments. Unlike traditional morphological studies, this approach sets aside the presumption of being objective, but also any fears of taking a stance, even though this may be criticised for being overly *thin*, or for not achieving the *thickness* that characterises most ethnography-based urban research.[2] What prevails is a discreet viewpoint in constant search of the right lens and the right focus to deduce specific characteristics and general features, to meticulously note regularities and repetitions, to record variations and alterations with precision. However, when necessary, this measured gaze is capable of quickly switching scale and perspective, even averting the eye to avoid misreading. The risk of misreading cannot be underestimated, and it is the foundation of the second filter applied to the selection of materials: some things cannot be investigated. The starting point for Ramondetti's research is physical spaces that seem recognisable; to some extent, they are similar to other known spaces. Indeed, this is why they were selected: their recognisability, that is, the ease of combining them with other spaces, in China and elsewhere, of establishing analogies and similarities, differences and contrasts. The objective of the selection is thus to gain familiarity with recognisable spaces and materials in order to develop an analysis without the presumption of understanding everything in great detail. At the same time, this prevents the observed object from being banished to the category of exceptionalism, where it is out of reach. We believe this quest for the right distance, the appropriate measure, the discretion of the gaze, and this attempt at familiarisation are anything but a search for easy shortcuts or simplistic expedients to normalise a situation otherwise beyond our comprehension. Rather, it is the distinctive feature of an investigation that is particularly fruitful in revealing those traits of contemporary urban China still concealed by the shroud of exceptionalism (often leading to stigmatisation) which prevails in Western literature.[3]

This book does not settle for an interpretation proposing exceptionalism as the explanation for the observed phenomena. It does not resort to the view of urban China as being "different from us". It does not stop at pointing out the similarities and then simply labelling them "with Chinese characteristics".[4] There are numerous reasons for this. In the first place, the research regards each and every space as an exception in itself (a principle which is equally valid in China and any other place in the world). This is backed up by the numerous samples upon which the research is based: specific locations that can accommodate diversity, friction, and conflict all within a single space. A second reason is grounded in the conviction that national borders are merely containers of convenience: they are not a fact, but a construct (political, institutional, legislative, and cultural), and are thus moot if the basis of the study is policies and projects (local, national, and supernational) rather than socio-spatial properties capable of revealing the features and characteristics of new urbanisations. A third reason is the hypothesis that regarding China from afar, with a touch of "nescience" that arises from the cultural gap, facilitates the construction of a useful dialogue between traditions, knowledge, and interpretative frameworks. This paves the way for a comparison between differences that renders our knowledge of the urban, inevitably circumstantial and partial, the object of a more generalised discourse open to the unexpected and surprising.[5] Based on this working hypothesis, the research endeavours to incorporate the observed phenomena into a framework of references and positions stemming from the international debate. The aim is to identify openings and prospects that allow us to discuss the space of contemporary China within a more general framework of issues, processes, and narratives that go beyond China itself and concern us too. We are well aware of how risky this is: urban China neither falls under nor fits into any of the established categories. It is obviously not part of the traditional "centre" of urban studies (the Western countries), nor can it be categorised under the global North/South divide, nor can it be pigeonholed in the *post-colonial approach* or *subaltern urbanism*.[6] Moreover, even though one may identify, describe, and represent "familiar spaces", the rationale that led to their construction; the role played by the inhabitants, the state, the government authorities; the impact of local, national, and international economies; and many other factors will always be radically beyond our grasp. Therefore, the resulting interpretative framework will never be entirely coherent, nor will it ever comfortably fit the established models. This emerges with clarity from the attempts to create synergies between Chinese urbanisation and the processes of global suburbanisation, urban diffusion, logistics standardisation, and infrastructural extractivism. China proves that coherent, inherently rigid frameworks are of no use; they are clearly unable to adequately describe the reality observed. However, a minimum of orientation is necessary: the numerous and diverse references to global urbanisation processes should be read in this light. At times they offer a safe haven, at other moments they open up new horizons, but they are never escape routes. Similarly, the adherence to disciplinary discourses is always critical and non-sectorial: open to debate consolidated research practices, while being aware that any methods, assumptions, knowledge, and, ultimately, any interpretative hypotheses, acquire meaning and validation only within the same discourses.

The hypothesis of this book is that the urbanisation processes in the Central Plains of China can be observed and discussed as acts of *enrichment*, conferring additional value to the space in terms of history, tradition, nature, art, and technology. This value transcends any use-value and exchange-value it may inherently have. Once again, this hypothesis is a risk, a challenge, since it harks back to the economy of *enrichment* theorised by Luc Boltanski and Arnaud Esquerre in the European context.[7] However, we believe this hypothesis is coherent with the strategy and the objective of the research, that is, to bring about collisions between distant worlds, to associate and dis-associate spaces and practices, to reveal both their radical uniqueness and their absolute ordinariness, and finally to go beyond the observed specificities by repositioning them in the general body of knowledge. Thus, *The Enriched Field* should stimulate debate on the urbanisation processes in the Central Plains, regardless of whether or not one agrees with the hypothesis that this is an attempt to rapidly and ubiquitously commodify and brand every single place and element. The space represented in Ramondetti's book provides strong arguments for this hypothesis, but seeks no approval. Rather, it is a position from which to start debating. More importantly, while based on the ongoing urbanisation in the Central Plains, it may be discussed either within or beyond the specificities of the Chinese context. After years of research carried out in China, we believe that this is a crucial starting point in studying today's urban transformations. This is true for any understanding of how the reconfiguration of certain global economic processes are playing out at the local level, and how spaces are being reshaped to become part of those processes. For scholars of urban transformation, the fact that half of the world's iPhones are produced in a single location—"iPhone City" in Zhengzhou—cannot be ignored. It cannot be ignored that today, China is the greatest construction site on the planet, with an unprecedented scale of urban growth, and that all this is reshaping socio-spatial relationships between urban and rural areas and challenging the cultures of urban planning and architecture. More importantly, these radical and extraordinary traits are not the sole reason for observing the ongoing spatial transformations in China. If anything, the opposite is the reason: the ordinariness of spaces and everyday practices. This ordinariness enables us to establish relationships of great familiarity and proximity, and to treat spaces and phenomena as if they were here and everywhere. However, in order to describe spaces and phenomena, it is necessary to immerse oneself in the field. For the last two years this field has been inaccessible, and there is now a vacuum in urban research that will not be easy to fill. Given the present situation, Ramondetti's book provides important perspectives for any debate today, and it will be a starting point for research once a return to the field is possible.

1 The literature on contemporary urban China is rich in studies that help us understand ways and forms of the ongoing transformations in national projects and policies. These numerous investigations involve many parts of the country and include both urban and rural areas. Despite of this, studies that attempt to reposition local and national specificities into broader theoretical frameworks are not common. Most research in this direction falls into two categories: focusing on the great urban conurbations (especially the Pearl River Delta and the metropolitan areas of Beijing and Shanghai), investigated in relation to emerging and evolving *global city regions* (cf. Scott, A. J. (2001). *Global City Regions: Trends, Theory, Policy*. Oxford University Press); or focusing on the spaces that result from suburbanisation processes and transformations in rural areas in comparison to other low density, diffuse, and rarefied urbanisations worldwide, for instance the studies on the development of *desakota* as theorised by McGee, T. G. (1991). The emergence of desakota regions in Asia: Expanding a hypothesis. In N. S. Ginsburg, B. Koppel and T. McGee (Eds.), *The Extended Metropolis: Settlement Transition in Asia* (pp. 3–26). University of Hawaii Press; and on the "introduction" of American *new urbanism* in China by Wu, F. (ed.) (2007). *China's Emerging Cities: The Making of New Urbanism*. Routledge. **2** *Thickness* and *thinness* refer to Clifford Geertz and the ethnographic and anthropological studies that develop and are debated in his position. See: Geertz, C. (1973). Thick description: Toward an interpretive theory of culture. In C. Geertz, *The Interpretation of Cultures: Selected Essays* (pp. 3–30). Basic; Gibson-Graham J. K. (2014). Rethinking the economy with thick description and weak theory." *Current Anthropology*. *55*(9); and Jackson, J. L. Jr. (2013). *Thin Description: Ethnography and the African Hebrew Israelites of Jerusalem*. Harvard University Press. **3** Over the last 20 years, "Chinese exceptionalism" has been the basis of a wide body of research that has influenced numerous studies on different urban phenomena. For instance, see: Friedman, J. (2005). *China's Urban Transition*. University of Minnesota Press; Logan, J. R. (2008). *Urban China in Transition*. Blackwell Publishing. **4** For instance, the many positions that deem policies, economies, and spatial organisation to have "Chinese characteristics", such as: Yeoh, E. K. (2010). Ethnoregional disparity, ethnoterritoriality and peripheral nationalism: Socioracial dilemmas in contemporary China. *International Journal of China Studies*, *1*(2), 569–644; and Timberlake, M., Wey, Y. D., Ma, X., & Hao, J. (2014). Global cities with Chinese characteristics. *Cities*, *41*, 162–170. **5** Regarding new methods for comparison between different contexts, see McFarlane, C. (2010). The comparative city: Knowledge, learning, urbanism. *International Journal of Urban and Regional Research*, *34*(4), 725–742; Robinson, J. (2011). Cities in a world of cities: The comparative gesture. *International Journal of Urban and Regional Research*, *35*(1), 1–23; and Robinson, J. (2016). Thinking cities through elsewhere: Comparative tactics for a more global urban studies. *Progress in Human Geography*, *40*(1), 3–29. **6** The issues arising from the positioning of China in the context of global urban studies have been explored and debated in our paper: Governa, F., & Sampieri, A. (2020). Urbanisation processes and new towns in contemporary China: A critical understanding from a decentred view. *Urban Studies*, *57*(2), 366–382. **7** Boltanski, L., & Esquerre, A. (2020). *Enrichment: A Critique of Commodities*. Polity Press.

Longhu Lake and the sub-CBD of Zhengdong New District, 2019.

References

A

Ahlers, A. L. (2014). *Rural Policy Implementation in Contemporary China: New Socialist Countryside*. Routledge.

Akhavan, M. (2017). Development dynamics of port-cities interface in the Arab Middle Eastern world—The case of Dubai global hub port-city. *Cities*, *60*, 343–352.

Allen, S. (1999). *Points and Lines: Diagrams and Projects for the City*. Princeton Architectural Press.

AlSayyad, N. (2001). *Hybrid Urbanism: On the Identity Discourse and the Built Environment*. Praeger.

Anand, N., Gupta, A., & Appel, H. (2018). *The Promise of Infrastructure*. Duke University Press.

Armstrong, W., & McGee, T. G. (1985). *Theatres of Accumulation: Studies in Asian and Latin American Urbanization*. Routledge Kegan & Paul.

Arup Engineering Consulting Company, Zhengzhou City Planning and Design Institute, & Kaifeng City Planning and Design Institute. (2009). *Master Planning of Zhengbian New District (2009–2020): Atlas*. Zhengzhou Municipality.

Arup Engineering Consulting Company, Zhengzhou City Planning and Design Institute, & Kaifeng City Planning and Design Institute. (2010). *Master Planning of Zhengbian New District (2009–2020): Atlas*. Zhengzhou Municipality.

B

Bablon, G., Ravis, T., Notkin, B., & Su, R. (2019). Stop this. *Domus*, *1038*, 856–861.

Bai, G. (2016). *Yanming Lake Town Government Work Report 2015*. Zhengzhou Municipal Affairs Service Network. http://zm.public.zhengzhou.gov.cn/02JB/202091.jhtml

Banham, R., & Day, J. (1971). *Los Angeles: The Architecture of Four Ecologies*. Fletcher & Son Ltd.

Barnett, E. (2012, March 29). Apple chief Tim Cook visits Foxconn factory in China. *The Telegraph*. https://www.telegraph.co.uk/technology/apple/9172974/Apple-chief-Tim-Cook-visits-Foxconn-factory-in-China.html

Barry, A. (2006). Technological Zones. *European Journal of Social Theory*, *9*(2), 239–253. https://doi.org/10.1177/1368431006063343

Baudrillard, J. (1968). *The System of Objects*. Verso Books.

Baudrillard, J. (1970). *The Consumer Society: Myths and Structures*. SAGE Publications Ltd.

Baudrillard, J. (1976). *Symbolic Exchange and Death*. SAGE Publications Ltd.

Ben-Joseph, E. (2005). *The Code of the City: Standards and the Hidden Language of Place Making*. MIT Press.

Berger, A. (2002). *Reclaiming the American West*. Princeton Architectural Press.

Berger, A. (2007). *Drosscape: Wasting Land in Urban America*. Princeton Architectural Press.

Berrizbeitia, A. (2002). Scales of undecidability. In J. Czerniak (Ed.), *CASE: Downsview Park Toronto* (pp. 116–125). Prestel Publishing.

Bianchetti, C. (2014). I vantaggi della continuità. *Anfione & Zeto*, *25*, 111–116.

Bolchover, J., Lange, C., & Lin, J. (2013). *Homecoming: Contextualizing, Materializing and Practicing the Rural in China*. Prestel Publishing.

Boltanski, L., & Chiapello, E. (2018). *The New Spirit of Capitalism*. Verso Books.

Boltanski, L., & Esquerre, A. (2020). *Enrichment: A Critique of Commodities*. Polity Press.

Bonino, M., & De Pieri, F. (2015). *Beijing Danwei: Industrial Heritage in the Contemporary City*. Jovis.

Bonino, M., Governa, F., Repellino, M. P., & Sampieri, A. (Eds.). (2019). *The City After Chinese New Towns: Spaces and Imaginaries from Contemporary Urban China*. Birkhäuser.

Bonomi, A. (1997). *Il Capitalismo Molecolare: La Società al Lavoro nel Nord Italia*. Einaudi.

Bosker, B., Knapp, R. G., & Ruan, X. (2013). *Original Copies: Architectural Mimicry in Contemporary China*. University of Hawaii Press.

Bourdieu, P. (1979). *Distinction: A Social Critique of the Judgement of Taste*. Routledge.

Branzi, A. (2006). *Weak and Diffuse Modernity: The World of Projects at the Beginning of the 21st Century*. Skira.

Bray, D. (2013). Urban Planning Goes Rural. Conceptualising the "New Village". *China Perspectives*, *2013*(2013/3), 53–62.

Brenner, N. (Ed.). (2014). *Implosions/Explosions: Towards a Study of Planetary Urbanization*. Jovis.

Brenner, N., & Katsikis, N. (2020). Operational landscapes: Hinterlands of the Capitalocene. *Architectural Design*, *90*(1), 22–31.

Bruegmann, R. (2006). *Sprawl: A Compact History*. University of Chicago Press.

Busquets, J., Yang, D., & Keller, M. (2019). *Urban Grids: Handbook for Regular City Design*. Oro Editions.

Busquets, J., & Yang, D. (Eds.). (2019). *Zhengzhou: From Rail-city to a Metro-polis*. Oro Editions.

C

Cai, A., Liu, Y., Liang, J., & Zhang, W. (2012). Research on the evolution and reconstruction of urban spatial structure in Zhengzhou. *Chinese Urban Studies, 19*(6), 54–60.

Cantrell, B. E., & Holzman, J. (2017). *Responsive Landscapes: Strategies for Responsive Technologies in Landscape Architecture*. Routledge.

Cao, C. (2019). *Zhengzhou Historical and Cultural City: Research on Strategic Planning of Protection and Development*. China Building Industry Press.

Caprotti, F. (2014). Critical research on eco-cities? A walk through the Sino-Singapore Tianjin Eco-City, China. *Cities, 36*, 10–17.

Carlisle, S., & Pevzner, N. (2019). Eating the crust. *Domus, 1033*, 276–285.

Castells, M. (1996). *The Rise of the Network Society*. Blackwell Publishing.

Cattoor, B., & De Meulder, B. (2011). *Figures Infrastructures: An Atlas of Roads and Railways*. SUN Architecture.

Central Committee of the Communist Party of China. (2016). *The 13th Five-Year Plan for Economic and Social Development of the People's Republic of China (2016–2020)*. Central Compilation and Translation Press.

Chan, K. W. (2013). China: Internal migration. In E. Ness (Ed.), *The Encyclopedia of Global Human Migration*. Blackwell Publishing.

Chen, Y., Wen, Y., & Li, Z. (2017). From blueprint to action: The transformation of the planning paradigm for desakota in China. *Cities, 60*, 454–465.

Chien, S.-S., & Gordon, I. (2008). Territorial competition in China and the West. *Regional Studies, 42*(1), 31–49.

China Labor Watch. (2019). iPhone 11 Illegally Produced in China. Apple allows supplier factory Foxconn to violate labor laws. *China Labor Watch*. http://www.chinalaborwatch.org/upfile/2019_09_06/Zhengzhou%20Foxconn%20English%2009.06.pdf

China National Bureau of Statistics. (2020). *China Statistical Yearbook 2020*. National Bureau of Statistics of China.

Clapson, M., & Hutchison, R. (2010). *Suburbanization in Global Society*. Emerald Publishing.

Cody, J. W. (1996). American planning in republican China, 1911–1937. *Planning Perspectives, 11*(4), 339–377.

Corboz, A. (1983). The Land as Palimpsest. *Diogenes, 31*(121), 12–34.

Corner, J. (2006). Terra fluxus. In C. Waldheim (Ed.), *The Landscape Urbanism Reader* (pp. 21–33). Princeton Architectural Press.

Corner, J. (2014). *The Landscape Imagination: Collected Essays of James Corner 1990–2010*. Princeton Architectural Press.

Corner, J., & MacLean, A. S. (2000) (Eds.). *Taking Measures Across the American Landscape*. Yale University Press.

Cosgrove, D. (2000). The measures of America. In J. Corner & A. S. MacLean (Eds.), *Taking Measures Across the American Landscape* (pp. 3–13). Yale University Press.

Coutard, O., & Rutherford, J. (2015). *Beyond the Networked City: Infrastructure Reconfigurations and Urban Change in the North and South*. Routledge.

Cowen, D. (2014). *The Deadly Life of Logistics*. University of Minnesota Press.

Craciun, M. (2001). Ideology. In R. Koolhaas, J. C. Chung, J. Inaba, & T. S. Leong (Eds.), *Great Leap Forward* (pp. 30–44). Taschen.

Cugurullo, F. (2016). Urban eco-modernisation and the policy context of new eco-city projects: Where Masdar City fails and why. *Urban Studies, 53*(11), 2417–2433.

D

De Geyter, X. (Ed.). (2002). *After-Sprawl: Research on The Contemporary City*. NAi Publishers.

de Solà-Morales, I. (1995). Urbanitè Intersticielle. *Inter Art Actuel, 61*, 27–28.

Donaghy, K. P. (2012). Urban environmental imprints after globalization. *Regional Environmental Change, 12*(2), 395–405.

Drori, G. S., Meyer, J. W., & Hwang, H. (2006). *Globalization and Organization: World Society and Organizational Change*. Oxford: Oxford University Press.

DuBois, T., & Li, H. (Eds.). (2016). *Agricultural Reform and Rural Transformation in China since 1949*. Brill.

E

Easterling, K. (2001). *Organization Space: Landscapes, Highways, and Houses in America*. MIT Press.

Easterling, K. (2002). Tomato world. *PRAXIS: Journal of Writing + Building, 4*, 116–123.

Easterling, K. (2014). *Extrastatecraft: The Power of Infrastructure Space*. Verso Books.

Easterling, K. (2021). *Medium Design: Knowing How to Work on the World*. Verso Books.

Ebanks, G. E., & Cheng, C. (1990). China: A unique urbanization model. *Asia-Pacific Population Journal, 5*(3), 29–50.

Ebbensgaard, C. L. (2020). Standardised difference: Challenging uniform lighting through standards and regulation. *Urban Studies, 57*(9), 1957–1976.

Entrikin, N. J. (1989). Place, region and modernity. In J. A. Agnew & J. S. Duncan (Eds.), *The Power of*

Place. Bringing Together Geographical and Sociological Imaginations (pp. 30–43). Unwin Hyman.

F

Fan, J., Sun, W., Zhou, K., & Chen, D. (2012). Major function oriented zone: New method of spatial regulation for reshaping regional development pattern in China. *Chinese Geographical Science, 22*(2), 196–209.

Fang, C., & Yu, D. (2016). *China's New Urbanization: Developmental Paths, Blueprints and Patterns*. Springer.

Fisher, J. C. (1962). Planning the city of Socialist man. *Journal of the American Institute of Planners, 28*(4), 251–265.

Fishman, R. (1990). America's new city. *The Wilson Quarterly, 14*(1), 24–55.

Food and Agriculture Organization of the United Nations. (2019). *FAOSTAT*. http://www.fao.org/faostat/en/#data/QC/

Furlong, K. (2021). Geographies of infrastructure III: Infrastructure with Chinese characteristics. *Progress in Human Geography*, 1–11.

G

Garnaut, R., Song, L., & Fang, C. (2013). *China: A New Model for Growth and Development*. ANU Press.

Glaeser, E., Huang, W., Ma, Y., & Shleifer, A. (2017). A real estate boom with Chinese characteristics. *Journal of Economic Perspectives, 31*(1), 93–116.

Gonghao, C., & Ma, L. J. (1999). Urbanization from below in China: Its development and mechanisms. *Acta Geographica Sinica, 54*(2), 106–115.

Goodchild, B. (1990). Planning and the modern/postmodern debate. *Town Planning Review, 61*(2), 119.

Gottman, J. (1987). *Megalopolis Revisited 25 Years Later*. University of Maryland Press.

Governa, F. (2019). Scaling up and scaling out. New towns and "the standpoint of an absence". In M. Bonino, F. Governa, M. P. Repellino, & A. Sampieri (Eds.), *The City After Chinese New Towns. Spaces and Imaginaries from Contemporary Urban China* (pp. 215–226). Birkhäuser.

Governa, F., & Sampieri, A. (2020). Urbanisation processes and new towns in contemporary China: A critical understanding from a decentred view. *Urban Studies, 57*(2), 366–382.

Graham, S. (2000). Constructing premium network spaces: Reflections on infrastructure networks and contemporary urban development. *International Journal of Urban and Regional Research, 24*(1), 183–200.

Graham, S., & Marvin, S. (2001). *Splintering Urbanism: Networked Infrastructures, Technological Mobilities and the Urban Condition*. Routledge.

Gregotti, V. (1966). *Il Territorio dell'Architettura*. Feltrinelli.

Greis, N. P. (2004). Integrated infrastructures for moving goods in the digital age. In Richard Hanley (Ed.), *Moving People, Goods and Information in the 21st Century: The Cutting-edge Infrastructures of Networked Cities* (pp. 31–45). Routledge.

Grosjean, B. (2010). *Urbanisation sans urbanisme: Une histoire de la ville diffuse*. Mardaga.

Gui, B. (2012). *Analysis of rationality of Zhengdong New District under the thought of Kisho Kurokawa* [Master's thesis]. Henan University.

H

Haiyan, L., & Stapleton, K. (2006). Chinese urban history: State of the field. *China Information, 20*(3), 391–427.

Hao, P. (2006). *Zhengzhou's City Planning and City Development since Modern Times* [Master's thesis]. Shaanxi Normal University.

Harvey, D. (1989). *The Condition of Postmodernity: An Enquiry into the Origins of Cultural Change*. Blackwell Publishing.

Hayden, D. (1979). *Seven American Utopias: The Architecture of Communitarian Socialism, 1790–1975*. MIT Press.

He, Q. (2000). The Land-Enclosure Movement of the 1990s. *The Chinese Economy, 33*(3), 57–88.

He, S., & Wu, F. (2007). Neighbourhood changes and residential differentiation in Shanghai. In F. Wu (Ed.), *China's Emerging Cities: The Making of New Urbanism* (pp. 185–209). Routledge.

He, W., & Zhang, G. (2007). Application of city metabolism theory in Zhengdong New Community planning. *Shanxi Architecture, 33*(23), 38–39.

Henan Province Bureau of Statistics. (2020). *Henan Statistical Yearbook 2020*. China Statistical Press.

Henan Province People's Government. (2012). *Foxconn Jiyuan Project signing ceremony held in Zhengzhou*. Portal of the Henan Province People's Government. http://www.henan.gov.cn/jrhn/system/2012/03/26/010298406.shtml

Henan Tengfei Engineering Cost Consulting Co., Ltd. (2015). *Yanming Lake Town People's Government, Zhongmu County announcement on the successful bid of Yanming Lake Town Leisure Agriculture Master Plan*. https://www.zh818.com/html/2015/8/27/9484658.html

Hong, L. (2021). *China in One Village: The Story of One Town and the Changing World*. Verso Books.

Hsing, Y. (2010). *The Great Urban Transformation: Politics of Land and Property in China*. Oxford: Oxford University Press.

Hsu, M.-L. (1996). China's urban development: A case study of Luoyang and Guiyang. *Urban Studies, 33*(6), 895–910.

Huang, Y. (2008). *Capitalism with Chinese Characteristics: Entrepreneurship and the State*. Cambridge University Press.

I

Isozaki, A., & Administrative Committee of Zhengdong New District. (2012). *Zhongyuan: Traces of Centuries and Future Steps*. La Biennale di Venezia.

ISTAT. (1994). *Struttura e Dimensione delle Imprese*. ISTAT.

J

Jackson, J. B. (1984). Concluding with landscapes. In J. B. Jackson (Ed.), *Discovering the Vernacular Landscape* (pp. 145–158). Yale University Press.

Jacobs, H. (2018, May 7). Inside 'iPhone City,' the massive Chinese factory town where half of the world's iPhones are produced. *Business Insider*. https://www.businessinsider.com/apple-iphone-factory-foxconn-china-photos-tour-2018-5

Jones, R. W., & Kierzkowski, H. (2001). Horizontal aspects of vertical fragmentation. In L. K. Cheng & H. Kierzkowski (Eds.), *Global Production and Trade in East Asia* (pp. 33–51). Springer.

K

Kasarda, J. D. (2018, August 13). China's Aerotropolis. The Zhengzhou Airport Economy Zone. *International Airport Review*. https://www.internationalairportreview.com/whitepaper/73497/chinas-aerotropolis-airport-economy/

Kasarda, J. D. (2019). The Zhengzhou Airport Economy Zone. A remarkable aerotropolis. *Site Selection*, 74–77.

Katsikis, N. (2014). Two Approaches to "World Management": C. A. Doxiadis and R. B. Fuller. In N. Brenner (Ed.), *Implosions/Explosions: Towards a Study of Planetary Urbanization* (pp. 480–534). Jovis.

Katsikis, N. (2018). The "other" horizontal metropolis: Landscape of urban interdependence. In P. Viganò, C. Cavalieri, & M. B. Corte (Eds.), *The Horizontal Metropolis Between Urbanism and Urbanization* (pp. 23–45). Springer.

King, A. D. (2004). *Spaces of Global Cultures: Architecture, Urbanism, Identity*. Routledge.

Kirkby, R. J. R. (1985). *Urbanisation in China: Town and Country in a Developing Economy, 1949–2000 AD*. Croom Helm.

Klingmann, A. (2007). *Brandscapes: Architecture in the Experience Economy*. MIT Press.

Knapp, R. G. (Ed.). (1992). *Chinese Landscapes: The Village as Place*. University of Hawaii Press.

Knapp, R. G., & Sheng, D. (1992). Changing Village Landscapes. In R. G. Knapp (Ed.), *Chinese Landscapes: The Village as Place* (pp. 47–72). University of Hawaii Press.

Koolhaas, R. (1995). Whatever Happened to Urbanism? In R. Koolhaas, O.M.A, & B. Mau (Eds.), *S, M, L, XL* (pp. 958–971). Monacelli Press.

Koolhaas, R., O.M.A, & Mau, B (Eds.). (1995). *S, M, L, XL*. Monacelli Press.

Koolhaas, R., Chung, J. C., Inaba, J., & Leong, S. T. (Eds.). (2001). *Great Leap Forward*. Taschen.

Koolhaas, R., Chung, C. J., Jeffrey, I., & Leong, S. T (Eds.). (2001). *Harvard Design School Guide to Shopping*. Taschen.

Krieger, A. (2019). *City on a Hill: Urban Idealism in America from the Puritans to the Present*. Belknap Press.

Kuhn, P. A. (2002). *Origins of the Modern Chinese State*. Stanford University Press.

Kurokawa, K. (1991). *Intercultural Architecture: The Philosophy of Symbiosis*. Aia Press.

Kurokawa, K. (2005). *Kisho Kurokawa: Metabolism and Symbiosis*. Jovis.

L

Lang, R. E. (2003). *Edgeless Cities: Exploring the Elusive Metropolis*. Brookings Institution Press.

Lee, C. C. M. (Ed.). (2016). *Common Frameworks: Rethinking the Developmental City in China*. Harvard University Graduate School of Design.

Lefebvre, H. (1991). *The Production of Space*. Blackwell Publishing.

Lem, S. (1970). *Solaris*. MON.

Li, K., Administrative Committee of Zhengdong New District, & Zhengzhou Urban Planning Bureau (Eds.). (2010a). *The Development and Partial Adjustments to the Master Plan of Zhengdong New District*. China Construction Industry Press.

Li, K., Administrative Committee of Zhengdong New District, & Zhengzhou Urban Planning Bureau (Eds.). (2010b). *The Masterplan of Zhengdong New District*. China Construction Industry Press.

Li, K., Administrative Committee of Zhengdong New District, & Zhengzhou Urban Planning Bureau (Eds.). (2010c). *The Special Planning of Zhengdong New District*. China Construction Industry Press.

Li, K., Administrative Committee of Zhengdong New District, & Zhengzhou Urban Planning Bureau (Eds.). (2010d). *The Urban and Architectural Design of Zhengdong New District*. China Construction Industry Press.

Li, K., Administrative Committee of Zhengdong New District, & Zhengzhou Urban Planning Bureau (Eds.). (2010e). *Urban Planning and the Architectural Designs for the CBD of Zhengdong New District*. China Construction Industry Press.

Li, Y., & Hu, Z. (2015). Approaching integrated urban-rural development in China: The changing institutional roles. *Sustainability*, *7*(6), 7031–7048.

Liang, S. Y. (2014). *Remaking China's Great Cities: Space and Culture in Urban Housing, Renewal, and Expansion*. Routledge.

Lin, G. C. S., & Ho, S. P. S. (2005). The state, land system, and land development processes in contemporary China. *Annals of the Association of American Geographers*, *95*(2), 411–436.

Lin, J. Y. (2011). China and the global economy. *China Economic Journal*, *4*(1), 1–14.

Liu, H., Yeerken, W., & Wang, C. (2015). Impacts of the Belt and Road Initiative on the spatial pattern of territory development in China. *Progress in Geography*, *34*(5), 545–553.

Liu, J., Sun, W., & Hu, W. (Eds.). (2017). *The Development of Eco Cities in China*. Springer Singapore.

Liu, J., & Xu, G. (2019). A policy discourse on new town development in contemporary China. In M. Bonino, F. Governa, M. P. Repellino, & A. Sampieri (Eds.), *The City After Chinese New Towns: Spaces and Imaginaries from Contemporary Urban China* (pp. 60–70). Birkhäuser.

Liu, Y. (Ed.). (1988). *Contemporary Zhengzhou Urban Construction*. Chinese Publishing.

Liu, Y., Zhao, R., & Xu, M. (2008). Analysis of Spatial Structure Changes of Zhengzhou. *Modern Urban Studies*, *3*, 61–66.

Lo, C.-P. (1980). Shaping socialist Chinese cities. A model of form and land use. In L. Chi-Keung & N. Giusbury (Eds.), *China: Urbanization and National Development* (pp. 130–155). University of Chicago Press.

Löfgren, O. (2014). Urban atmospheres as brandscapes and lived experiences. *Place Branding and Public Diplomacy*, *10*(4), 255–266.

Lubin, G. (2011, October 25). Black market lenders say money is drying up around China's most famous ghost city. *Business Insider*. https://www.businessinsider.com/black-market-ordos-ghost-city-2011-10

Lyster, C. (2016). *Learning from Logistics: How Networks Change our Cities*. Birkhäuser.

M

Ma, L. J. C. (2005). Urban administrative restructuring, changing scale relations and local economic development in China. *Political Geography*, *24*(4), 477–497.

Machor, J. L. (1987). *Pastoral Cities: Urban Ideals*. University of Wisconsin Press.

Marx, L. (1964). *The Machine in the Garden: Technology and the Pastoral Ideal in America*. Oxford University Press.

Marx, L. (1991). The American Ideology of Space. In S. Wrede & W. H. Adams (Eds.), *Denatured Visions: Landscape and Culture in the Twentieth Century* (pp. 62–78). Museum of Modern Art.

McFarlane, C., & Rutherford, J. (2008). Political infrastructures: Governing and experiencing the fabric of the city. *International Journal of Urban and Regional Research*, *32*(2), 363–374.

Mehrotra, R., Vera, F., & Mayoral, J. (2017). *Ephemeral Urbanism: Does Permanence Matter?* ARQ Ediciones.

Mendel, P. (2006). The making and expansion of international management standards: The global diffusion of ISO 9000 quality management certificates. In G. S. Drori, J. W. Meyer, & H. Hwang (Eds.), *Globalization and Organization: World Society and Organizational Change* (pp. 137–166). Oxford: Oxford University Press.

Miller, T. (2012). *China's Urban Billion: The Story Behind the Biggest Migration in Human History*. Zed Books.

Ministry of Finance of the People's Republic of China. (2015a). *Announcement of Bidding for the Greening Construction Project of Zhugu Community, Zhongmu County, Phase I*. Ministry of Finance of the People's Republic of China. http://www.ccgp.gov.cn/cggg/dfgg/gkzb/201503/t20150305_5043997.htm

Ministry of Finance of the People's Republic of China. (2015b). *Yanminghu Town People's Government of Zhongmu County Announces Tendering for the Leisure Agriculture Master Planning Project of Yanminghu Town*. Ministry of Finance of the People's Republic of China. http://www.ccgp.gov.cn/cggg/dfgg/gkzb/201507/t20150731_5640477.htm

Ministry of Finance of the People's Republic of China. (2017). *Announcement of the results of the phase II of the project of Zhugu Community, Yanminghu Town, Zhongmu County*. Ministry of Finance of the People's Republic of China. http://www.ccgp.gov.cn/cggg/dfgg/zbgg/201708/t20170831_8779116.htm

Ministry of Finance of the People's Republic of China. (2018). *Notice of tender for the Zhugu Community, Yanming Lake Town, Zhongmu County comprehensive cultural service centre*. Ministry of Finance of the People's Republic of China. http://www.ccgp.gov.cn/cggg/dfgg/gkzb/201503/t20150305_5043997.htm

Morton, T. (2016). *Dark Ecology: For a Logic of Future Coexistence*. Columbia University Press.

Mostafavi, M., & Doherty, G. (2016). *Ecological Urbanism*. Lars Müller Publishers.

Mozingo, L. A. (2011). *Pastoral Capitalism: A History of Suburban Corporate Landscapes*. MIT Press.

N

National People's Congress. (2010, December 2). *Delegates of the National People's Congress inspect the planning and construction of Zhengzhou New District*. National People's Congress (NPC) of the People's Republic of China official. http://www.npc.gov.cn/zgrdw/npc/xinwen/dfrd/henan/2010-12/02/content_1607521.htm

O

Oakes, T. S. (2019). China's urban ideology: New towns, creation cities, and contested landscapes of memory. *Eurasian Geography and Economics*, *60*(4), 400–421.

Oi, J. C. (1992). Fiscal reform and the economic foundations of local state corporatism in China. *World Politics*, *45*(1), 99–126.

P

Phelps, N. A., & Wu, F. (2011). *International Perspectives on Suburbanization: A Post-Suburban World?* Palgrave Macmillan.

Picon, A., & Ratti, C. (2019). Everything becomes data. *Domus*, *1039*, 1000–1005.

Q

Qin, F. K. (2009). *Kisho Kurokawa's planning of Zhengdong New District* [Master's thesis]. Suzhou University.

R

Ren, X. (2011). *Building Globalization: Transnational Architecture Production in Urban China*. University of Chicago Press.

Ren, X. (2013). *Urban China*. John Wiley & Sons.

Repellino, M. P. (2019). Exhibition Halls. In M. Bonino, F. Governa, M. P. Repellino, & A. Sampieri (Eds.), *The City after Chinese New Towns. Spaces and Imaginaries from Contemporary Urban China* (pp. 133–142). Birkhäuser.

Romero, H., Méndez, M., & Smith, P. (2012). Mining Development and Environmental Injustice in the Atacama Desert of Northern Chile. *Environmental Justice*, *5*(2), 70–76.

Rossi, A. (1982). *The Architecture of the City*. MIT Press.

Rowe, P. G. (1991). *Making a Middle Landscape*. MIT Press.

Rowe, P. G., & Kan, H. Y. (2016). China's townization plan and its implications. In C. C. M. Lee (Ed.), *Common Frameworks: Rethinking the Developmental City in China* (pp. 210–225). Harvard University Press.

Roy, A., & Ong, A. (Eds.). (2011). *Worlding Cities: Asian Experiments and the Art of Being Global*. John Wiley & Sons.

Rozelle, S., & Hell, N. (2020). *Invisible China: How the Urban-rural Divide Threatens China's Rise*. University of Chicago Press.

S

Sampieri, A. (2019). The city is available. Chinese new towns as a backup space. In M. Bonino, F. Governa, M. P. Repellino, & A. Sampieri (Eds.), *The City after Chinese New Towns. Spaces and Imaginaries from Contemporary Urban China* (pp. 204–214). Birkhäuser.

Schlosberg, D. (2009). *Defining Environmental Justice: Theories, Movements, and Nature*. Oxford University Press.

Sclar, E. (2019). *Zoning: A Guide for 21st-Century Planning*. Routledge.

Secchi, B. (1989). *Un progetto per l'urbanistica*. Einaudi.

Secchi, B. (2000). *Prima lezione di urbanistica*. Laterza.

Secchi, B. (2005). *La città del ventesimo secolo*. Laterza.

Secchi, B., & Viganò, P. (2014). Isotropia e Porosità: Progetti manifesto. *Anfione & Zeto*, *25*, 19–24.

Sennett, R. (2009). *The Craftsman*. Yale University Press.

Sennett, R. (2018). *Building and Dwelling: Ethics for the City*. Allen Lane.

Shachar, B.-O. (2013, March 4). China's Real Estate Bubble [Video]. *60 Minutes*. CBS News.

Shepard, W. (2015). *Ghost Cities of China: The Story of Cities without People in the World's Most Populated Country*. Zed Books.

Sheppard, E., Leitner, H., & Maringanti, A. (2013). Provincializing global urbanism: A manifesto. *Urban Geography*, *34*(7), 893–900.

Shin, H. B. (2007). Residential redevelopment and social impacts in Beijing. In F. Wu (Ed.), *China's Emerging Cities: The Making of New Urbanism* (pp. 163–184). Routledge.

Sieverts, T. (2003). *Cities without Cities: An interpretation of the Zwischenstadt*. Routledge.

Simone, A. (2004). People as infrastructure: Intersecting fragments in Johannesburg. *Public Culture*, *16*(3), 407–429.

Skinner, G. W. (1977). *The City in Late Imperial China*. SMC Publishing.

Sklair, L. (2005). The transnational capitalist class and contemporary architecture in globalizing cities. *International Journal of Urban and Regional Research*, *29*(3), 485–500.

Sklair, L. (2006). Iconic architecture and capitalist globalization. *City*, *10*(1), 21–47.

Smith, N. R. (2021). *The End of the Village. Planning the Urbanization of Rural China*. University of Minnesota Press.

Soja, E. W. (2000). *Postmetropolis: Critical Studies of Cities and Regions*. Blackwell Publishing.

Soja, E. W. (2010). *Seeking Spatial Justice*. University of Minnesota Press.

Su, M. (2009). *China's Rural Development Policy: Exploring the "New Socialist Countryside"*. FirstForumPress.

Swyngedouw, E. (2017). More-than-human constellations as immuno-biopolitical fantasy in the urbicene. *New Geographies*, *9*, 20–27.

T

Teyssot, G. (Ed.). (1999). *The American Lawn*. Princeton Architectural Press.

The Economist. (2015, March 12). Aerotropolitan ambitions. *The Economist*. https://www.economist.com/china/2015/03/12/aerotropolitan-ambitions

Thomas, J. L. (2000). Holding the middle ground. In R. Fishman (Ed.), *The American Planning Tradition. Culture and Policy* (pp. 33–64). Woodrow Wilson Center Press.

Thün, G., Velikov, K., McTavish, D., Ripley, C., McMorrough, J., & Fishman, R. (2015). *Infra-Eco-Logi Urbanism: A Project for the Great Lakes Megaregion*. Park Books.

Tian, Y. Y., & Wong, C. (2007). Large urban redevelopment projects and sociospatial stratification in Shanghai. In F. Wu (Ed.), *China's Emerging Cities: The Making of New Urbanism* (pp. 210–231). Routledge.

Timberlake, M., Wei, Y. D., Ma, X., & Hao, J. (2014). Global cities with Chinese characteristics. *Cities*, *41*, 162–170.

Tout, D. (1990). The Horticulture Industry of Almería Province, Spain. *The Geographical Journal*, *156*(3), 304–312.

Tunnard, C., & Pushkarev, B. (1964). *Man-made America: Chaos or Control*. Yale University Press.

V

Viganò, P. (2014). *Territorialism*. Harvard University Press.

Viganò, P. (2016). *The Territories of Urbanism: The Project as Knowledge Producer*. Routledge.

Viganò, P., Fabian, L., & Secchi, B. (Eds.). (2016). *Water and Asphalt: The Project of Isotropy*. Park Books.

Viganò, P., Cavalieri, C., & Corte, M. B. (Eds.). (2018). *The Horizontal Metropolis Between Urbanism and Urbanization*. Springer.

W

Waldheim, C. (2006) (Ed.). *The Landscape Urbanism Reader*. Princeton University Press.

Waldheim, C. (2016). *Landscape as Urbanism: A General Theory*. Princeton University Press.

Wang, F.-L. (2005). *Organizing Through Division and Exclusion: China's Hukou System*. Stanford University Press.

Wang, M. Y., Kee, P., & Gao, J. (Eds.). (2014). *Transforming Chinese Cities*. Routledge.

Wang, X. (2007). Study on Zhengzhou and Kaifeng integrated development under the background of rising of central area of China. *Areal Research and Development*, *26*(6), 28–34.

Wang, X. (2020). *Blockchain Chicken Farm: And other Stories of Tech in China's Countryside*. Farrar Straus & Giroux.

Wang, X., Feng, D., Yang, Y., Du, J., & Zhang, H. (2013). The construction of Zhengzhou airport: The Economic Comprehensive Experimental Zone and the spatial organization of Growth Triangle in Zhengzhou–Kaifeng–Xuchang. *Areal Research and Development*, *32*(6), 172–176.

Wang, X., & Tomaney, J. (2019). Zhengzhou. Political economy of an emerging Chinese megacity. *Cities*, *84*, 104–111.

Weller, R., Hoch, C., & Huang, C. (2017). *Atlas for the End of the World*. http://atlas-for-the-end-of-the-world.com/

Wen, J. (2006, April 6). New Socialist Countryside. What Does It Mean? *Beijing Review*. http://www.bjreview.com.cn/special/third_plenum_17thcpc/txt/2008-10/10/content_156190.htm

Wigley, M. (1999). The electric lawn. In G. Teyssot (Ed.), *The American Lawn* (pp. 155–195). Princeton Architectural Press.

Williams, A. (2017). *China's Urban Revolution: Understanding Chinese Eco-Cities*. Bloomsbury Academic.

Wong, C. P. (2000). Central-local relations revisited the 1994 tax-sharing reform and public expenditure management in China. *China Perspectives*, 52–63.

Wu, F. (2003). Globalization, place promotion and urban development in Shanghai. *Journal of Urban Affairs*, *25*(1), 55–78.

Wu, F. (Ed.). (2006). *Globalization and the Chinese City*. Routledge.

Wu, F. (Ed.). (2007). *China's Emerging Cities: The Making of New Urbanism*. Routledge.

Wu, F. (2015). *Planning for Growth: Urban and Regional Planning in China*. Routledge.

Wu, F. (2016a). State dominance in urban redevelopment: Beyond gentrification in urban China. *Urban Affairs Review*, *52*(5), 631–658.

Wu, F. (2016b). China's emergent city–region governance: A new form of state spatial selectivity through state-orchestrated rescaling. *International Journal of Urban and Regional Research*, *40*(6), 1134–1151.

Wu, Y., Zhang, W., Shen, J., Mo, Z., & Peng, Y. (2018). Smart city with Chinese characteristics against the background of big data: Idea, action and risk. *Journal of Cleaner Production*, *173*, 60–66.

Wyman, L. (2002). Replascape™. In R. Koolhaas, C. J. Chung, I. Jeffrey, & S. T. Leong (Eds.). (2001). *Harvard Design School Guide to Shopping* (pp. 618–631). Taschen.

X

Xiao, Z. (Ed.). (2016). *China Environment and Development Review: The Rural Eco-Environment of China*. Paths International Press.

Xu, J., & Yeh, A. G. O. (2005). City repositioning and competitiveness building in regional development: New development strategies in Guangzhou, China. *International Journal of Urban and Regional Research*, *29*(2), 283–308.

Xu, J., & Yeh, A. G.-O. (2009). Decoding urban land governance: State reconstruction in contemporary Chinese cities. *Urban Studies*, *46*(3), 559–581.

Xue, C. Q. L., & Wang, Y. (2010). The decision-making and implementation of a multifaced project: Rethinking Kisho Kurokawa planning of Zhengdong New District. *Architect, 146*, 14–20.

Xue, C. Q. L., Sun, L. L., & Tsai, L. (2011). The architectural legacies of Kisho Kurokawa in China. *The Journal of Architecture, 16*(3), 415–442.

Xue, C. Q. L., Wang, Y., & Tsai, L. (2013). Building new towns in China: A case study of Zhengdong New District. *Cities, 30*, 223–232.

Y

Yang, D. (2014). *Townization: In Search of New Paradigm of Urbanization in China* [Doctoral dissertation]. Harvard University Graduate School of Design.

Ye, X. (2009). China's urban–rural integration policies. *Journal of Current Chinese Affairs, 38*(4), 117–143.

Yeh, A. G.-O., & Wu, F. (1996). The new land development process and urban development in Chinese cities. *International Journal of Urban and Regional Research, 20*(2), 330–353.

Yeh, A. G.-O., & Wu, F. (1999). The transformation of the urban planning system in China from a centrally-planned to transitional economy. *Progress in Planning, 51*(3), 167–252.

Z

Zhang, C. (2007). *Urban Spatial Structure's Evolvement Research of Zhengzhou City* [Doctoral dissertation]. Zhengzhou University.

Zhang, C., Song, X., & Zeng, F. (2010). Urban spatial structure's evolvement of Zhengzhou city from 1948 to 1978. *Shanxi Architecture, 36*(11), 34–35.

Zhang, L., & Zhao, S. X. B. (1998). Re-examining China's "urban" concept and the level of urbanization. *The China Quarterly, 154*, 330–381.

Zhao, D. (2013). *The Competitive Strategy of Zhengdong New District* [Doctoral dissertation]. Hebei University.

Zhengzhou City Planning Administration. (1989). *Zhengzhou City Zoning Plan Atlas*. Zhengzhou Municipality.

Zhengzhou Municipal Bureau of Statistics. (2019). *Zhengzhou Yearbook 2019*. Zhengzhou Ancient Book Publishing.

Zhengzhou Municipal Bureau of Urban and Rural Planning. (2018). *National Aviation Economic Zone Planning Innovation and Practice: Documentary Work of Zhengzhou Airport Economic Comprehensive Experimental Zone*. People's Publishing House.

Zhengzhou Municipal Statistics Bureau. (2018). *Zhengzhou Statistic Data*. Zhengzhou Municipality. http://tjj.zhengzhou.gov.cn/

Zhengzhou Municipality. (2009). *Solicitation for Spatial Development Strategic Planning Scheme of Zhengbian New District*. Zhengzhou Municipality.

Zhu, J. (2009). *Architecture of Modern China: A Historical Critique*. Routledge.

Zhu, J. (2012). Study on evolution of Zhengzhou's urban planning and spatial structure from 1906 to 1957. *China City Planning Review, 21*(1), 66–72.

Zukin, S. (1996). *The Cultures of Cities*. Blackwell Publishing.

Index of Places

Illustration Credits

Cover photography by Leonardo Ramondetti, 2019.
Pages 6–7 photography by Leonardo Ramondetti, 2019.

Exploring the Central Plains of China

Maps and Data, pages 33–58.

Fig. 1 Drawing by Leonardo Ramondetti.

Figs. 2, 3, 6, 9, 12, 15 Maps drawn by Leonardo Ramondetti, based on satellite images, GIS information, and data archives from OpenStreetMap (OSM) and the global land cover datasets provided by the International Geosphere Biosphere Programme (IGBP-DIS), the University of Maryland (UMD), the European Commission Joint Research Centre (GLC2000), and the MODIS land cover map.

Figs. 4, 5, 7, 8, 10, 11, 13, 14, 16, 17, 18 Infographics drawn by Leonardo Ramondetti, based on data retrieved from the Henan Province Bureau of Statistics. (2020). *Henan Statistical Yearbook 2020*. China Statistical Press.

Policies, Plans, and Projects, pages 59–98.

Figs. 1, 2, 5, 6, 7, 8, 10, 11, 13, 14, 15, 16, 17, 18, 19, 20, 21 Historical images of Zhengzhou retrieved from https://www.henandaily.cn and http://www.sohu.com (accessed on December 10th, 2021).

Figs. 3, 4, 12, 22 Plans published by Zhengzhou municipality.

Fig. 9 Project published by the South China University of Technology (SCUT).

Figs. 23, 24, 25 Plans, schemes, and views by Kisho Kurokawa published in: Li, K., Administrative Committee of Zhengdong New District, & Zhengzhou Urban Planning Bureau (Eds.). (2010e). *Urban Planning and the Architectural Designs for the CBD of Zhengdong New District*. China Construction Industry Press.

Fig. 26 Photography by Leonardo Ramondetti, 2019.

Figs. 27, 28, 29, 32, 33 Plan and views published by Zhengzhou municipality in the book: Zhengzhou Municipality. (2009). *Solicitation for Spatial Development Strategic Planning Scheme of Zhengbian New District*. Zhengzhou municipality.

Figs. 30, 31 Views by the Zhengzhou Design Institute.

Fig. 34 Drawing by Arata Isozaki published in: Isozaki, A., & Administrative Committee of Zhengdong New District. (2012). *Zhongyuan: Traces of Centuries and Future Steps*. La Biennale di Venezia.

Fig. 35 Beijing Tsinghua Planning and Design Institute, 2014. Source: https://hn.leju.com (accessed on December 10th, 2021).

Artefacts and Structures, pages 99–200.

Figs. 1, 2, 5, 8, 9, 10, 13, 15, 16, 17, 21, 23, 24, 25, 28, 30, 31, 35, 36, 40, 43, 46, 48, 53, 56, 57, 62, 63, 66, 67 Maps, plans, and architectural drawings by Leonardo Ramondetti, based on information retrieved from fieldwork activity, official sources, OpenStreetMap (OSM), and Google Earth.

Figs. 3, 4, 11, 12, 18, 19, 20, 22, 26, 27, 29, 33, 34, 38, 39, 42, 44, 45, 49, 50, 51, 52, 54, 55, 58, 59, 60, 61, 64, 65, 69, 70, 71, 72, 73 Photographs taken in 2017 and 2019 by Leonardo Ramondetti.

Figs. 6, 7, 14, 68 Tables and graphs by Leonardo Ramondetti, based on: Zhengzhou Municipal Bureau of Statistics. (2019). *Zhengzhou Yearbook 2019*. Zhengzhou Ancient Book Publishing; and official sources.

Figs. 32, 37, 41, 47 Axonometric views by Cinzia Stella and Leonardo Ramondetti.

Pages 220–221 photography by Leonardo Ramondetti, 2019.

Acknowledgements

This book has benefited from the help and support of many people and institutions. First, I offer my sincere thanks to the following people who have been extremely influential, not only in my work, but also in my personal life. Angelo Sampieri has always been a pillar of support, offering constant encouragement, incomparable insights, and timely contributions. Francesca Governa's invaluable suggestions and thought-provoking questions have stimulated my critical thinking immensely. Astrid Safina helped me see Chinese urbanisation so much more clearly and shared many of my experiences. Over the past few years, these outstanding individuals have all become friends and supporters, as well as honest critics.

This book would not have been possible without the backing of the research project "Rescaling the Belt and Road Initiative: Urbanization Processes, Innovation Patterns and Global Investments in Urban China" (2020–2023) at the Politecnico di Torino and Università di Macerata; and the joint research project "CeNTO—Chinese New Towns: Negotiating Citizenship and Physical Form" (2015–2019) by the Politecnico di Torino, Tsinghua University of Beijing, and École Polytechnique Fédérale of Lausanne (EPFL), which culminated in the publication of *The City After Chinese New Towns. Spaces and Imaginaries from Contemporary Urban China* edited by Michele Bonino et al. (Basel: Birkhäuser, 2019). I wish to express my profound gratitude to the coordinators of the respective research projects, Francesca Governa (Politecnico di Torino—DIST) and Michele Bonino (Politecnico di Torino—DAD), who have inspired so many people with their passion for China.

Between 2016 and 2019, I was given opportunities to conduct fieldwork in China, to work as a visiting Ph.D. researcher at Tsinghua University in Beijing, and to discuss the provisional outcomes of my research in international workshops, seminars, and conferences. For this, I thank Prof. Umberto Janin Rivolin, the coordinator of the Ph.D. programme in Urban and Regional Development at Politecnico di Torino, Prof. Andrea Bocco, the head of the Interuniversity Department of Regional and Urban Studies and Planning, and Prof. Zhong Ge, my contact person at Tsinghua University. During my time in China, I discussed my work with several scholars at the Tsinghua University of Beijing and the South China University of Technology in Guangzhou (SCUT). I am especially grateful to Prof. Liu Jian (Tsinghua University) and Dr. Xuefei Han (post-Ph.D. at SCUT) for their suggestions. I also thank Prof. Xianguang Li (Henan University), Arch. Song Yuan Liu (Zhengzhou Design Institute), Prof. Ying Li (Zhengzhou University), and Ms. Zhou Lulu (Zhengzhou University) for supporting my fieldwork in Zhengzhou, and for sharing documents and valuable materials for this work. I am also grateful to the photographer Samuele Pellecchia (Prospekt Photographers), my travelling companion in Beijing, Zhengzhou, and Guangzhou.

I would not have been able to achieve so much without the invaluable contributions of several scholars who I met over the last four years. Above all, I am grateful to Pierre-

Alain Croset (Politecnico di Milano), Giuseppe Bertrando Bonfantini (Politecnico di Milano), Timothy Oakes (University of Colorado Boulder), Xuefei Ren (Michigan State University), and Matteo Robiglio (Politecnico di Torino), with whom I discussed the main hypothesis of my Ph.D. dissertation. As a member of the organising committee of the seminars *The City after Chinese New Towns* and *How to Study Contemporary China?* (February–May 2019) at the Politecnico di Torino, I had the opportunity to be in contact and discuss my research with several specialists whose observations greatly inspired my work. I would like to thank Christopher C. M. Lee (GSD Harvard), Florence Graezer Bideau (EPFL), Guanghui Ding (Beijing University of Civil Engineering and Architecture), Yang Dingliang (GSD Harvard), Carine Henriot (UTC), and Austin Williams (Kingston University London).

I have also greatly benefited from the feedback of organisers and participants at the conferences, workshops, and seminars at which I presented my work, including the conference *Regional Governance, Industrial Restructuring and Sustainable Development*, organised by the Regional Studies Association at Peking University (Beijing) (June 29th – July 1st, 2018); the conference *China's New Urban Agenda: An International Dialogue on Sustainable Development* organised by the Manchester Urban Institute at the University of Manchester (October 30th – November 3rd, 2018); the seminar *Wording Urban Diffusion* organised by the Diffuse Cities & Urbanization Network (DCUN) and the research group Vocabularies of Architectural and Urban Design across Time (CNRS-AUSSER) at the National School of Architecture of Paris Belleville (November 21st, 2018); and the conference *Cities and Infrastructures* organised by Olivier Coutard (CNRS-LATTS) and Daniel Florentin (Mines ParisTech) at the Mines ParisTech campus in Fontainebleau, France (September 6th – 8th, 2021). I am especially grateful to Thomas Sieverts for his esteemed advice on my work.

This book, more than most, greatly benefits from the challenging environment of the Interuniversity Department of Regional and Urban Studies and Planning (DIST) and my colleagues in the China Room research group: Mauro Berta, Alberto Bologna, Edoardo Bruno, Francesco Carota, Giorgia Cestaro, Valeria Federighi, Filippo Fiandanese, Camilla Forina, Francesca Frassoldati, Silvia Lanteri, Xian Lu, Marta Mancini, Matteo Migliaccio, Monica Naso, Lidia Preti, Maria Paola Repellino, Marco Santangelo, Ahmed Sohrab, and Ling Xiang. I also express my gratitude to my colleagues at the Ph.D. programme for Urban and Regional Development at the Politecnico di Torino.

Finally, this book is dedicated to my parents, my family, and Marianna with great admiration, profound gratitude, and much love.

This research was carried out over more than three years before the COVID-19 outbreak. Since that time, the world has been turned upside down, and even now it is not possible to tell how this tragic event will affect our lives in the coming months and years. In spite of this, I believe that the issues and hypothesis of this work are still important matters today.

About the Author

Leonardo Ramondetti, Ph.D. in Urban Planning and Regional Development, is a post-doctoral researcher at the Interuniversity Department of Regional and Urban Studies and Planning (DIST) at the Politecnico di Torino and Università di Torino. His field of research is contemporary urban design theory and planning culture, with a particular focus on the Chinese context.

Proofreading: Thomas O'Byrne
Copy editing: Ada Anastasia
Project management: Ria Stein
Layout, cover design: Jenna Gesse
Typography: hawemannundmosch

Print: Beltz Grafische Betriebe GmbH
Paper: Magno Natural, 120 g/m²
Lithography: LVD Gesellschaft für Datenverarbeitung mbH

Library of Congress Control Number: 2022931031

Bibliographic information published by the German National Library
The German National Library lists this publication in the Deutsche Nationalbibliografie; detailed bibliographic data are available on the Internet at http://dnb.dnb.de.

ISBN 978-3-0356-2491-5
e-ISBN (PDF) 978-3-0356-2492-2

P.O. Box 44, 4009 Basel, Switzerland
Part of De Gruyter

Printed on acid-free paper produced from chlorine-free pulp. TCF ∞

Printed in Germany

9 8 7 6 5 4 3 2 1

www.birkhauser.com

This project was realised within the framework of the research project "Rescaling the Belt and Road Initiative: Urbanization Processes, Innovation Patterns and Global Investments in Urban China" (2020–2023) carried out at the Politecnico di Torino and Università di Macerata. It involved a number of research partners to whom I would like to express my gratitude, particularly the Interuniversity Department of Regional and Urban Studies and Planning (DIST) and the China Room research group at Politecnico di Torino.